Be A Better Reader

Level E

Seventh Edition

Nila Banton Smith

Globe Fearon Educational Publishers
A Division of Simon & Schuster
Upper Saddle River, New Jersey

Pronunciation Key

Symbol	Key Word	Respelling
a	act	(akt)
ah	star	(stahr)
ai	dare	(dair)
aw	also	(awl soh)
ay	flavor	(flay vər)
e	end	(end)
ee	eat	(eet)
er	learn	(lern)
	sir	(ser)
	fur	(fer)
i	hit	(hit)
eye	idea	(eye dee ə)
y	like	(lyk)
ir	deer	(dir)
	fear	(fir)
oh	open	(oh pen)
oi	foil	(foil)
	boy	(boi)
or	horn	(horn)
ou	out	(out)
	flower	(flou ər)
oo	hoot	(hoot)
	rule	(rool)
yoo	few	(fyoo)
	use	(yooz)

Symbol	Key Word	Respelling
u	book	(buk)
	put	(put)
uh	cup	(kuhp)
ə	a as in along	(ə lawng)
	e as in moment	(moh mənt)
	i as in modify	(mahd ə fy)
	o as in protect	(prə tekt)
	u as in circus	(ser kəs)
ch	chill	(chil)
g	go	(goh)
j	joke	(johk)
	bridge	(brij)
k	kite	(kyt)
	cart	(kahrt)
ng	bring	(bring)
s	sum	(suhm)
	cent	(sent)
sh	sharp	(shahrp)
th	thin	(thin)
z	zebra	(zee brə)
	pose	(pohz)
zh	treasure	(treszh ər)

Be A Better Reader, Level E, Seventh Edition
Nila Banton Smith

Copyright © 1997 by Globe Fearon Educational Publisher. One Lake Street, Upper Saddle River, New Jersey 07458. All rights reserved. No part of this book may be kept in any information storage or retrieval system, transmitted or reproduced in any form or by any means without the prior written permission of the publisher.

Printed in the United States of America

9 10   00 01

C12
ISBN 0-8359-1928-5

Acknowledgments
We wish to express our appreciation for permission to use and adapt copyrighted materials.

The dictionary definitions in this book are reprinted with permission of Macmillan Reference USA, a Division of Simon & Schuster, from WEBSTER'S NEW WORLD DICTIONARY, Student Edition. Copyright © 1976, 1981, 1983, by Simon & Schuster Inc. Universal Press for "Woodpeckers in Summer Frolic" by David Nava Monreal from SIGHS AND SONGS OF AZTLAN. Copyright © 1975. Moore Publishing Company for "Long Distance" by Carole Gregory from NINE BLACK POETS. Copyright © 1968. "First Snow" from SURE SIGNS: NEW AND SELECTED POEMS, by Ted Kooser, © 1980. Reprinted by permission of the University of Pittsburgh Press. "In the beginning was the" from THE SIDEWALK RACER AND OTHER POEMS OF SPORTS AND MOTION by Lillian Morrison. Copyright © 1965, 1967, 1977 by Lillian Morrison. Used by permission of Marian Reiner for the author. "For a Hopi Silversmith" by Joy Harjo from THE FIRST SKIN AROUND ME. Copyright © 1976. Reprinted by permission of Joy Harjo. "Point Clearview" cartoon by Courtney Smith is reprinted by permission from *National Parks* magazine, September/October 1981. Copyright © 1981 by National Parks and Conservation Association. "Welcome to Overcrowded Park" by Langley © *The Christian Science Monitor.*

Photo Credits
p. 12: Library of Congress; **p. 19:** (*left*) Chris Bruun from the National Audubon Society/Photo Researchers, (*center*) Jeff Foott/Bruce Coleman, (*right*) Stouffer Productions/Animals, Animals; **p. 32:** Mitchell Campbell/DPI; **p. 61:** The Bettmann Archive; **p. 62:** (*left*) W. Brindle/Photo Researchers, (*right*) Pat Witherspoon from the National Audubon Society/Photo Researchers; **p. 63:** Taranga Zoo, Sydney, Tom McHugh/Photo Researchers; **p. 122:** Yoav Levy/Phototake; **p. 128:** Santa Fe Railway; **p. 133:** (*left*) Britton-Logan/Photo Researchers, (*right*) Ward Wells/DPI; **p. 139:** (*both*) Michael Fogden/Animals, Animals.

Contents

For more than thirty years, *Be A Better Reader* has helped students improve their reading skills. *Be A Better Reader* teaches the comprehension and study skills that you need to read and enjoy all types of materials—from library books to the different textbooks that you will encounter in school.

To get the most from *Be A Better Reader*, you should know how the lessons are organized. As you read the following explanations, it will be helpful to look at some of the lessons.

In each of the first four lessons of a unit, you will apply an important skill to a reading selection in literature, social studies, science, or mathematics. Each of these lessons includes the following seven sections.

Skill Focus

This section teaches you a specific skill. You should read the Skill Focus carefully, paying special attention to words that are printed in boldface type. The Skill Focus tells you about a skill that you will use when you read the selection.

Word Clues

This section teaches you how to recognize and use different types of context clues. These clues will help you with the meanings of the underlined words in the selection.

Reading a Literature, Social Studies, Science, or Mathematics Selection

This section introduces the selection that you will read and gives you suggestions about what to look for as you read. The suggestions will help you understand the selection.

Selection

The selections in the literature lessons are similar to those in a literature anthology, library book, newspaper, or magazine. The social studies selec- tions are like chapters in a social studies textbook or encyclopedia. They often include maps and tables. The science selections, like a science textbook, include special words in boldface type and sometimes diagrams. The mathematics selections will help you acquire skill in reading mathematics textbooks.

Recalling Facts

Answers to the questions in this section—the first of three activity sections—can be found in the selection. You will sometimes have to reread parts of the selection to do this activity.

Interpreting Facts

The second activity includes questions whose answers are not directly stated in the selection. For these questions, you must combine the information in the selection with what you already know in order to *infer* the answers.

Skill Focus Activity

In the last activity, you will use the skill that you learned in the Skill Focus section at the beginning of the lesson to answer questions about the selection. If you have difficulty completing this activity, reread the Skill Focus section.

The remaining lessons in each unit give you practice with such skills as using a dictionary, an encyclopedia, and other reference materials; using phonics and syllabication aids in recognizing new words; locating and organizing information; and adjusting reading rate. Other reading skills that are necessary in everyday experience are also covered, such as reading a bus schedule and a menu.

Each time that you learn a new skill in *Be A Better Reader*, look for opportunities to use the skill in your other reading at school and at home. Your reading ability will improve the more you practice reading!

Lesson 1

Setting and Plot

Reading a Literature Selection

▶ **Background Information**

In this story, two teenagers suddenly find themselves in a dangerous situation in which even the smallest action could have tragic consequences.

▶ **Skill Focus**

Setting is the place and time of the events in a story. The setting of a story can be as ordinary as a kitchen or as dramatic as a racetrack. The time can be now, the distant past, or years from now.

Setting often influences a story's **plot**, or action. It can add to the conflict around which the plot revolves.

Read the paragraph below. Look for details of setting that influence the story's plot.

It was not the safest neighborhood. In fact, it was no place for two out-of-town teenagers at two o'clock in the morning. As Lucille and Jerry huddled under the dimly lit metal roof of the bus shelter, a dog approached. Its growl and menacing eyes frightened Lucille and Jerry.

In this paragraph, the setting helps to create a conflict. Such phrases as *not the safest neighborhood, under the dimly lit metal roof,* and *two o'clock in the morning* describe an isolated, dark setting and create tension. Once the ferocious dog confronts the teenagers, the reader can expect the plot to move quickly. Suddenly, there is a conflict.

A different setting, however, could lead to a story with a different plot.

The questions below will help you see how setting influences plot.

1. Where and when do the story's events take place?
2. What details of the setting help develop the conflict?
3. How would a different setting affect the story's plot and conflict?

▶ **Word Clues**

When you read a word that you do not know, look for context clues to help you. Context clues are nearby words and phrases that help make the meaning clearer. Read the following sentences.

All that we have to do is follow those ski lift pylons back to the base lodge. Those posts will be our markers.

If you don't know the meaning of the word *pylons,* the word *posts* in the second sentence can help you. The words *pylons* and *posts* are synonyms. A pylon is a post, or a column, used as a support.

Use **synonym** context clues to find the meanings of the three underlined words in the selection.

▶ **Strategy Tip**

As you read "Storm on Alyeska," look for details that describe the two settings of the story. Note that a space between paragraphs signals a change in setting. How do the elements of nature affect the outcome of the story?

Storm on Alyeska

Marina surveyed the glacier proudly. The light glinted off its folds, as thin, wispy veils of crystalline snow curled and skimmed across its surface. Because this was her favorite place, Marina was eager to show it to her friend, Tom. "It's incredibly beautiful, isn't it, Tom?" she asked.

"Well, it isn't the Arctic, but it certainly is spectacular," Tom agreed.

"Yes!" shouted Marina, throwing her arms out as if she were attempting to embrace the scene before her. "I don't know of anyone else who's come to Portage Glacier on cross-country skis along that rugged trail, Tom. Because everyone usually takes the ski lift up here, this is an accomplishment. Maybe they'll put us in the record books, like that person from the lower forty-eight who ate 130 prunes in two minutes."

"I can see it now," laughed Tom. "'Woman Sets Cross-Country Record on Mount Alyeska.'" Then, checking the sky, he added, "I think that we should head back now, or we'll set a quick-freeze record for the mountain as well. I don't think I'd like to be featured in that headline. Since we can still catch it, why don't we take the last ski lift back from the glacier?"

"Oh, Tom," laughed Marina. "You're not in Barrow, up above the Arctic Circle, anymore. You're not on pipeline patrol on the permafrost. You're here in lower Alaska. You can relax."

"It's a glacier-covered mountain, the sun will soon go down, and a wind is coming up. At home, we don't take nature for granted. We're Inuits, and we're supposed to understand terrible weather."

Marina bristled. "I know this mountain. I work here on weekends. All that we have to do is follow those ski lift pylons back to the base lodge. Those posts will be our markers. Come on, I'll race you!"

Tom grinned. "How can I resist a challenge? I'll be right behind you, and if you can get us back to the lodge in record time, I'll admit that you haven't gone completely soft on your Arctic heritage."

Marina and Tom set off across the edge of the glacier field. As they disappeared over the line of the slope, the light changed. Clouds scudded across a sky that was rapidly turning leaden and yellow-gray. Snow began to fall.

At a police station in Girdwood, near Mount Alyeska, Chief Ellanna slammed the door shut against the now-swirling snow and stamped his boots on the rubber mat. He strode down the hall and into the squad room.

"We've got a truck jackknifed across the highway, cars stranded everywhere," he growled, "and my snowmobile had to get stuck in a drift."

He unzipped his parka and sat behind the desk. "We can't do much as long as the wind keeps up," he grunted. "How do we stand, Sergeant?"

"Your wife called about an hour ago, Chief. She said that your daughter and her friend, Tom, were expected home two hours

ago. She's afraid they're lost in the storm on Mount Alyeska," reported Sergeant Price.

"Sergeant, call my wife back. See if she's heard from them."

Just then, Officer Casey walked into the squad room to give the chief an update on rescue operations. Officer Casey, holding a sheaf of papers, glanced at the stack in her hands and read from it. "Mrs. Tift's lined up 20 vehicles from the Snowmobile Club. Pat Mooney over at the rescue squad has a dozen snowshoe experts coming in. About 30 rescue units can be at the ski lodge in about an hour. That should be enough help to cover all possible storm emergencies."

Chief Ellanna nodded. "Have you called Anchorage?"

"The U. S. Weather Bureau reports that winds are slowing down just south of there," Officer Casey responded. "But they say that it will be three hours or more before the winds die down here."

Sergeant Price walked back into the squad room. "Chief, no word yet about your daughter and her friend. No one's seen them since they headed up the mountain."

The police chief glanced up at the clock and scowled. The reason that he frowned was clear when he said, "We've got at least three hours to wait. Visibility is so poor that we can't even send up helicopters to look for them. It'll also be dark soon. This is bad. Tom and Marina have already been out there too long. I just wish we had some idea where they were headed."

Tom's hands were almost numb, and his feet throbbed with pain. While he had the foresight to wear heavy gear, he neglected to take along a pair of snow goggles. The blizzard had shrunk visibility until he could barely make out the dark shadows of thick trees a few feet ahead.

Suddenly, Marina materialized right in front of him; he almost collided with her. When she appeared, she was leaning on her ski poles, peering into the flying, whirling snow.

"They should be here! I don't know why they're not! This is ridiculous. Pylons don't get up and walk away."

"Are you sure we've come in the right direction?" asked Tom.

"Positive. I have this mountain memorized. Let's keep going. The pylons must be a bit farther on." Marina bent forward and pushed off, breaking a slow path through darkening woods.

At that point, Tom didn't care about finding the pylons. A little frightened, he just wanted to be safe and warm. The frigid open stretches of the Arctic Circle, where he lived, seemed more hospitable and comfortable than this rugged, forested mountain resort. In the Arctic, he knew what to expect. Now he had to depend on Marina and her knowledge of the mountain. He didn't like depending on someone else. He liked to be able to depend on himself. Nevertheless, he set off after Marina.

She blamed herself for their predicament—she had taken the mountain for granted.

"How long has it been now?" wondered Marina desperately. It was so much colder than before. She blamed herself for their predicament—she had taken the mountain for granted. It was now obvious that they had missed the pylons, as well as the trail that the posts marked. Their only hope was to continue downhill. If only she and Tom could reach the highway, she thought.

Tom caught up with her. "Now what?" he yelled. "Where are we? Do you have another great plan?"

Marina's eyebrows were caked with snow. She tried to wipe them, but her gloves were clumsy and stiff. She took one off—and it slipped from her fingers to the ground.

"Marina—your glove! Don't!" shouted Tom. As he shouted, the wind swept the glove down the slope. "I'll get it," he yelled, as he unthinkingly launched down the slope. "How could Marina take her glove off?" he muttered as he tried to keep it in sight.

"Not that way, Tom!" Marina bellowed, skiing after him. She was in time to watch, horrified, as he tumbled into a craggy, narrow, rock-strewn ravine. She couldn't believe Tom's foolish action.

The CB radio in the police station squad room crackled and brought Chief Ellanna bolt upright. A message was coming in from one of the police snowmobiles out on patrol. "This is Big Tlingit to Smokey. I'm stuck down here at mile 39 on the highway. I just saw two skiers near the road, but they veered off into a wooded area. Could they be your daughter and her friend?"

Chief Ellanna immediately directed units to move in the direction of the woods near mile 39. The Chief sighed. At least they had been seen alive!

"Sergeant Price, call my wife. Tell her we think that we've found Marina and Tom."

Tom couldn't move. He knew his leg was broken. At least he knew that it was when he was conscious, but he kept drifting off. He couldn't understand why he wasn't colder. He could swear someone had covered him with a feathery, fresh-smelling blanket. He kept trying to tell Marina something. Maybe if he could joke with her, she wouldn't think things were so awful. If only he hadn't gone off after that glove . . .

Chief Ellanna was the last to reach the ravine. As he jumped out of his snowmobile, he saw a blanket-wrapped figure on a stretcher.

He ran toward it as another figure stumbled toward him.

"Dad!" Marina screamed hoarsely. "It was my fault! Poor Tom."

"Marina, are you all right? What happened to Tom?" asked the relieved chief.

The doctor ran up to them. "Just one minute. Now that I've seen to your friend—I think he'll recover—I want to check your hands."

Marina's father looked with concern at his daughter's hands. They were not only vivid red with the early signs of frostbite, but also torn and bleeding. "What . . . ?" he began to inquire but was interrupted by the doctor.

"She bruised her hands as she tore pine boughs from a tree to shelter her friend. It must have been very painful. It's a good thing that the storm did not last any longer than it did."

"Oh Dad . . . Tom . . ." Marina choked, "even then, he kept trying to keep up my spirits."

As her father draped a thermal blanket over her shoulders, Marina realized the mistake she had made. She would never again take nature for granted. As they walked to the snowmobile, the brilliant glittering stars of the Arctic sky peered through a rift in the clouds.

RECALLING FACTS

Write the answers to the following questions on the lines provided. You may go back to the selection to find an answer.

1. Unlike Marina, Tom wants to take the last ski lift back to the lodge.
   a. Why does Tom want to use the lift?

   _____

   _____

   b. Why does Marina not want to go back on the lift?

   _____

   _____

   _____

2. What effect does the weather have on the search for the lost skiers?

   _____

   _____

3. At different times, Tom and Marina think the other does something foolish.
   a. What does Marina do that Tom thinks is foolish?

   _____

   _____

   b. What does Tom do that Marina thinks is foolish?

   _____

   _____

4. Draw a line to match each word with its meaning.

   sheaf   emerged

   scowled   grimaced

   materialized   bundle

Not all the questions about a selection are answered directly in the selection. For the following questions, you will have to figure out answers not directly stated in the selection. Write the answers to the questions on the lines provided.

1. The following statements are either fact or opinion. Fill in the space between the lines in front of each statement that expresses a fact.

‖ **a.** Mount Alyeska is in lower Alaska.

‖ **b.** The Arctic is more dangerous than Mount Alyeska.

‖ **c.** Marina is unable to locate the ski lift pylons.

2. a. How is Mount Alyeska similar to the Arctic? ———————————

———————————

   b. How is it different? ———————————

3. Is Tom more cautious than Marina? Explain. ———————————

———————————

———————————

———————————

———————————

4. Why is Tom so concerned when Marina takes off her glove?

———————————

5. Why do you think Tom agrees to go along with Marina's plan even though he sees that a storm is approaching?

———————————

———————————

6. What might Marina and Tom learn from the experience on the mountain?

———————————

———————————

SKILL FOCUS

A story's setting often provides the elements of conflict around which the plot develops.

1. The action in this story takes place in two separate places during a snowstorm.

   a. What are the two settings?

———————————

———————————

b. How does the action differ in each setting?

_____

_____

_____

c. In which setting does most of the action take place?

_____

d. What is the story's conflict?

_____

_____

e. How does this setting influence the conflict?

_____

f. How is the conflict resolved?

_____

2. How do the following details of setting affect the plot of the story?
   a. As Marina and Tom raced over the edge of the glacier field, the sunlight changed, clouds scudded across the sky, and snow began to fall. The blizzard had reduced visibility.

_____

_____

   b. To wipe her snow-caked eyebrows, Marina took off one of her stiff and clumsy gloves— and dropped it. The wind swept the glove down the slope. In an attempt to get it, Tom tumbled into a narrow ravine and was injured.

_____

_____

3. Consider the second setting in this story. Why do you think the author includes it?

_____

_____

_____

_____

4. Suppose the time and place of this story were different. How would a different setting affect the story?

_____

_____

_____

_____

▶ Real Life Connections Compare Mount Alyeska with your own geographic area. How are they the same? How are they different?

Reading a Flow Chart

Reading a Social Studies Selection

▶ **Background Information**

The state of Alaska is valued today for its natural resources, important location, and wilderness areas. Throughout much of its history, however, Alaska was exploited and neglected. The people who originally lived in this vast, beautiful region respected the land and lived in harmony with the animals. Russian trappers arrived in Alaska in 1784. Primarily interested in getting rich, these trappers hunted extensively with little regard for the future and slaughtered Alaska's wildlife. After the Russians, American trappers and traders came to Alaska. They also had little interest in conserving the natural resources. Later, the United States government ignored Alaska's needs as a developing region. Finally, in 1959, Alaska achieved statehood.

▶ **Skill Focus**

A **flow chart** shows the important stages, or steps, in a process. In a flow chart, a block or box represents each stage. Information in each block or box explains the stage represented. Connecting the boxes are arrows or lines that

1784 –1867
Russian fur traders establish and maintain the first white settlement in Alaska on Kodiak Island.

→

1867
United States purchases Alaska from Russia.

show the flow, or movement, from one stage to another.

Two stages in the history of Alaska are shown on the flow chart above.

The following questions will help you read a flow chart.
1. What process does the chart describe?
2. How does the chart show the order and movement of events?
3. What period of time does the chart cover?
4. How are the events on the chart related?

▶ **Word Clues**

When you read a word that you do not know, look for context clues to help you understand it. Context clues are words near the unknown word that make its meaning clearer. Read the sentence that follows.

Many of the native inhabitants were forced to provide the Russians with free labor; others died from the diseases that Russian traders spread among the <u>indigenous</u> population.

If you do not know the meaning of the word *indigenous,* the words *native, inhabitants,* and *population* can help you. You can figure out the meaning of *indigenous* by reading the details in the sentence. By doing so, you can infer, or figure out, that *indigenous* means "originally living in an area."

Use **detail** context clues to find the meanings of the three underlined words in the selection.

▶ **Strategy Tip**

Preview "Alaska's Struggle to Statehood" by reading the headings. As you read the selection, refer to the flow chart, which traces Alaska's history from settlement to statehood. If necessary, review the steps in the Skill Focus for reading a flow chart.

Alaska's Struggle to Statehood

January 3, 1959, was a time of celebration for the people of Alaska who had struggled long and hard for statehood. Nearly a century had passed since 1867, when the United States purchased Alaska from Russia. For many years, Alaska suffered from the neglect and prejudice of the "lower forty-eight." Statehood marked a new era of pride and privilege for Alaskan citizens.

The Russians Arrive in Alaska

The native people of Alaska—the Inuits and the Aleuts—lived for centuries in the Alaskan wilderness. They survived by hunting and fishing the plentiful Alaskan wildlife on the land and in the coastal waters.

In 1725, however, an event took place in far away Russia that forever changed the native Alaskans' way of life. In that year, Peter the Great, Czar of Russia, ordered a Danish-born officer in his navy named Vitus Bering to explore the North Pacific. Bering's mission was to see if Asia and North America were connected by land. Bering fulfilled this mission when his ships passed through a channel between Asia and North America, known today as the Bering Strait.

On a second voyage in 1741, Bering's party sighted the southeastern coast of Alaska and landed on Kayak Island in the Alexander Archipelago. When Bering's ship returned to Russia, it was loaded with the rich furs of sea otters. The value of these furs drew many Russian hunters and fur traders to Alaska. Not until 1784, however, did Russian fur traders establish the first settlement on Kodiak Island, in the Gulf of Alaska. By 1799, Russia established the Russian-American Fur Company.

The growth of the Russian fur trade brought little prosperity to Alaska's people. Many of the native inhabitants were forced to provide the Russians with free labor; others died from the diseases that Russian traders spread among the indigenous population.

At the same time, the growth of the Russian fur trade meant disaster for Alaska's fur-bearing animals. The seals and sea otters living in Alaskan waters were slaughtered by the millions, and their skins were wasted in dyeing.

Many were destroyed simply to keep the world price of furs high.

By 1820, the Russians, having failed to use the area's great natural wealth, were losing control of the Alaskan fur trade. Not only were the animals becoming scarce, but the United States and Britain had entered the fur trade. This competition was cutting into Russian profits. In 1824 and 1825, Russia signed treaties with the United States and Britain that drew the southern boundary of Russian territory in America at about latitude 54 degrees.

The United States Buys Alaska

By the 1850s, Russia, having lost interest in Alaska, wanted to abandon the area. Secretary of State William H. Seward saw an opportunity to buy Alaska for the United States. In 1867, he negotiated a treaty with the Russians to purchase Alaska for $7.2 million. At that price, Alaska sold for about two cents an acre.

Seward, a man of vision, understood that Alaska contained great wealth in its natural resources. Also committed to the expansion of the United States, he realized that the acquisition of Alaska would help the United States become a world power.

✔ Most Americans at the time thought Seward had been a fool to waste $7.2 million on an "icebox." Alaska was soon called Seward's Folly, Walrussia, Icebergia, and the Polar Bear Garden. The *New York Tribune* stated in an editorial, "We may make a treaty with Russia, but we cannot make a treaty with the North Wind or the Snow King." In short, most Americans, basing their opinions on ignorance and prejudice, thought that Alaska was a total wasteland of ice and snow.

Supporters of Seward, however, knew better. American whalers and seafarers were aware of the wealth in Alaska's waters. American scientists and explorers who had traveled to Alaska realized the potential of the country's natural resources. Several legislators supported Seward's belief that Alaska's location would help make the United States a stronger nation.

After months of debate, the U. S. Congress finally approved Seward's treaty. The American flag flew over Alaska, but little else happened.

For the next 17 years, the United States made no effort to provide Alaska with a government.

The Great Gold Rush

Alaska was largely ignored by the U.S. government until the wealth of its natural resources was realized. In the 1870s and 1880s, the salmon industry in Alaska became profitable; soon after, large canneries were built. Prospectors had also begun to find gold in Alaska's wilderness. By 1884, Congress set up a government for Alaska and gave it district status.

By the turn of the century, Alaska was in the headlines of newspapers across the United States. The great Gold Rush was on. Thousands of Americans hastened to Alaska to strike it rich. In only a few years, the population of Alaska swelled to ten times its original size. A few individuals became millionaires overnight. But many more remained as <u>impoverished</u> as they had been when they came to Alaska with nothing but dreams. Some died a harsh death, seeking riches that they never found.

The Gold Rush of 1897–1898 did much more for Alaska than make a few of its citizens rich. It drew national attention to the district and forced the U.S. government to provide it with more laws. By 1906, Alaska elected its first delegate to Congress. Although the delegate could not vote, he spoke for Alaskan interests in Congress.

✘ One of the most important influences on Alaska during this time was a U.S. judge named James Wickersham. He traveled throughout Alaska by dogsled or slow river steamer, bringing law and order to the district. Elected Alaska's delegate to Congress in 1908, Judge Wickersham pushed the Act of 1912 through Congress. This act gave Alaska an elected legislature and made it a U.S. territory. He served Alaska in Congress for seven terms and introduced the Alaska Statehood Bill as early as 1916. Because of his early support of statehood, he is known in Alaska as the state's first citizen.

World War II (1939–1945) greatly changed the United States' view of Alaska. The territory became an important military base in the war against Japan and the Axis powers. In 1942, the Alaska Highway was built, providing an artery for transporting military supplies. That same year, the Japanese occupied three Alaskan islands, the only part of North America to be invaded during the war. Alaska's <u>strategic</u> importance to the United States could no longer be ignored. Its geographic location was vital to the nation's defense. After World War II, Alaskans began to make serious attempts to win statehood.

Statehood at Last

✘ The people of Alaska wanted statehood for many reasons. As a territory, Alaska had a delegate to Congress who could only observe and speak, but not vote. Alaskan citizens could not vote for the president of the United States, even though the president appointed their territorial officials. Alaska also had little control over its own legislature, since it did not have the rights of a state.

Congress <u>repudiated</u> the Alaska Statehood Bill several times during the period between 1916 and 1957. Although pressures from the fishing industry and conservative senators blocked statehood votes for several years, both the House and the Senate finally approved Alaskan statehood in 1958. On the night of the Senate vote, jubilant Alaskans celebrated the victory that they had wanted for so long. They danced in the streets, set bonfires, and even dyed a river in Fairbanks gold. On January 3, 1959, President Dwight D. Eisenhower declared Alaska the forty-ninth state.

By 1898, prospectors were racing to Alaska. The two women in this photograph faced a hazardous journey over treacherous mountain passes. Their equipment had to be carried or hauled along.

Alaska: From Settlement to Statehood

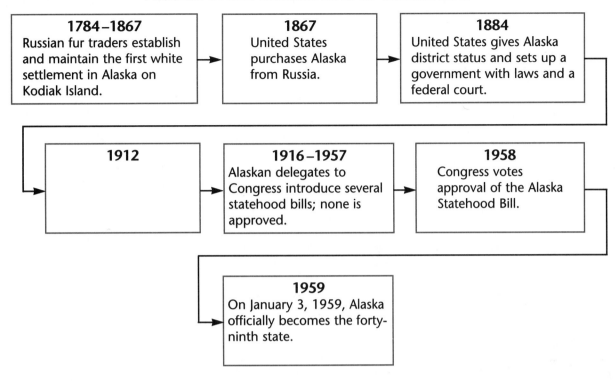

| **1784–1867**
Russian fur traders establish and maintain the first white settlement in Alaska on Kodiak Island. | **1867**
United States purchases Alaska from Russia. | **1884**
United States gives Alaska district status and sets up a government with laws and a federal court. |

| **1912** | **1916–1957**
Alaskan delegates to Congress introduce several statehood bills; none is approved. | **1958**
Congress votes approval of the Alaska Statehood Bill. |

| **1959**
On January 3, 1959, Alaska officially becomes the forty-ninth state. |

RECALLING FACTS

Write the answers to the following questions on the lines provided. You may go back to the selection to find an answer.

1. Write the cause for the effect stated below.

Cause —————————————————————————————

————————————————————————————————————

Effect Most Americans thought Seward was a fool to pay $7.2 million for Alaska.

2. Contrast the privileges of a state and a territory by filling in the blanks in the sets of descriptions below.

State elects voting members of Congress

Territory ————————————————————————————

State citizens vote in presidential elections

Territory ————————————————————————————

State controls its state legislature as one of its states' rights

Territory ————————————————————————————

3. Reread the two paragraphs in the selection that are marked with Xs. In each paragraph, underline the sentence that best states its main idea and then circle at least three details that support the main idea.

4. Complete each statement with the correct words below.

repudiated   strategic   impoverished

   a. The ————————— villagers appreciated the food and medical supplies donated by the Red Cross.

   b. The suspected robbers lied when they ————————— their story.

   c. The army base was built in a ————————— location on the coast.

INTERPRETING FACTS

Not all questions about a selection are answered directly in the selection. For the following questions, you will have to figure out answers not directly stated in the selection. Write the answers to the questions on the lines provided.

1. a. How did Americans view Seward's purchase of Alaska in 1867? Explain.

   _____

   _____

   b. How do Americans view Seward's purchase of Alaska today?

   _____

   _____

2. Reread the section titled "The United States Buys Alaska." Then, in the space below, write one example of how opinion was used to oppose the purchase of Alaska.

   _____

   _____

   _____

3. From 1867 to 1884, Alaska did not have a government or a set of laws. What effect did this neglect have on the region and its population?

   _____

   _____

4. What is the meaning of the phrase "lower forty-eight"?

   _____

5. Reread the paragraph with a check mark next to it. Write a sentence describing its main idea.

   _____

   _____

Use the selection and the flow chart on page 15 to answer the questions below.

1. What process does the flow chart describe? _____

_____

    a. With what event does the flow chart begin? _____

    b. With what event does the flow chart end? _____

    c. What event occurred in 1912? Write your answer in the appropriate box on the flow chart.

    d. How many stages does the flow chart show? _____

2. How does the flow chart show the order and movement of events?

_____

_____

3. What period of time does the flow chart cover? _____

    a. What period does the first stage on the flow chart cover? _____

    b. What event took place in 1867? _____

    c. During what period of time did Alaska attempt to achieve statehood? _____

    d. In what year did Congress approve the bill for Alaskan statehood? _____

4. How are the events on the chart related? _____

_____

    a. Which nation owned Alaska before the United States? _____

    b. During which period as a U.S. possession did Alaska not have a government?

    _____

    c. What status did Alaska have before it became a territory? _____

    d. What approval did Alaska need to become a state? _____

5. A flow chart shows a step-by-step process. Complete the statement below.

    After its **purchase** by the United States, Alaska became a **district** and then a _____

    before becoming a _____ .

6. How is a flow chart helpful in following the stages of a process?

_____

_____

_____

▶ **Real Life Connections** How would your daily life be affected if your area were taken over by foreign invaders?

Inferences

___ Reading a Science Selection ___

▶ Background Information

Although a large portion of Alaska has extremely cold winters, the state teems with wildlife. This selection discusses some interesting methods that animals employ for coping with Alaska's harsh winter.

▶ Skill Focus

Sometimes you can **infer**, or figure out, information that is not directly stated in a selection.

Read the following paragraph. Think about the inferences that you can make.

> Winter weather conditions sometimes cause a hard crust to form on deep snow. Wolves can often run over the crust without breaking through it. Heavier animals, such as deer, usually break through the crust and sink into the softer snow beneath it.

What happens to wolves and deer when deep snow forms a hard crust? Clues from the paragraph can help you make inferences about the answer to this question. The paragraph tells you two clues. First, wolves can often run over the crust without breaking through it. Second, deer usually break through the crust and sink into the softer snow beneath it.

Using these two clues, you can infer that deer cannot run as fast as wolves when deep snow forms a hard crust. A deer has to lift its legs out of deep snow with every step, while a wolf runs easily over the flat surface of the hard crust.

You could infer other things from this paragraph. If you know that deer have sharp hoofs, you could infer that their hoofs break through the crust more easily than the wolves' paws. If you know that wolves hunt deer, you could infer that wolves are more often successful in catching deer when deep snow forms a hard crust.

If you go through the following steps, you will find it easier to infer information.

1. Read the selection carefully.
2. Think about what you've read. Be sure that you understand the information that is stated in the selection.
3. Read again and look for clues to information not stated in the selection.
4. Combine the information stated in the selection with information that you already know. Use clues to help you make inferences.

▶ Word Clues

Read the sentences below. Look for context clues that explain the underlined word.

> In Alaska, as well as in other cold areas, low temperatures can put some animals in a <u>predicament</u>, or difficult situation.

If you do not know the meaning of the word *predicament,* the phrase *or difficult situation* can help you. The phrase *or difficult situation* is an appositive phrase. An appositive phrase explains a word coming before it and is set off by commas or dashes.

Use **appositive phrases** to find the meanings of the three underlined words in the selection.

▶ Strategy Tip

As you read "Hibernation," remember to use clues stated in the text, and information that you already know, to make inferences. Think about the inferences that you can make. Also think about relationships among the ideas stated in the selection.

Hibernation

1. In Alaska, as well as in other cold areas, low temperatures can put some animals in a predicament, or difficult situation. Even more serious than the cold itself is the lack of food that the cold causes. Directly or indirectly, all animals depend on plants for food, and plants either die or stop growing in extreme cold.

2. Animals deal with harsh weather conditions and with the lack of food in various ways. Some animals, including many birds, simply migrate to more hospitable places for the winter. Many insects die, but they leave hardy eggs in the ground, in water, or attached to rocks and trees to hatch the following spring. Still other animals, including frogs and some mammals, fatten up just before going into a deep sleeplike state called **hibernation**. The decreasing temperatures and shorter days of autumn help trigger hibernation.

Hibernation of a Cold-Blooded Animal

3. After feeding well all summer and autumn, the wood frog is fat and ready for hibernation. It crawls under a log or rock. At first, its body temperature is normal, that is, very close to the temperature of the air around it. Then, as the air temperature drops, so does the wood frog's body temperature. The frog's respiration, or breathing, slows to only a few breaths a minute. Its heartbeat also decreases. Its body is now working only hard enough to keep it alive. The

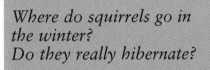

Where do squirrels go in the winter?
Do they really hibernate?

wood frog remains in this state until the temperatures warm up in the following spring. In this state of being only slightly alive, the frog can survive a normal winter with the food that its body can store. The rock or log protects it from being eaten at a time when it cannot protect itself.

4. Compared to most other frogs, the wood frog is a little unusual because it hibernates on land. Most frogs bury themselves in the mud at the bottom of a lake or pond when they hibernate. While hibernating, many frogs absorb the small amount of oxygen that they need through their thin, moist skin.

Hibernation of a Warm-Blooded Animal

5. Ground squirrels hibernate in underground burrows, where the air temperature in winter is warmer than the temperature above ground. However, even with the insulation of the ground, hibernation for the ground squirrel is more drastic, or extreme, than it is for a frog or other cold-blooded animal. The ground squirrel, like other warm-blooded animals, has a constant body temperature that is often much higher than its surroundings. So, as its body temperature approaches the air temperature in the burrow, it may descend, or fall, as much as 30 degrees Celsius. Scientists have found that some hibernating mammals go through a few test runs before they go fully into hibernation. The

Wood frog

Hibernating ground squirrel

Dormant bear

animal's temperature drops a few degrees, comes back to normal, then drops and returns to normal again.

6. Eventually, the ground squirrel goes into hibernation, and its body temperature drops to within a degree of the air temperature of its burrow. Now other changes occur. The ground squirrel's heartbeat, normally about 150 beats per minute, slows to 5 beats per minute. The animal's respiration also drops from about 200 breaths a minute to 4 or 5 breaths per minute. The ground squirrel's position during hibernation also helps it to survive the winter. It stays curled in a tight ball, with its head tucked between its hind feet and its tail over its head. This position helps the animal retain some of its body heat and thus stay alive. Should the animal's body temperature fall to near freezing, an internal monitor, or warning device, causes the animal to awaken and shiver violently. The shivering raises the squirrel's body temperature.

7. To survive hibernation, an animal must produce enough heat to keep its body from freezing. The fuel for heat production comes from the body fat stored by the animal during the summer and autumn. Scientists have found something interesting about the fat supplies of hibernators. Most animal fat is white, but the fat of hibernating animals is brown. Burning white fat produces some heat, but it also gives off chemical energy that can be used to fuel body functions. When brown fat is burned, however, most of it is turned into heat. During hibernation, much of an animal's body heat is lost to its surroundings. The heat produced by the fat keeps the animal alive.

Dormancy

8. When people think of hibernating animals, they usually think first of bears. Bears remain inactive during winter, and they may sleep and do without food for three months or more. Yet bears do not really hibernate. A characteristic of hibernation is that the animal's body temperature drops to nearly that of its surroundings. This drastic temperature drop does not occur in bears, nor do a bear's heart rate and breathing rate decrease as greatly as those of true hibernators. As a result, scientists prefer to call a bear's winter state **dormancy** rather than hibernation. If warm weather occurs during a bear's winter rest period, it may awaken and leave its den for a while to feed. Two other animals that go into winter dormancy are raccoons and skunks.

9. Near the end of the female bear's dormancy, usually in late January or February, her cubs are born. Most often born in pairs, the cubs are blind and almost helpless at birth, but they are able to nurse from their sleeping mother. By the time spring arrives, the cubs' eyes are open, and the young animals are large enough to follow their mother into the world outside the den.

RECALLING FACTS

Write the answers to the following questions on the lines provided. You may go back to the selection to find an answer.

1. What is hibernation?

_____

_____

2. What happens to an animal when it hibernates?

_____

_____

_____

3. What helps to trigger hibernation?

_____

_____

4. How is the hibernation of a wood frog different from the hibernation of most other frogs?

_____

_____

_____

5. How does the position of a hibernating ground squirrel help it to survive?

_____

_____

6. What happens to a hibernating ground squirrel if its temperature falls close to freezing? Why?

_____

_____

_____

7. Why are bears not considered true hibernators?

_____

_____

_____

_____

8. What do bears sometimes do during warm periods in winter?

_____

_____

9. How long can bears go without food in winter?

_____

_____

10. Complete each sentence with the correct word from the list below.

drastic   descend   monitor

   a. Temperatures sometimes quickly

   _____ during a blizzard.

   b. Quitting her job was a _____ move.

   c. The proper kind of _____ can tell of an approaching storm.

INTERPRETING FACTS

Not all the questions about a selection are answered directly in the selection. For the following questions, you will have to figure out answers not directly stated in the selection. Fill in the space between the lines next to the correct answer.

1. Unlike birds, ground squirrels don't migrate because
   - a. squirrels cannot travel great distances.
   - b. birds can store more brown fat than squirrels can store.
   - c. they can grow thick, warm feathers.

2. If a winter is very severe, and spring comes very late,
   - a. some animals that do not usually hibernate, such as raccoons, would go into a state of dormancy.
   - b. some hibernating animals might die from starvation.
   - c. some hibernating animals would become overheated and wake up.

3. Which characteristics would you expect a hibernating bat to have?
   - a. a body temperature far above its surroundings, a lowered heart rate, and stored brown fat
   - b. a body temperature near its surroundings, increased heart and breathing rates, and stored white fat
   - c. a body temperature near its surroundings, lowered heart and breathing rates, and stored brown fat

4. A person hiking in the remote woods during an unusually warm winter might
   - a. stumble upon a newly born bear cub.
   - b. encounter a bear looking for food.
   - a. see many deer, but not many raccoons or skunks.

For each of the paragraphs listed, decide which statement can be inferred. Put a check mark next to the statement or statements. On the lines that follow, write the phrase or sentence that has the clue you found. Then explain how you inferred the information.

Paragraph 1 (check one)

—— Animals that eat plants depend on them indirectly.

—— Animals that eat plants depend on other animals directly.

—— Animals that eat plant-eating animals depend on plants indirectly.

Clue ————————————————————————

————————————————————————

Explanation ————————————————————

————————————————————————

Paragraph 3 (check one)

—— A cold-blooded animal's temperature changes with the temperature of its surroundings.

—— A cold-blooded animal's temperature never varies.

—— A cold-blooded animal's temperature remains high all winter.

Clue ————————————————————————

————————————————————————

Explanation ————————————————————

————————————————————————

Paragraph 5 (check one)

—— A warm-blooded animal can control its body temperature only in summer.

—— Unless a warm-blooded animal is hibernating, its temperature does not change with the air temperature.

—— When temperatures are very low, a warm-blooded animal cannot hibernate because its body temperature changes.

Clue ————————————————————————

————————————————————————

Explanation ————————————————————

————————————————————————

Paragraph 6 (check two)

—— Some ground squirrels hibernate in the fall.

—— The heartbeats of hibernating and nonhibernating ground squirrels have been counted.

—— All hibernating animals have the same breathing rate.

—— A hibernating animal that does not have an internal temperature monitor could freeze to death.

Clue ——

——

Explanation ——————————————————————————————————

——

Clue ——

——

Explanation ——————————————————————————————————

——

Paragraph 7 (check one)

—— Hibernating animals need less chemical energy for body functions than nonhibernating animals.

—— Hibernating animals store less body fat than nonhibernating animals.

—— Animals have equal amounts of white fat and brown fat.

Clue ——

——

——

Explanation ——————————————————————————————————

——

——

Paragraph 8 (check one)

—— Bears sleep lightly during winter.

—— Bears do not have an internal temperature monitor.

—— The winter activity of bears seems to be controlled by outside temperature.

Clue ——

——

Explanation ——————————————————————————————————

——

▶ **Real Life Connections** Find out which animals in your geographic area truly hibernate for the winter.

Word Problems

Reading a Mathematics Selection

▶ **Background Information**

Word problems usually describe a situation, supply information about the situation, and ask you to use the information to solve a problem.

Some word problems are long and supply a lot of information. However, you don't always need all the information that you're given in order to solve the problem. Sometimes it's easier to solve a word problem when you know what information you *don't* need. That way, you don't lose time thinking about something that won't help you solve the problem anyway.

Some word problems supply too little information. These problems cannot be solved because you don't have all the facts that you need to arrive at an answer. Some of the skill involved in solving word problems is being able to recognize when you're not given enough information to solve the problem.

When solving a word problem, it helps to read the problem twice before you begin to work on it. The first time, read to get a general sense of the information you're being given and what

you're being asked to do. The second time, read to be sure that you understand the information and know what the question is. After carefully reading the problem, you'll understand it better. Once you have a clear sense of the problem, you're ready to start solving it.

▶ **Skill Focus**

Use the following five steps in solving word problems.

1. Read the problem. Be sure that you are familiar with all the words, especially the labels that are used with each number. Think about the question that is being asked. Try to picture in your mind the information that is given. Read the problem again carefully to be sure that you understand the question.
2. Decide how to find the answer. It may be helpful to write a sentence about each fact that is given in the problem. Is enough information given? Is extra information given? Decide which operations to use to solve the problem. If you decide that two operations are necessary, write two mathematical sentences, or equations.

3. Estimate the answer. Use rounded numbers to make an estimate for each equation.
4. Carry out the plan and solve each equation.
5. Reread the problem. Then write the complete answer. Is the answer logical? How close is it to your estimate?

▶ **Word Clues**

Look for key words for each operation necessary to solve a problem. Some phrases, such as *how much more,* show that you have to compare groups, or subtract. Some words, such as *total,* show that you have to combine groups, or add.

▶ **Strategy Tip**

After you read each problem in the following selection, decide whether the problem has extra information or not enough information to solve it. In the problems that you can solve, you will have to perform two mathematical operations.

Solving Word Problems

Alaska is the largest and most northern state in the United States. The word problems in the selection contain facts about Alaska.

Use the following five steps in solving word problems.
1. Read the problem.
2. Decide how to find the answer.
3. Estimate the answer.
4. Carry out the plan.
5. Reread the problem.

READ THE PROBLEM

In 1867, the United States purchased all 1,524,640 square kilometers of Alaska for $7,200,000. Just 102 years later, oil companies bought the leasing rights to only 6,760 square kilometers for $900,040,000, and they had to put up 20% of the price as a down payment. How much more than the original purchase price of Alaska was the down payment for the oil lease?

Read the problem again. Be sure that you know the label used with each number fact. Are there any words that you do not know? If so, look them up in a dictionary to find their meanings. What question does the problem ask? Often the last sentence of the problem asks the question: *How much more than the original purchase price of Alaska was the down payment for the oil lease?*

DECIDE HOW TO FIND THE ANSWER

The problem gives you many number facts, including dates, areas, costs, and a percentage. Written as separate sentences, the facts are as follows:
1. The United States bought Alaska in 1867.
2. The area of Alaska is 1,524,640 square kilometers.
3. The cost of Alaska was $7,200,000.
4. Oil leases were sold 102 years after 1867.
5. Leases covered 6,760 square kilometers.
6. The oil leases cost $900,040,000.
7. The down payment on the oil leases was 20% of the purchase price.

The problem gives enough facts for it to be solved. In fact, it gives more than enough information. When extra information is given, decide which facts are not needed and cross them out. In this problem, facts 1, 2, 4, and 5 are not necessary to answer the question.

You need to do two arithmetic operations to find the answer. First, you need to find out the size of the down payment. To do this, take 20% of the cost of the lease. To find a percentage of a number, you can change the percentage to a decimal and multiply. This is your equation. The letter d represents the amount of the down payment.

$$0.20 \times 900,040,000 = d$$

Second, you need to find how much more than Alaska's original purchase price the down payment was. The key phrase is *how much more.* When a problem asks "how much more," you must subtract. This is your equation:

$$d - 7,200,000 = a$$

In this equation, the letter d represents the down payment, the answer to the first operation. The letter a represents the difference between the down payment for the oil lease and the original purchase price of Alaska. This is the answer that you are seeking.

ESTIMATE THE ANSWER

Use rounded numbers to make an estimate. Round 900,040,000 to the nearest million and estimate.

$$0.20 \times 900,000,000 = 180,000,000$$

For the second operation, use the estimate from the first operation and round 7,200,000 to the nearest million.

$$180,000,000 - 7,000,000 = 173,000,000$$

Your estimate is $173,000,000.

CARRY OUT THE PLAN

Do the arithmetic.
First operation: $0.20 \times 900,040,000 = d$
$$180,008,000 = d$$
Second operation:
$$180,008,000 - 7,200,000 = a$$
$$172,808,000 = a$$

REREAD THE PROBLEM

After rereading the problem, write the complete answer. The down payment for the oil lease was $172,808,000 more than the original purchase price of Alaska. How close is your answer to your estimate? If your answer is not close to your estimate, start over.

Use the five steps to solve the next problem.

Read: In 1897, at the start of the Klondike Gold Rush, two ships sailed from Alaska to San Francisco within two days. One ship brought $400,000 in gold, and the other carried $700,000 in gold. The Klondike Gold Rush continued for about five years. What was the total dollar value of gold taken from the Klondike during those years?

Read the problem again. Try to picture the action of the problem. Make sure that you understand the sequence of events. What question does the problem ask? *What was the total dollar value of gold taken from the Klondike during those years?* Make sure that you know which years the problem refers to. The question is about the five years of the Klondike Gold Rush, which started in 1897.

Decide: The problem includes three number facts. The facts are as follows:

1. In 1897, one ship brought $400,000 in gold into San Francisco.
2. In 1897, another ship brought $700,000 in gold into San Francisco.
3. The Klondike Gold Rush continued for about five years.

The question cannot be answered by using just these facts. You know about only two shiploads of gold early in the Gold Rush. Obviously, much more gold was found later, or the gold rush would not have lasted five years. More information is needed to solve the problem.

If you decide that a word problem does not have enough information to answer the question, then you cannot go on to Step 3. At this point, you can only decide what facts you need. If you knew the total amount of gold for each of the five years, you could solve the problem.

In real-life situations, you might be able to find the information that you need in the library. If you found the missing information, you could complete Steps 3–5. In fact, you might even find that someone else has already worked out the answer to the problem.

RECALLING FACTS

Write the answers to the following questions on the lines provided. You may go back to the selection to find an answer.

1. What are the five steps used to solve word problems?

   a. _____

   b. _____

   c. _____

   d. _____

   e. _____

2. What should you do if you do not have enough information to solve a word problem?

   _____

   _____

3. How should you keep track of the number facts presented in a problem?

   _____

   _____

4. What should you do if you find that you have extra information in a problem?

   _____

   _____

5. If a problem contains the key phrase *how much more,* which operation do you most often use to solve the problem?

   _____

Not all the questions about a selection can be answered with information directly from the selection. For the following questions, you will have to figure out answers not directly stated in the selection. Write the answers on the lines provided.

1. One of the steps used in problem solving could be done in a different order from the one given. Which step is it?

   _____

   _____

2. Why do you think a word problem might have extra information?

   _____

   _____

   _____

3. In real-life situations, why might a problem not have enough information for you to solve it?

   _____

   _____

   _____

   _____

   _____

   _____

SKILL FOCUS

To solve these word problems, you have to use two mathematical operations. You may find it helpful to write a sentence for each number fact given. Use another sheet of paper for your sentences. Some problems have extra information. For these problems, cross out the facts that are not needed and solve the problem. Some problems do not give enough information. For these problems, describe the facts that are needed in the **Decide** space.

1. **Read:** The lowest temperature ever recorded in Alaska is –62°C. The highest temperature ever recorded in Alaska is 38°C. In January, the average low temperature in Anchorage is –14°C. In August, the average high is 18°C. Which is greater: the difference between the average low January temperature in Anchorage and the lowest temperature ever recorded in Alaska, or the difference between the average high August temperature in Anchorage and the highest temperature ever recorded in Alaska?

Decide: _____

Estimate: _____

Carry Out: _____

Reread: _____

_____

_____

2. **Read:** Alaska is wider from east to west than any other state. The part of the state called the Alaska Peninsula begins at Iliamna Lake and is about 885 kilometers long. The Aleutian Islands extend another 2,415 kilometers from the end of the peninsula. How far is it from one end of the state to the other?

Decide: _____

_____

Estimate: _____

Carry Out: _____

Reread: _____

3. **Read:** Many of the mountains in Alaska are volcanic, including the 3,083-meter Iliamna Peak that overlooks Cook Inlet, along with Redoubt Volcano. Redoubt Volcano is 25 meters taller than Iliamna Peak. Mount Katmai is 1,068 meters shorter than Iliamna Peak. How tall are Redoubt Volcano and Mount Katmai?

Decide: _____

Estimate: _____

Carry Out: _____

Reread: _____

4. **Read:** During the Klondike Gold Rush, a ship took miners to Skagway. From Skagway, the miners traveled on foot to Lake Bennett, where they took boats across the lake. The miners then continued another 800 kilometers to Dawson City. Eventually, a railway was built from Skagway. The railway ended 438 kilometers from Dawson City. How much of the distance from Skagway to Dawson City did the new rail line save?

Decide: _____

_____

Estimate: _____

Carry Out: _____

Reread: _____

5. **Read:** In area, Alaska is about one fifth the size of the rest of the United States. Yet Alaska does not have many people. Its population is about 550,000, compared with a total United States population of about 249,000,000. Approximately what would Alaska's population be if it were half as densely populated as the rest of the United States?

Decide: _____

Estimate: _____

Carry Out: _____

Reread: _____

_____

_____

Real Life Connections Use the five steps that you have learned in this lesson to complete an upcoming math assignment in school. On which step did you rely most heavily?

Syllables

To pronounce long words, divide the words into syllables. Then pronounce each syllable until you can say the whole word. There are several different ways of deciding how a word should be divided.

Guide 1: Compound Words

One of the easiest guides to use in dividing words is the one for a compound word. Because a compound word is made up of two words, it must have at least two syllables. Always divide a compound word into syllables by separating it between the two smaller words first. If one or both of the smaller words in a compound word have more than one syllable, it may be necessary to use another guide. However, you can pronounce most compound words if you divide them into two words.

newspaper   news paper

Read each of the following compound words. Divide the word into two syllables, writing each of the two smaller words separately on the line to the right of the compound word.

1. airport ———————
2. earthquake ———————
3. sailboat ———————
4. northwest ———————
5. horseback ———————
6. cardboard ———————

Guide 2: Words with Double Consonants

Another guide that you may use is for words with double consonants. Divide the word into two syllables between the two consonants and read each syllable.

current   cur rent

Use Guide 2 to divide the following words into syllables. Write each syllable separately on the line to the right of the word.

1. ribbon ———————
2. appeal ———————
3. arrange ———————
4. happen ———————
5. mammal ———————
6. message ———————

Guide 3: Words with a Prefix or Suffix

A prefix or suffix always has at least one sounded vowel. Therefore, a prefix or suffix always contains at least one syllable. You can divide a word that has a prefix or suffix between the prefix or suffix and the root word.

replace   re place   yearly   year ly

Divide each of the words below into two syllables between the prefix or suffix and the root word. Write each syllable separately on the line to the right of the word.

1. unfair ———————
2. healthy ———————
3. mistake ———————
4. foolish ———————
5. reread ———————
6. kindness ———————

Guide 4: Words with Two Consonants Between Two Sounded Vowels

A word that has two consonants between two sounded vowels is usually divided into syllables between the two consonants.

circus   cir cus

Divide each of the words below into two syllables by writing each syllable separately on the line to the right of the word.

1. basket ———————
2. system ———————
3. order ———————
4. absorb ———————
5. perhaps ———————
6. surface ———————

Guide 5: Words with One Consonant Between Two Sounded Vowels

Guide 5a: A word that has one consonant between two sounded vowels, with the first vowel long, is usually divided into syllables before the consonant.

famous   fa mous

Guide 5b: A word that has one consonant between two sounded vowels, with the first vowel short, is usually divided into syllables after the consonant.

solid   sol id

Say each of the words below to yourself. If the first vowel is long, use Guide 5a to divide it into two syllables. If the first vowel is short, use Guide 5b. Write each syllable separately on the line to the right of the word.

1. native ———————
2. damage ———————
3. credit ———————
4. second ———————
5. value ———————
6. total ———————

Guide 6: Words with Blends

The word *zebra* has two consonants between two sounded vowels. Because *br* is a consonant blend, you do not divide between the two consonants. The letters *br* should be treated as one consonant. When dividing the word *zebra* into syllables, use Guide 5a.

ze bra

If three consonants are in the middle of a word, two of the consonants may be a blend, or digraph. You treat the blend, or digraph, as one consonant. For example, *concrete* has a *cr* blend. You divide the word between the consonant and the blend.

con crete

Circle the blend (digraph) in each of the words below. Then divide the word into two syllables by writing each syllable separately on the line to the right of the word.

1. children ———————
2. country ———————
3. degree ———————
4. subtract ———————
5. secret ———————
6. complex ———————

When a word ends in *-le*, the *-le* and the consonant before it make up a syllable, as in *ti tle*.

Divide each of the words below into two syllables by writing each syllable separately on the line to the right of the word.

1. bundle ———————
2. trouble ———————
3. ankle ———————
4. candle ———————
5. cradle ———————
6. tremble ———————

Fact and Opinion

As you read books, newspapers, or magazines, you should be able to distinguish facts from opinions. A statement of **fact** is information that can be proven to be true. A statement of **opinion** is a personal belief or feeling.

As you read the following paragraphs, think about which statements are facts and which are opinions.

Alaska's Climate

When Secretary of State William H. Seward bought Alaska from Russia in 1867, many Americans thought that it was a land of nothing but snow and ice. Yet this region, which became the forty-ninth state in 1959, is not a frozen wasteland at all. It is a scenic state that is rich in fish, minerals, timber, and oil. Alaska, the largest of the 50 states, actually has a variety of climates.

Some areas of Alaska are very mild, considering the state's high northern latitude, or its closeness to the Arctic Circle. The southeastern and south-central parts of Alaska have a damp but mild climate, with cool summer temperatures averaging about 56°F. Rain, snow, and other precipitation is heavy in this region, with low clouds and long periods of drizzle. Only a duck would be happy spending time on Baranof Island, which receives about 221 inches of precipitation annually—more precipitation than any place in the continental United States.

Like southeastern Alaska, the climate of southwestern Alaska is mostly cool and wet throughout the year. Summer temperatures there are cooler than in the southeast, but winter temperatures are similar.

The interior of Alaska is characterized by warm summers with temperatures as high as 80°F and cold winters with temperatures dropping as low as –60°F. The Alaskan Arctic region has temperatures similar to those of the interior. The northernmost settlement of North America, Barrow, is located four degrees south of the Arctic Circle. Here the average high temperature in July is just 47°F and the average low temperature in January is –11°F.

Due to Alaska's high northern latitude, its summer days vary in length from its winter days considerably more than in any other region of the United States. At the Arctic Circle on December 21, the shortest day of the year, the sun appears at the horizon at noon and then quickly disappears. With so little sun seen from late November until late January, living in Barrow can be depressing. During the summer, however, the days are so long that Alaska, not Norway, should be called the land of the midnight sun. At the Arctic Circle on June 21, the longest day of the year, the sun never sets at all! After two gloomy winter months in almost total darkness, Barrow gets too much sunlight. From early May to early August, the sun does not set at all.

Read the following statements based on the selection. On the line before each statement, write *F* if it is a statement of fact or *O* if it is an opinion.

—— 1. Alaska is a scenic state.

—— 2. Baranof Island receives more precipitation than any place in the continental United States.

—— 3. Only a duck would be happy on Baranof Island.

—— 4. December 21 is the shortest day of the year.

—— 5. Very little sun is seen in Barrow from late November until late January.

—— 6. Barrow is depressing in the winter.

—— 7. Barrow gets too much sunlight from early May to early August.

—— 8. In July, Barrow has an average high temperature of 47°F.

Stated or Unstated Main Idea

When you read a chapter in a textbook, the main idea of each paragraph may be stated in a sentence. Sometimes, however, the main idea of a paragraph is not stated in one of the sentences. If so, you need to use the information in the paragraph to **infer**, or figure out, the main idea. To do so, you need to ask yourself what the paragraph is about.

Read the following paragraph about birds. Because the main idea is not stated, you need to infer the main idea.

During late autumn, you have probably noticed large flocks of birds filling the skies. The change of seasons prompts some birds to migrate south for the winter. Each autumn, migrating birds leave the colder regions or climates and migrate to warmer regions. Then, in the spring, these same birds migrate north.

Underline the phrase that tells what this paragraph is about.
a. the feeding habits of animals   **b.** the seasons of the year   **c.** the reasons birds migrate

If you chose answer **c**, you are correct. The paragraph tells why birds migrate. The following sentence is a main idea sentence for this paragraph.

Every autumn, as it gets colder, birds migrate to warmer climates.

Read the following selection about salmon.

The Migration of Salmon

1. Most fish live all their lives either in the saltwater of the ocean or in freshwater inland. A few species, such as salmon, are unique in that they live part-time in both kinds of water. Although born in freshwater streams, most salmon spend part of their lives in saltwater. To spawn, or lay and fertilize eggs, they return to the stream in which they hatched.

2. Alaskan salmon tend to spawn during the summer or autumn, after their journey up the Yukon River. The migration of salmon from the ocean to the streams of their birth may cover as much as 2,000 miles (3,200 kilometers) and take up to several months. High dams present obstacles. To help the salmon in their journey upstream, dam builders have constructed artificial waterfalls, called fish ladders. Upon returning to its birthplace, each female salmon lays from 2,000 to 10,000 eggs. These round jellylike eggs are laid in the gravel beds of shallow streams, where the males fertilize them. All five species of Pacific salmon spawn only once and die soon afterward. Thus, the migration from the ocean back to freshwater means death.

Salmon swimming upstream

3. After three or four months, when spring is near, the eggs hatch. For several weeks, the young salmon feeds on a part of the egg yolk that remains attached to its stomach. By the time it has eaten the "baby food" of the yolk sac, the young salmon is strong and active. Some species of salmon immediately struggle to

emerge from the shelter of the gravel and leave the freshwater for the ocean. Other salmon spend as much as three years in the freshwater before migrating downstream toward the ocean.

4. As the young salmon head toward the ocean, polluted water may kill many of them. They are swept over waterfalls and bruised on the rocks below. Many young salmon are eaten by predators. Because of the many dangers, only a small number of salmon reach the ocean after leaving the stream.

5. Zoologists know that most salmon return to spawn in the same stream in which they hatched. According to zoologists, adult salmon have the sensitivity to respond to the chemical characteristics of "their" streams. Once the salmon reach the coast, each adult seems able to locate its spawning stream by remembering its odor. It then follows the scent inland.

6. The Chinook salmon is the largest of the five species of Pacific salmon. When it is about four years old, this fish spends the summer migrating over 2,000 miles (3,200 kilometers) up the Yukon River. Although most Chinooks are about 3 feet (91 centimeters) long and weigh about 22 pounds (10 kilograms), some have been known to weigh as much as 100 pounds (45 kilograms).

7. Fresh from the ocean, the red Chinook becomes paler and more streaked as it travels upriver. The females become round and plump. The males become thin and their snouts become hooked. As the spawning season approaches, the salmon stop eating completely. They are able to live off fat that they have stored in their bodies when they lived in the ocean.

8. When males and females reach their birthplaces, they mate. In the shallow streambed, the mating fish dig a hole, deposit the eggs in the hole, fertilize the eggs there, and cover them with gravel. Soon after spawning, the exhausted parents die, never to return to the ocean.

9. Fish, particularly salmon and trout, are plentiful in the streams of southeastern Alaska. In fact, Alaska usually leads the states in the value of fish caught by the fishing industry. The state's annual fish catch is about $1.25 billion. The salmon catch alone makes up close to two-thirds of this figure. Fishing for salmon is one of the major industries of Alaska.

A. In paragraphs 1, 4, 5, 6, and 9, the main ideas are stated. Underline the main idea sentence in each of these paragraphs.

B. In paragraphs 2, 3, 7, and 8, the main ideas are not stated. For each of these paragraphs, do the following:

1. Underline one of the phrases below that tells what the paragraph is about.
2. Write a main idea sentence on the lines provided.

Paragraph 2

a. spawning in summer
b. migrating to lay and fertilize eggs
c. traveling for several months

_____
_____
_____

Paragraph 7

a. round and plump look
b. the spawning season
c. changes in salmon

_____
_____
_____

Paragraph 3

a. the eggs hatch in spring
b. the "baby food" of the yolk sac
c. from fertilized egg to adult salmon

_____
_____
_____

Paragraph 8

a. a one-way trip
b. shallow streambeds
c. fertilizing the egg

_____
_____
_____

Driver's License Application

In learning to drive a car, you are acquiring a skill that requires a great deal of ability, concentration, and responsibility. Before learning to drive, you must apply for a learner's permit. After learning to drive, you are ready to apply for a driver's license. A **driver's license application** is a written form that asks for information about yourself and about anything that will affect your ability to drive a car or other vehicle, such as a motorcycle or truck.

Study the application for a driver's license on the next page. Then answer the following questions.

A. Fill in the circle next to the phrase that correctly completes each sentence.

1. The address where the applicant receives mail is —————.
   - ○ not given on the application
   - ○ 481 Fairlawn Drive, Cedarhurst, N.Y.
   - ○ 62 Pinecrest Road, Floral Park, N.Y.
   - ○ 62 Pinecrest Road, Cedarhurst, N.Y.

2. The applicant didn't fill in section 8 on the form because —————.
   - ○ she has not changed her address
   - ○ her name has changed
   - ○ she has no physical disabilities or problems
   - ○ she doesn't presently have a driver's license

3. The sections on the right of the application that all applicants must fill out are —————.
   - ○ A and B   ○ B and D   ○ A and D   ○ C and D

4. If an applicant filled in section 8a on the left of the application to amend, or change, a current license, the reason may have been that the applicant —————.
   - ○ has a name change
   - ○ plans to drive a motorcycle
   - ○ has a new address
   - ○ now wears glasses

5. A licensed driver needs to fill in section C if he or she —————.
   - ○ has a license from another state
   - ○ has to wear eyeglasses
   - ○ is under 18 years old
   - ○ has ever been treated for a heart ailment

B. Use the information on the application to answer each question.

1. Who filled out the application? ———————————————————

2. In what year was she born? —————— How old is she now? ———————————

3. Has she had a license before? —————————— How do you know? ———————
   _____

4. Where is the only place that the applicant shouldn't print? —————————————

5. Why didn't the applicant have to fill out section A on the right of the application?
   _____

6. Why do you think a license requires the applicant's height and eye color?
   _____

7 Each state issues its own drivers' licenses. Explain what the reciprocity section on the application allows for. _____

_____

8. If the applicant had been convicted of a speeding violation, which question on the right would she have to answer yes? _____

MV-44T APPLICATION FOR DRIVER'S LICENSE
PLEASE PRINT WITH BLUE OR BLACK INK IN WHITE SPACES AT ARROWS

Last Name | First | Middle Initial
1 *Gillis* | *Elizabeth* | *J.*

NM

Date of Birth | Month | Day | Year | Sex
2 | *3* | *29* | *77* | M Ⓕ

BS

Number and Street (Mailing Address)
3 *62 Pinecrest Road*

ST

City or Town | State | ZIP Code
4 *Floral Park* | *New York* | *11005*

CT

County of Residence | Legal Address if different from Mailing Address
5 *Queens* | *481 Fairlawn Drive*

CY | *Cedarhurst, New York 11516*

Has your address changed since your last license was issued? ☐ Yes ☒ No
6

Height | Eyes | Med. or Psych. | Restriction Stamps
7 *5'6"* | *brn* |

PD

RS

If you are presently a licensed driver, enter the motorist identification number exactly as it appears on your license.
8

MI

TO AMEND YOUR LICENSE, FILL IN THIS SECTION

(a) For a change of name, print former name exactly as it appears on your present license.

Last Name | First | Middle Initial

(b) For a change of license type: FROM: _____

TO: _____

(c) To remove the following restriction _____

(d) To add the following restriction _____

(e) If other than above, give change and reason _____

ANSWER ALL QUESTIONS WHICH APPLY TO YOU

A *Learner's Permit or Original for persons under 18 years old.*
CONSENT OF PARENT OR GUARDIAN
I am the parent or guardian of the applicant named and I hereby consent to the issuance of a permit or license to said applicant.
Signature of Parent or Guardian _____
Relationship to Applicant _____ Date _____

B *All applicants must answer all questions in this section.*
For a duplicate, renewal or amended license, have the conditions mentioned below occurred <u>since</u> your last license was issued? For an original or reciprocity license, have the conditions mentioned <u>ever</u> occurred?

WRITE YES or NO

1. Have you had or been treated for a convulsive disorder, epilepsy, fainting or dizzy spells, or any condition which caused unconsciousness? . . . . *No*
2. Have you been treated for a heart ailment? . . . . *No*
3. Have you had any mental illness for which you have been confined to a public or private institution or hospital? . . . . *No*
4. Have you been confined to an institution or received medical treatment for alcoholism? . . . . *No*
5. Have you been confined to an institution or received treatment for narcotic addiction? . . . . *No*

If you answered "Yes" to any of the questions above, obtain Form MV-80 from your Motor Vehicle Issuing Office.

6. Have you been found guilty of ANY crime, offense, or traffic infraction (except parking violations), or forfeited bail in any court either in this state or elsewhere? . . . . *No*

If yes, give details below. If more space is needed use Form MV-22.
Date | Crime, Infraction, Offense | Court & Location

7. Are you currently on probation or parole as the result of a felony conviction or a misdemeanor conviction which has a sentence of one year or more? . . . . *No*
8. Do you have any physical disability or have you suffered the loss of, or the loss of the use of a leg, hand, foot, or eye? *No*
If yes, give details below.
9. Have you ever had a license, permit, or license privilege to operate a motor vehicle refused, suspended, revoked, or canceled, or an application for a driver's license denied in this state or elsewhere? . . . . *No*
If yes, give reasons below. If accident was involved, give date and place.
10. Have you operated a vehicle while under suspension or revocation? . . . . *No*
If yes, give the most recent date of such operation.
Give details, with dates, here:

C *Reciprocity*
I request that the road test be waived based on my possession of the following current out-of-state or military license; if not current, license is within one year of expiration date.
Type of License _____ This license was issued by the state of _____
Driver License No. _____ Expiration Date _____

D *All Licenses*
I, the undersigned, state that the information I have given in the foregoing application is true to the best of my knowledge and belief.
SIGN HERE **X** *Elizabeth J. Gillis* _____
Sign Name in Full — A married woman must use her own first name.

Lesson 9

Theme

Reading a Literature Selection

▶ **Background Information**

What bits and pieces of someone's past influence a person's important choices in life? How can childhood events affect a person's future? As the main character in this story relives some early events in her life, she discovers important things about herself.

▶ **Skill Focus**

Theme is the meaning or message in a work of literature. In many stories, the theme is directly stated by the narrator of the story or by one of the story's characters. In fables, the theme is directly stated at the end of the story.

In most stories, however, the author does not directly state the theme. Instead, the reader must think about the characters and plot to **infer**, or figure out, the theme.

Clues to the theme can be found throughout the story: in the title, in the dialogue, in the thoughts and actions of the main characters. Sometimes even the setting contributes to the theme. As you read, use these elements

as keys to inferring the theme.

Sometimes an author writes a story just to entertain. This kind of story may not have a theme. However, when an author uses a story to make a statement about life, society, or the world, the story does have a theme.

The following questions will help you infer a story's theme.

1. What does the title of the story mean? Why is it appropriate?
2. What does the dialogue reveal about the main character?
3. What does the main character learn about himself, herself, or others as the plot unfolds?
4. What is the story's theme?

▶ **Word Clues**

Read the sentences below. Look for context clues that explain the underlined word.

" . . . I do miss him and Mum when I'm here at school, but a month on that wretched, dust-ridden station of ours in the middle of the <u>outback</u> is

almost more than I can bear. The interior is so removed from everything. It really is frontier country . . . "

If you do not know the meaning of the word *outback,* the word *interior* in the sentence that follows can help you. The words *outback* and *interior* are synonyms. Outback is another name for the interior, or frontier country, of Australia. The word *outback* describes the vast, rugged inland regions of Australia.

Use **synonym** context clues to find the meanings of the three underlined words in the story.

▶ **Strategy Tip**

As you read " A Change on the Air," pay attention to the dialogue, the attitudes of the characters, and the personality contrasts among the characters. Use the questions in the Skill Focus to help you infer the theme of the story.

A Change on the Air

Kirsty and Celia meandered slowly around the perimeter of the opera house, its spectacular arches soaring above Sydney's wide harbor. The two young women had just finished their afternoon classes at the Animal Health Center. The day was the kind that would make anyone delight in life and relish the bustle of Sydney, perched on the east coast of the Australian continent. A fresh sea breeze had swept away the stifling heat and humidity. For a few hours at least, the air would be crisp and clear. The sky held a few cottony clouds, leaving the sea a clean azure. The bright sails of a score of small boats dotted the harbor while skyscrapers lining the bay gleamed in the sun.

"What are you doing for the holidays?" asked Kirsty idly.

"My parents are flying in from our station with my two brothers. I'm so eager to see them! They want to look for some new sheep-shearing equipment and do some shopping and see some plays—things they can't do back on the ranch. What are your plans?"

"Dad wants me home. I do miss him and Mum when I'm here at school, but a month on that wretched, dust-ridden station of ours in the middle of the outback is almost more than I can bear. The interior is so removed from everything. It really is frontier country. There's nothing for hundreds of miles but sheep, hills, and scrub trees. I don't think I was aware of the <u>isolation</u>, the remoteness of it all, until I came here to Sydney, but I learned quickly enough."

"I'm from a sheep station, too, remember," reminded Celia. "But, unlike you, I'm homesick. I'd just as soon my parents had me fly home for the holidays instead of their coming here. I've never figured out why you've turned on the outback so. I can't wait to get my degree, go home, and set up practice."

"That's the other thing!" exclaimed Kirsty. "After I graduate, I don't want to head for the back-of-beyond. I want to do research on animals here in Sydney. No country practice for me!"

"So," Celia said, "you'll practice in the city someday."

"Yes, but it will be difficult to convince Dad," said Kirsty. "It was difficult enough trying to persuade him to send me to veterinary school." Kirsty tossed a small flat stone at the water. It skipped twice before it slipped below the clear surface. "Now I know he'll want me to practice on the station. I don't know how to break it to him that I plan to practice here."

"My dad took some persuading, too. At first, he didn't understand what I saw in veterinary medicine, but when he realized that animals have always been a part of all our lives, he changed his mind," said Celia. "I can't wait to take care of them! I think of all those dear lambs in the spring . . . "

"Ugh!" groaned Kirsty. "You're so sentimental. It probably comes from growing up with the soft life," she teased. "After all, you may have lived on a station, but you had companions nearby. You even went to school!"

"Oh, Kirsty, you went to school, too!" Celia reminded her.

Kirsty almost exploded. "The School of the Air! Some school! Can you imagine what it was like getting your lessons in the mail and knowing your teacher and classmates only as voices on a two-way radio?"

"I suppose not," said Celia, "and you certainly haven't talked much about it."

"Well," said Kirsty, "Let's get a cup of tea and I'll tell you what it was like to go to school on the air."

The young women strode along the Sydney boulevards until they found a welcoming restaurant. They entered and were seated in a cozy booth. In the booth to their left were <u>boisterous</u> neighbors, a group of noisy students from a nearby secondary school in their uniforms with regulation blazers, striped ties, and knee socks.

On the other side sat a young man drawing on a pad of paper. From where she was sitting, Kirsty could see that his artwork was very <u>intricate</u>, very detailed. He seemed content to be by himself. Kirsty glanced at him and marveled how at that moment he seemed so self-sufficient, so quietly self-confident.

When the waitress brought their tea, Celia broke the silence. "So. The School of the Air—tell me what it's like."

"I loved it, and I hated it," said Kirsty. "I loved it because it was a lifeline to the outside. I could discuss my lessons with a teacher who cared about me. I could talk to other kids. I even had one particular chum. We became friends when our lessons were mixed up in the mail. One of my corrected lessons went to him, and one of his, to me. Our call letters were on the lessons, so we began talking to each other on the radio, sometimes for hours."

"Then why do you say you hated it?"

"It wasn't enough!" cried Kirsty impatiently. "Can you imagine what it's like never to meet your best friend? To know you're part of a class, but never to set eyes on your classmates? I think that's why I now want to live smack in the center of things, surrounded by people I can see as well as hear," she said.

The students in the booth on the left got up and departed, loudly discussing the chances of the local rugby team for a city championship. On the right, the young man had stopped his idle sketching. He was still, and his eyes were closed. He seemed to be concentrating on something. A distant sound, perhaps? The girls paid no attention.

The two friends became silent. Kirsty, staring at the flecks of tea suspended in her cup, hated to admit even to herself: As much as going home for vacation was hard, leaving again for school was even more difficult. By the end of her stay, she was used to the smell and taste of the dust in her throat and to the sharp tang of the sheep smell in her nostrils. She was used to the solitude and the vast crimson sunsets that spread across the sky. But being accustomed to something wasn't the same as liking it. Probably, she thought, she was feeling guilty about not wanting the same things that her parents wanted. Certainly she couldn't really love the outback!

Her reverie was broken by her friend. "Stop daydreaming, Kirsty, and tell me why you decided to become a veterinarian."

Kirsty replied, "That one's easy. My invisible friend, Jack—from the School of the Air—made me realize it. He had a dog, a dog that he adored. I heard about that silly creature every day on the wireless," she chuckled.

"Then one day it became ill. Its eyes were dull, and it was listless. Jack told me about it on the radio. He was so upset. I got out one of my dad's books on animal care. I read symptoms of various diseases to Jack over the air, and he checked them against the dog's symptoms. We spent every spare minute for two days trying to find out what was wrong. We didn't succeed; the dog died. Jack was desolate, so upset about his loss. We read poems and stories about dogs to each other over the radio as a sort of memorial service, the best we could do since Jack lived hundreds of miles away. I never met Jack," Kirsty continued slowly, "but he and his dog made me angry at how helpless we were in the outback. So, I decided to come to Sydney and study medicine. I realized how much I had wanted to save that dog, whatever its name was."

"Its nickname was Chuck," the young man in the booth said excitedly. "His real name was Prince Charles the Second . . ."

". . . because his ears stuck out!" shouted Kirsty gleefully. "You're Jack! You must be!"

"I couldn't help overhearing your voice, Kirsty! It was like a bolt from the blue. At first I couldn't figure out why your voice was so familiar! Then it came to me. Still, I wasn't

> *By the end of her stay, she was used to the smell and taste of the dust in her throat . . .*

sure until you started to talk about Chuck."

Kirsty was speechless. She sat motionless and stared at the blond, windburned young man. He wasn't what she had once pictured, but the voice was unmistakable. It hadn't changed much since their school days.

Jack went on, "I couldn't help thinking as I listened to you that you're not telling Celia the whole story. Remember," he prodded, "those poems about the outback and the sun setting across scarlet hills? It seems to me," he said, "that they were written by a budding veterinarian of my acquaintance."

Kirsty blushed. "I don't know what you're saying."

Jack said, "What I'm saying is that you seem to be denying your past, as if you are afraid to admit that you might actually like living in the outback. Maybe it isn't for you. Perhaps Sydney is where you belong, but shouldn't you give the outback a fair chance?"

Celia was nodding as Kirsty gazed at her new-found old chum.

"And just what makes you such an expert?" demanded Kirsty.

Calmly, Jack replied, "I've been through this all myself. I came to Sydney to get into broadcast journalism. But those tugs from home, from the outback, kept pulling at me. What was I to do? As you can guess, not many radio newscasts originate from the outback."

"So what did you do?" asked Kirsty.

"I ended up on the air after all. I live here in Sydney and have two jobs—one as a news reporter on the local radio station, and one as a teacher of current events on the School of the Air," was his response. "The school now broadcasts from a studio not far from here."

"You're really fortunate, Jack. Broadcasting is helping you keep in touch with the outback," responded Kirsty.

"That's right," said Celia. "Teaching on the air is your link to your past."

"Exactly," said Jack. "Oh, Kirsty, go home for the month and give the outback a chance. You don't have to give it up totally. You may discover it's more a part of you than you know."

"Well, maybe a week or two . . . I just don't know."

RECALLING FACTS

1. Describe the setting of this story.

_____

_____

2. Describe the setting of Kirsty's childhood.

_____

_____

3. a. How are Kirsty and Celia alike?

_____

_____

   b. How do they differ?

_____

_____

_____

4. What influenced Kirsty's decision to become a veterinarian?

_____

_____

5. Fill in the circle next to the word that correctly completes each sentence.

   a. The police had to calm the celebrating crowd when it became ———.
      ○ small ○ boisterous ○ desolate

   b. Hundreds of tiny connecting knots make lace very ———.
      ○ intricate ○ woven ○ wiry

   c. Great distances between stations in the outback contribute to its ———.
      ○ dustiness ○ isolation ○ schools

1. Identify each of the following statements as fact or opinion. Write *F* for fact or *O* for opinion.

    _____ The outback is wretched.

    _____ Much of the outback is isolated.

    _____ The outback is not the place for Kirsty.

2. Why do Kirsty and Celia feel so differently about returning to the outback?

    _____

    _____

3. Kirsty's father expects her to return to the outback after graduation. Do you think he expects too much of her? Explain.

    _____

    _____

    _____

4. Once Kirsty has her medical degree, will she practice in the outback or in the city? Use details from the story to support your answer.

    _____

    _____

5. What does the title "A Change on the Air" mean?

    _____

    _____

SKILL FOCUS

The following questions will help you to infer the story's theme.

1. Dialogue reveals that Kirsty faces two problems.
    a. What is the more immediate problem facing Kirsty?

    _____

    _____

    b. What is the long-term problem facing her?

    _____

    _____

    _____

2. In facing these problems, Kirsty learns about herself.
   a. At first, Kirsty thinks she hates the outback. Why?

   _____

   _____

   _____

   b. Later, Kirsty discovers her real feelings about the outback. What are they?

   _____

   _____

   _____

   c. How does Celia feel about returning to the outback? Explain.

   _____

   _____

   _____

   d. How does Jack feel about the outback? Explain.

   _____

   _____

   _____

   e. Kirsty talks with and listens to Celia and Jack. What is the effect of her conversations?

   _____

   _____

   _____

   f. Are Kirsty's problems resolved by the end of the story? Explain.

   _____

   _____

   _____

3. Kirsty, Celia, and Jack all come from the outback, which influences some of their decisions. Celia and Jack, who know how they feel about the outback, try to help Kirsty decide how she really feels. What is the author saying about decision making? What is the story's theme?

   _____

   _____

   _____

   _____

   _____

   _____

▶ **Real Life Connections** Would a School of the Air be popular in your community? Explain why or why not.

Comparing and Contrasting

___ Reading a Social Studies Selection ___

▶ Background Information

Australia is made up of tropical forests, rolling grasslands, and barren deserts. Climate and geography influence where and how its people live. As a result, the lives of city people and country people are as different as the landscapes they inhabit.

This selection compares and contrasts city and country living, the two main lifestyles of the Australian population. The four maps provide comparisons and contrasts about population distribution, agriculture, and average temperatures.

▶ Skill Focus

When reading, you will often need to compare or contrast people, places, or events. To **compare**, look for similarities. To **contrast**, look for differences.

One way to compare and contrast two or more topics is to put the similarities and differences into visual form. For instance, maps often use colors or shades of a color to highlight similarities and differences. Maps can thus compare or contrast different regions, or the same region at different times. Rainfall maps can show the amounts of rain in different regions at the same time of the year, or in the same region at different times. Population maps can show the number of people living in a particular region over a span of years, or in several regions at the same time.

In addition to maps, you can use information in the text to fully understand comparisons and contrasts. By studying the information presented in the text and on the maps, you will be able to draw conclusions about the information presented.

Use the following steps when looking for comparisons and contrasts.

1. Preview the maps before reading the selection. What is the purpose of each map? What do the colors represent?
2. Read the selection to understand the topics being compared and contrasted.
3. As you read, refer to the maps to locate the regions discussed in the text.
4. Finally, draw conclusions based on information in both the maps and the text.

▶ Word Clues

Read the sentence below. Look for context clues that explain the underlined word.

> For most people, Australia brings to mind images of kangaroos bounding across the open countryside and rugged people working on sheep <u>stations</u>, or ranches, in the isolated interior.

If you don't know the meaning of the word *stations*, the word following *or* can help you. In Australia, stations are ranches in the rugged inland regions of the country. The word *stations* is explained in an appositive phrase set off by a comma.

Use **appositive phrases** to find the meanings of the three underlined words in the selection.

▶ Strategy Tip

In reading textbooks, you may find words that are difficult to say. These words are often respelled to help you pronounce them. In this selection, *grazier* is respelled (GRAY zər). The pronunciation key on page 2 will help you.

Australia: Land of Contrasts

For most people, Australia brings to mind images of kangaroos bounding across the open countryside and rugged people working on sheep stations, or ranches, in the isolated interior. Yet, this stereotype describes only a part of Australia's diverse population and landscape. Australia is a vast country. The land is both fertile and barren; the people are both rural and urban.

European settlers began arriving in Australia over 200 years ago. They found the land already populated by aboriginal people whose ancestors had settled there 30,000 years earlier. Through the years, white settlers seized the most desirable land and drove its aboriginal inhabitants into remote areas of the country. Since 1976, however, the Australian government has been restoring some tribal lands to the aboriginal people. Today many of Australia's aboriginals remain in remote areas and prefer their traditional way of life. About half of the Aboriginal population lives in cities and towns.

Down Under

Australia lies between the Indian and South Pacific Oceans. Because the entire country is in the Southern Hemisphere, Australia is referred to as being "down under" the equator.

✗ ✗ Australia's geographic features divide it into three main regions. The Eastern Highlands extends from north to south along the east coast. Of the three regions, this area has the highest elevations, the greatest amount of rainfall, and the most forests and grasslands. Its natural attractions make it the most populated area as well. The Central Lowlands runs north to south through the eastern interior. The land is low and flat, with many rivers cutting through it. Covering the western two-thirds of the country is the Western Plateau. Much of this land is desert, but some areas support enough grass to graze livestock.

The Coastal Cities

✔ Of Australia's total population, about 89 percent live in cities and towns. Approximately 65 percent of the people live in cities in the southeastern coastal region, which has the best climate in the country. Because most of the Eastern Highlands lies away from the equator's Torrid Zone, the region has very cool temperatures and receives a plentiful amount of rainfall. The

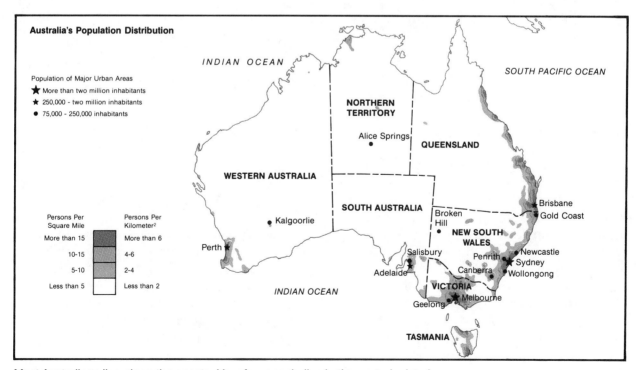

Australia's Population Distribution

Population of Major Urban Areas
★ More than two million inhabitants
★ 250,000 - two million inhabitants
● 75,000 - 250,000 inhabitants

Persons Per Square Mile	Persons Per Kilometer²
More than 15	More than 6
10-15	4-6
5-10	2-4
Less than 5	Less than 2

INDIAN OCEAN

SOUTH PACIFIC OCEAN

NORTHERN TERRITORY

Alice Springs

QUEENSLAND

WESTERN AUSTRALIA

SOUTH AUSTRALIA

Kalgoorlie

Perth

Broken Hill

Brisbane
Gold Coast

NEW SOUTH WALES

Salisbury

Adelaide

Penrith
Canberra

Newcastle
Sydney
Wollongong

INDIAN OCEAN

VICTORIA

Geelong   Melbourne

TASMANIA

Most Australians live along the coasts. Very few people live in the vast, dry interior.

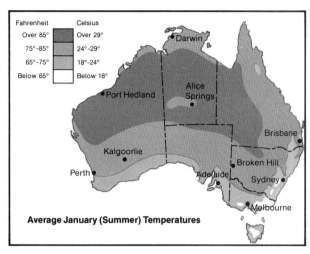

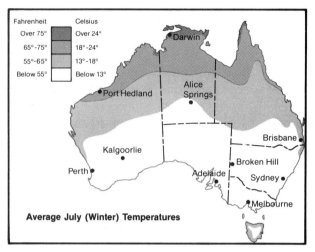

Because Australia lies south of the equator, its seasons are opposite those in the Northern Hemisphere.

environs, or areas surrounding the cities, display a luxuriant beauty rather than a scorched barrenness.

From the earliest years of settlement by Europeans, Australia's coastal cities have been important centers of life. Each state capital is the oldest settlement in the state. Dating back to the days when Australia was a British colony, these settlements were all founded at the mouths of rivers and situated on good harbors.

City Life

The downtown business areas of the cities are the old sections. Crowded with traffic, they share in the crime and pollution of all large cities. The people in Australia's cities are a typical mix of urban employees. The majority of Australians belong to the middle class and enjoy a high standard of living.

Australians do not live in urban high-rise apartments or condominiums. They prefer the suburbs outside the city centers, where the focus of their leisure time is the outdoors. The beautiful, sunny climate makes outdoor living attractive almost year-round. The suburbs were designed with plenty of open areas for cricket grounds, tennis courts, and parks. Because most of the cities are coastal, people can also go to the beaches on the weekends to swim or surf. An important aspect of the Australian national character is a love of sports, competition, and outdoor life.

> *Australians call the vast interior of their country—a huge stretch of dry grassland—the outback.*

The Isolated Interior

Australians call the vast interior of their country—a huge stretch of dry grassland—the outback. Only 11 percent of the people live in Australia's interior. The climate keeps it from being more populated. Many parts are semi-arid areas, with too little rainfall to support much plant or animal life.

Australia's rural economy is based on agriculture. Only five percent of the farmland is suited for growing crops. The land is used so efficiently, however, that Australian farmers are able to feed the nation and still export large amounts of wheat and sugar.

Most of the farmland in Australia is used for sheep and cattle grazing. Australia is the world's leading producer and exporter of wool. It is also a major producer of beef. Sheep and cattle roam over vast areas of grasslands. One underline{grazier} (GRAY zər), or station owner, may own up to 1,000 square miles (2,600 square kilometers) of grazing land.

Country Life

The Australian outback is renowned for its sprawling, open spaces and its stark, sunlit beauty. Vast distances isolate the people of the outback from those of the bustling, congested coastal cities. The lives of people in the outback center on their occupations as wheat farmers, cattle graziers, sheep shearers, or silver miners.

A typical homestead in the Australian

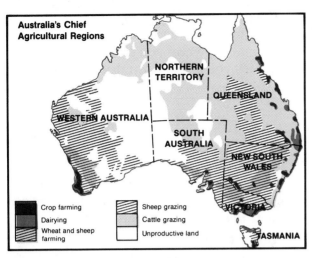

Australia's Chief Agricultural Regions

NORTHERN TERRITORY

QUEENSLAND

WESTERN AUSTRALIA

SOUTH AUSTRALIA

NEW SOUTH WALES

VICTORIA

TASMANIA

Crop farming
Dairying
Wheat and sheep farming
Sheep grazing
Cattle grazing
Unproductive land

Dry grassland covers most of the interior. In contrast, fertile cropland lies along the coastal areas.

outback is the sheep station. An individual station can cover thousands of square miles. The grazier lives in a big but modest house, usually surrounded by a wide porch. Nearby are sheep pens and a blacksmith shop, as well as housing for the sheep shearers (SHIR ərs) and other workers on the station.

✗ While life is isolated in the country, the standard of living there is as high as in the city. Rural homes have electricity, telephones, air conditioning, and other amenities, or conveniences, of modern life. Most graziers own light airplanes for convenient transportation.

The real hardships of country life come from drought and bush fires. A long, dry spell can mean death for livestock and financial ruin for station owners. A raging fire can spread across millions of acres of the outback, destroying everything in its path.

While life in Australia's outback is filled with its own kind of rewards and beauty, most Australians clearly prefer city life.

RECALLING FACTS

1. Reread the paragraph that has an X next to it. Underline the sentence that states its main idea.

2. Reread the paragraph in the selection marked with an XX. Underline the sentence that best states its main idea. Then circle three details that support the main idea.

3. Answer each question by writing *yes* or *no* on the line provided.
   a. Could a traffic controller find a job in a city and its environs? _____
   b. Would a pioneer be impressed by the amenities of modern living? _____
   c. Is a grazier the owner of an Australian sheep station? _____

INTERPRETING FACTS

1. If travelers wanted to go to the coolest part of Australia at the coolest time of year, where and when would they go? Circle the correct choices.

   west   south   January   July

2. Which state in Australia do you think has the highest population? Why?

   _____

   _____

3. Write one cause for the effect below.

Cause _____

_____

_____

_____

Effect Rather than live in apartments, most Australians own their own homes, with yards and gardens.

Lesson 10 *Comparing and contrasting* **45**

4. Read the facts listed below. Then write a generalization based on these facts.

Facts

a. Australia is the world's leading producer of wool.

b. Australia is a major exporter of beef.

c. Australia is rich in mineral resources.

Generalization

_____

_____

_____

_____

5. Only five percent of the land is suited for growing crops, but Australia exports large amounts of wheat and sugar. What does this tell you about Australian farmers?

_____

_____

_____

6. Read the paragraph with a check mark next to it. Then underline the phrase below that tells what the paragraph is about.

a. coastal towns and cities

b. densely populated cities

c. densely populated state capitals

SKILL FOCUS

Use both the selection and the maps to answer the following questions.

A. Use the population map on page 43 to answer the questions below.

l. a. Write the names of the two cities with the largest populations in Australia.

_____

b. Are these cities on the coast or in the interior? _____

2. a. Write the names of the three cities with populations of 250,000 to 2 million.

_____

b. Are these cities on the coast or in the interior? _____

3. a. Write the names of six of the cities with populations between 75,000 and 250,000.

_____

_____

b. Are most of these cities near the coast or in the interior? _____

4. a. Write the names of the three states or areas with the most people per square mile.

_____

b. In which parts of the country are they located? _____

5. Write the names of the state and the territory with the fewest people per square mile.

_____

B. Use the temperature maps on page 44 to complete the chart below. The first entry is done for you.

Average Temperatures				
City	**Coastal Interior (check one)**		**Average Summer Temperature**	**Average Winter Temperature**
Syndey	✔		65° – 75°F (18° – 24°C)	Below 55°F (13°C)
Adelaide				
Perth				
Broken Hill				
Kalgoorlie				
Alice Springs				

C. Compare the population map and average temperature maps.

1. Broken Hill, Kalgoorlie, Alice Springs, Sydney, Adelaide, and Perth all have the same average winter temperatures. Yet, Sydney, Adelaide, and Perth have larger populations than the other three cities. Why?

_____

_____

2. In one or two sentences, tell how temperature relates to population distribution in Australia.

_____

_____

D. Use the agricultural regions map on page 45 to answer the questions below.

1. Which two types of agriculture are found only near Australia's coast and along its rivers?

_____

2. Which type of agriculture is prevalent in the northeastern region and the central interior?

_____

3. Which two kinds of agriculture are found in the interior of New South Wales?

_____

4. In which part of the country is the greatest amount of unproductive land?

_____

E. Compare the population map and the agriculture map. What kind of agriculture is practiced in the least populated areas of the country? Explain.

_____

_____

▶ **Real Life Connections** How would your life be different if you lived in Australia? How would it be the same?

Cause and Effect

▬ Reading a Science Selection

▶ **Background Information**

In any given place, animals depend on plants and on other animals in complex feeding relationships. Scientists call these feeding relationships food chains. The concept of food chains helps scientists understand the causes and effects in feeding relationships. For example, if a plant that is eaten by a certain animal suddenly dies off, then the animals that depend on that plant will not have enough food and might also begin to die. Seeing fewer of these animals, scientists may realize that the plant is disappearing and may act faster to help save it. Similarly, if there is not enough rain, and very few new plants grow, scientists will know in advance that the animals that need this plant to survive may not have enough food. Knowing this before the animals start to die of starvation, scientists might be able to do something to help the animals that feed on the plant.

▶ **Skill Focus**

A cause is a reason, condition, or situation that makes an event happen. An

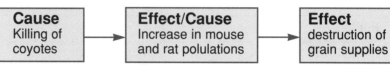

| **Cause** Killing of coyotes | → | **Effect/Cause** Increase in mouse and rat polulations | → | **Effect** destruction of grain supplies |

effect is the result of a cause. For example, an animal searches for food when it is hungry. The hunger is the cause, and the search for food is the effect.

One effect can have many causes. Similarly, one cause can produce many effects.

Sometimes an effect can be the cause of another effect, forming a chain of causes and effects. Read the following paragraph.

> In farming and ranching areas, people often kill coyotes. Without coyotes to keep their numbers under control, mouse and rat populations increase dramatically. These rodents then destroy grain supplies.

The increase in the mouse and rat populations, the effect of the first cause, is also the cause of the destruction of grain supplies. The diagram above shows this chain of causes and effects.

Causes and effects are often directly stated in textbooks. Sometimes, however, you have to infer, or figure out, a cause or an effect.

▶ **Word Clues**

Read the following sentences. Look for context clues to help you understand the underlined word.

> Unlike rabbits, which are herbivores, dingoes are very underlinedeffective hunters. Scientists think that dingoes turned many natural food chains upside down because they are such capable hunters.

If you don't know the meaning of the word *effective*, the word *capable* in the next sentence can help you. The words *effective* and *capable* are synonyms.

Use **synonym** context clues to find the meanings of the three underlined words in the selection.

▶ **Strategy Tip**

As you read "Food Chains," look for causes and effects. Try to understand how energy is passed through food chains and how the introduction of new animals can affect food chains. Study the diagrams, labels, and captions carefully.

Food Chains

Kangaroos jump from place to place, eating grass and shrubs. Foxes and dingoes lurk in the shadows, waiting for a joey, a baby kangaroo, to stray from its mother. Insects are also active, some feeding on the plants and some on other insects. Mouselike animals pounce on and devour any insects they can catch, while unusual-looking cats stalk the mice.

Although this scene takes place in Australia, the description could apply to the relationships in any area. You need only change the names of the organisms, that is, of the individual animals or plants. The description is that of an **ecosystem,** which is a group of organisms and their physical surroundings.

A basic fact of life is that all organisms must have energy, or food, to survive. Plants make their own food. They use the energy of sunlight to convert carbon dioxide and water to glucose and oxygen. The glucose is used as food or stored for later use. Because plants can make their own food, they are called **producers.**

Unlike plants, animals must get their food from other living things. Organisms that consume, or eat, other organisms are referred to as **consumers.** They are the second type of organisms in an ecosystem.

The third type of organisms in an ecosystem are the **decomposers.** Decomposers are organisms that break down organic material, which is dead plants and animals, and return it to the soil, where producers reuse it. This process is known as decay. Examples of such decomposers are one-celled organisms called bacteria and fungi, such as mushrooms.

Relationships in a Food Chain

Scientists use the concept of a **food chain** to describe the feeding relationships among organisms in an ecosystem. The first organism in a food chain is always a producer, usually a plant. The organism that eats the producer is called a **primary consumer.** Usually, a primary consumer is a **herbivore** (HUR bə vor), which is an animal that eats plants. The organism feeding on the primary consumer is a **secondary consumer.** The food chain can also contain higher levels. For example, a **tertiary consumer** eats a secondary consumer, and a **quaternary consumer** eats a tertiary consumer. Secondary,

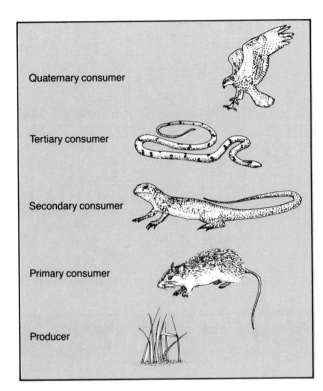

Figure 1. This diagram shows the feeding relationships in a food chain.

tertiary, and quaternary consumers are **carnivores** (KAR nə vorz) or **omnivores** (OM nə vorz). A carnivore is an animal that eats meat. An omnivore is an animal that eats both meat and plants. See Figure 1.

When one consumer feeds on another, the relationship is called a **predator–prey** relationship, regardless of which level consumers they are. The predator is the organism that eats, and the prey is the organism that is eaten. When a frog eats an insect, for example, the frog is the predator, and the insect is the prey. When a bird eats a frog, the bird is the predator, and the frog is the prey.

Most ecosystems contain many overlapping food chains. For example, birds, fish, and frogs may all eat insects. In turn, birds and raccoons may both eat frogs. These overlapping food chains are called **food webs.**

Energy Flow in a Food Chain

Food chains provide information about the flow of energy through an ecosystem. Look at the vertical arrows in the food chain shown in Figure 2. They point *from* the producers *to* the

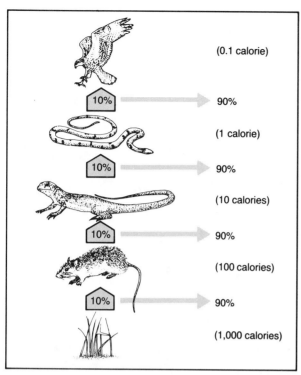

(0.1 calorie)

10% → 90%

(1 calorie)

10% → 90%

(10 calories)

10% → 90%

(100 calories)

10% → 90%

(1,000 calories)

Figure 2. This diagram shows the energy flow in a food chain.

consumers and *from* the prey consumers *to* the predator consumers.

Each arrow represents a loss of 90 percent of the energy from the level below it. For example, suppose that a herbivore eats plants that supply 1,000 calories of energy. As the herbivore carries on its life functions, it burns up 900 of the 1,000 calories. Only 100 calories of energy from the plants become part of the herbivore's body. These 100 calories are stored in body tissues.

When a secondary consumer eats the herbivore, it gets only 100 of the original 1,000 calories. The secondary consumer burns up 90 of these calories, and only 10 calories become part of its body. The tertiary consumer that preys on the secondary consumer gets only 10 of the original 1,000 calories, and so on up the food chain.

The energy loss in a food chain explains certain characteristics of ecosystems. For one thing, it explains why most ecosystems contain many producers but very few tertiary and quaternary consumers. In most food chains, the number of organisms at each level is in balance with all others. The predators keep the number of herbivores low enough for the producers to support the herbivores. This balance enables a healthy ecosystem to supply enough energy for all the organisms that it contains.

The food chain concept helps scientists to understand each organism's place in a natural ecosystem. When an organism that is not normally present in a food chain is brought in, or introduced, serious consequences can occur. In Australia, for instance, a rancher imported twelve pairs of European rabbits in 1859 as a source of food and skins. However, not many predators preyed on rabbits in Australia, and by 1950 an estimated one billion rabbits roamed the Australian countryside. This huge rabbit population destroyed great areas of grasslands, threatening both the sheep and cattle industries, as well as the food chains of the native organisms, such as the kangaroos. Scientists brought the rabbit population under control by introducing a viral disease of rabbits, myxomatosis (mik sə mə TOH sis), which killed more than 90 percent of the rabbits.

A similar situation occurred between 3,000 and 6,000 years ago. At that time, the Australian Aborigines introduced wild dogs, called dingoes, that had no natural predators. Unlike rabbits, which are herbivores, dingoes are very effective hunters. Scientists think that dingoes turned many natural food chains upside down because they are such capable hunters. Competition from dingoes may have been responsible for causing many native Australian animals, including the Tasmanian devil, to become extinct.

Symbiosis

Ecosystems include a particular kind of relationship called **symbiosis** (sim by OH sis), which means living together. Symbiosis often involves a special feeding relationship. One of the most unique relationships among all living things occurs between a fungus, which is a decomposer, and an alga, which is a producer. These two organisms live together in an extraordinary permanent bond. They form a discrete group of living things called **lichens** (LY kənz). In lichens, the fungus absorbs the water that the alga needs to make its own food. In turn, the fungus obtains food from the alga, which it uses to meet its needs for energy. This type of symbiosis, in which both organisms benefit, is called **mutualism.**

In a second type of symbiosis, known as **commensalism,** one organism benefits from the relationship, and the other neither benefits nor is harmed. An example is the relationship between two kinds of fish, the remora and the shark. A disk on top of the remora's head acts like a suction cup to attach the fish to the body of the shark. The remora benefits by getting transportation through the ocean and leftovers from the shark's meals. The shark is not harmed.

Possibly the most familiar type of symbiosis is **parasitism** (PAR ə sit izm). In this type of association, one organism, the parasite, gets its food from the living tissues of another organism, the host. While the parasite benefits, the host is harmed or even killed. Hookworms, tapeworms, and roundworms are examples of parasites. These worms live in the intestines of larger animals, where they feed on the nutrients that the animals have eaten. Parasites can severely weaken their hosts and sometimes kill them.

The study of food chains can provide a great deal of information about an ecosystem. This information can lead to insights into the interactions among organisms in their natural settings. These insights may eventually help scientists to recommend ways to restore ecosystems whose natural balance has been disturbed.

RECALLING FACTS

1. What are the three types of organisms in an ecosystem?

   _____

2. What is a primary consumer?

   _____

3. Name the type of food eaten by each of the following groups of animals: herbivore, carnivore, omnivore.

   _____

   _____

4. What is the name given to the relationship in which one consumer feeds on another?

   _____

5. How much energy is lost from one level of a food chain to the next higher level?

   _____

6. What caused the dramatic increase in the number of rabbits in Australia?

   _____

7. What kind of symbiosis does a lichen show?

   _____

8. Describe the relationship, called commensalism, between a remora and a shark.

   _____

   _____

   _____

9. How is parasitism different from other kinds of symbiosis?

   _____

   _____

   _____

10. What do parasitic worms get from their hosts?

    _____

11. Complete each sentence by filling in the correct word below.

    extinct   unique   discrete

    a. The car was unlike any other; it was truly _____.

    b. If a type of animal no longer exists, it is _____.

    c. Clearly separate and unconnected, the groups were _____.

Circle the letter next to each correct answer.

1. How much of the original energy in a food chain does a secondary consumer receive?
   a. 1/10th of it
   b. 1/100th of it
   c. 1/1000th of it

2. Which organism would be present in the smallest numbers in the following food chain?

   plants ⟶ mice ⟶ snakes ⟶ hawks

   a. plants
   b. mice
   c. snakes
   d. hawks

3. Which level in a food chain represents the greatest amount of available food energy?
   a. producers
   b. primary consumers
   c. secondary consumers
   d. tertiary consumers

4. The organisms listed below are involved in symbiotic relationships. Which organism could survive quite well, and probably better, without the relationship?
   a. the fungus in a lichen
   b. the remora in the shark-remora relationship
   c. the host of parasitic worms

5. How did the introduction of rabbits in Australia affect kangaroos?
   a. Rabbits ate young kangaroos.
   b. Rabbits competed with kangaroos for the same food.
   c. Rabbits became the main prey for kangaroo predators.

6. If all the insects suddenly disappeared from an ecosystem, which other organisms would be affected?
   a. frogs
   b. birds
   c. fish
   d. all of the above

A. To answer the following questions, you need to think about cause and effect patterns in food chains and feeding relationships. You may need to reread sections of the selection and review the diagrams. Use the headings to help locate information. For some of the questions, you will have to infer causes or effects.

1. What caused dingoes to upset food chains in Australia?

_____

_____

2. What would be the effect on a food chain if all the decomposers died?

_____

_____

_____

3. What would be the effect on a food chain if there were an increase in the number of producers?

_____

_____

_____

4. What could cause a natural decrease in the number of primary consumers in a food chain?

_____

5. What could cause an increase in the total amount of energy available in a food chain?

_____

6. What would be the effect on a food chain if there were a sudden rise in the number of quaternary consumers?

_____

_____

_____

_____

B. Three chains of causes and effects can be made from the events listed below. Together, these chains describe food chains. To show the chains, first draw an arrow from an event in the first column to an event in the second column. Then draw an arrow to the event in the third column.

Cause	Effect/Cause	Effect
Rabbits were introduced into Australia, but they had no natural predators.	Herbivores die.	Primary consumers decrease in number.
Drought kills many plants.	The rabbit population exploded.	Secondary consumers cannot get enough food.
Tertiary consumers die out.	Secondary consumers increase in number.	Huge grassland areas were destroyed.

▶ Real Life Connections What evidence of a food chain is visible in your geographic area? Which animals serve as predators? Which are prey?

Word Problems

— Reading a Mathematics Selection

▶ Background Information

Australia is both a continent and a nation. As the last continent to be explored by Europeans, it still seems new to many people. Because of its isolation, Australia is inhabited by life forms that are different from those found elsewhere in the world.

Word problems about Australia often reflect the differences between Australia and the other parts of the world. For example, a word problem about Australian animals might mention such creatures as the kangaroo, koala, or wombat, which are common in Australia but are found in few other places.

A word problem about Australian industry might include information about sheep and cattle ranching, wheat and sugar farming, or mining. Also, word problems about Australia might mention Aborigines (the native people of this huge country), sheep or cattle stations (*station* is the Australian term for *ranch*), the School of the Air (which uses two-way radio to educate children who live on remote stations), or the outback, which is uniquely Australian.

▶ Skill Focus

Use the following five steps in solving word problems.

1. Read the problem. Be sure that you are familiar with all the words used in the problem. Think about the question that is being asked. Try to picture the information given in the problem. Carefully read the problem again to be sure that you understand the question.

2. Decide how to find the answer. It may be helpful to write a sentence about each fact given in the problem. Often you may need to use two or more operations for a single problem. If, for example, three operations are involved, you need to write three equations to find the answer. Be sure to look for key words that can help you decide which operations to use in the equations.

3. Estimate the answer. Use rounded numbers to make an estimate for each equation.

4. Carry out the plan. Solve each equation.

5. Reread the problem. Then write the complete answer. Is the answer logical? How close is the answer to your estimate?

▶ Word Clues

Look for key words for each operation. The word *per*, for example, is often used with ratios. If your car gets 14 kilometers per liter of gas, the ratio of kilometers to liters is 14 to 1. The word *per* usually indicates that either multiplication or division should be used for part of a problem.

▶ Strategy Tip

When word problems require two or more operations, decide on the order in which to solve the parts of the problem. When you figure out how to get the answer to the first part, think about how to solve the next part, and so on.

Solving Word Problems

Use the following five steps to solve word problems.

1. Read the problem.
2. Decide how to find the answer.
3. Estimate the answer.
4. Carry out the plan.
5. Reread the problem.

READ THE PROBLEM

Australia is about the size of the continental United States, with an area of nearly 8,000,000 square kilometers. With an average population density of only 1.75 persons per square kilometer, most of the land is sparsely populated. In fact, sheep, an important product of Australia, outnumber people 18 to 1. A single sheep rancher in Australia cares for about 4,000 sheep. About how many sheep ranchers are there in Australia?

Read the problem again. Be sure that you know the label for each number in the problem. Are there any words that you do not know? If so, look them up in a dictionary to find their meanings. What question does the problem ask you to figure out? Often the question is asked in the last sentence at the end of the problem, as is the case in this problem: *About how many sheep ranchers are there in Australia?*

DECIDE HOW TO FIND THE ANSWER

The problem provides a number of facts about Australia. Written as separate sentences, the facts are as follows:

1. Australia's area is 8,000,000 square kilometers.
2. The population density is 1.75 persons per square kilometer.
3. There are 18 sheep for every person.
4. A single sheep rancher can take care of 4,000 sheep.

Be sure that you understand how the population density, the area, and the number of people are related. The density of 1.75 persons per square kilometer means that, on the average, 1.75 persons live in each square kilometer.

You have to do three arithmetic operations to find the answer. First, you must find the total number of people in Australia by multiplying the population density, by the area. Then, to find the total number of sheep, multiply the number of sheep per person by the number of persons. Finally, you need to divide the total number of sheep by the number of sheep that each rancher can take care of. Each of the operations can be shown as an equation. Let p be the number of people, s be the number of sheep, and r be the number of ranchers.

$$8,000,000 \times 1.75 = p$$

$$18 \times p = s$$

$$s \div 4,000 = r$$

ESTIMATE THE ANSWER

Before you estimate, think about the following questions:

1. Will the number of people be greater or less than the number of square kilometers?

2. Will the number of sheep be greater or less than the number of people?

3. Will the number of ranchers be greater or less than the number of sheep?

There should be more people than square kilometers, more sheep than people, and fewer ranchers than sheep. Also, because not all the people in Australia are sheep ranchers, a logical answer would show that there are fewer ranchers than people.

Once you have thought about these relationships, use rounded numbers to estimate the answer more closely.

$$8,000,000 \times 2 = 16,000,000$$

$$20 \times 16,000,000 = 320,000,000$$

$$320,000,000 \div 4,000 = 80,000$$

CARRY OUT THE PLAN

Do the arithmetic.

First operation:	$8{,}000{,}000 \times 1.75 = p$
	$14{,}000{,}000 = p$
Second operation:	$18 \times 14{,}000{,}000 = s$
	$252{,}000{,}000 = s$
Third operation:	$252{,}000{,}000 \div 4{,}000 = r$
	$63{,}000 = r$

REREAD THE PROBLEM

After rereading the problem, write the complete answer in sentence form: *There are about 63,000 sheep ranchers in Australia.*

While this number is lower than the estimate of about 80,000 ranchers, the difference is to be expected. In both of the multiplication equations, the numbers were rounded up, or increased. In the division equation, no further rounding took place. The estimate should therefore be greater than the actual number. Moreover, although there are 14,000,000 people in Australia, only 63,000 of them are sheep ranchers. This difference also tends to confirm the answer because it is logical that not all of the people are ranchers.

Use the five steps to solve the following problem.

Read: Some people tend to think that all the mammals in Australia are marsupials. Marsupials are pouched mammals that do not live in Europe and Asia and that are represented in the Americas only by opossums. Yet, when the European explorers reached Australia, there were 110 species of nonmarsupial mammals, mostly bats, rats, and mice. Furthermore, there were two species of egg-laying mammals. The rest of the 235 species of mammals in Australia, however, were marsupials, including many species of kangaroos. The various species of kangaroos made up 36.6% of the marsupials.

How many different species of kangaroos were there?

Make sure that you know what all the words mean. If you do not understand the words *mammal, marsupial,* or *species,* look them up in a dictionary.

Decide: The question asks for the number of kangaroo species. You know the percentage of all the marsupial species that kangaroos represented, but you do not know the total number of all marsupial species. To find that number, you need to subtract the number of nonmarsupial species from the total number of mammal species. You do not, however, know the number of nonmarsupial species. To find that information, you must add the various nonmarsupial species. This problem therefore requires three operations. The equations are as follows:

$$110 + 2 = n$$
$$235 - n = m$$
$$m \times 0.366 = k$$

Notice that you must change the percentage, 36.6%, to the decimal 0.366. In the first equation, 110 is the number of nonmarsupial species. The number 2 is the number of egg-laying species. The letter n stands for the total number of species of nonmarsupial mammals. The letter m stands for the total number of marsupial species. The letter k stands for the number of kangaroo species.

Estimate:

$$110 + 2 = \text{about } 110$$
$$235 - 110 = 125$$
$$120 \times \tfrac{1}{3} = 40$$

Carry Out:

$$110 + 2 = 112$$
$$235 - 112 = 123$$
$$123 \times 0.366 = 45.0 \text{ to the nearest tenth}$$

Reread: There were 45 species of kangaroos.

The number 45 is reasonably close to the estimate of 40.

RECALLING FACTS

1. Other than comparing the answer with your estimate, what commonsense test should you apply to your answer?

2. What must be done to the percentage before it can be used in an equation?

3. Which operation or operations does the word *per* in a problem indicate?

_____

_____

4. The first time you read a problem, what should you be sure of?

_____

_____

5. The second time you read a word problem, what should you be sure of?

_____

_____

6. If you read a problem and don't understand a word, what should you do?

_____

_____

INTERPRETING FACTS

1. The density of ants at a picnic is 50 per square meter, and the picnic area covers 16 square meters. How would you find the total number of ants?

_____

2. A problem asks how many people work at home in a community of 10,000 people. Would you estimate the answer to be greater or less than 10,000?

_____

3. To solve a problem, you need to multiply 7,893 by 5,648. You estimate the answer by rounding the numbers to 8,000 and 6,000. Would you expect the answer to the problem to be greater or less than the estimate?

_____

4. What would be a good way to estimate the answer to 6,000,000 divided by 2,000?

_____

SKILL FOCUS

To solve each of the word problems on this page and the next, you will need to use three mathematical operations.

1. Read Unlike the United States, Australia did not become independent from Britain in one step. The state of Victoria declared its independence in 1853. Three years later, South Australia also got self-government. It was another 55 years before Western Australia became independent. However, the Commonwealth of Australia had actually been declared 10 years before Western Australia became independent. In what year did Australia become a commonwealth?

Decide _____

Estimate _____

Carry Out _____

Reread _____

2. **Read** Immediately after World War II, 218,000 displaced Europeans were admitted to Australia. In the period from 1947 through 1971, the government aided 1,850,000 immigrants by paying for their passage, while an equal number came on their own. Of all the people who came, however, about 1,418,000 decided to return home or to travel elsewhere. By 1971, a fifth of all Australians were immigrants who had come to the country since the end of World War II. What was the total population of Australia in 1971?

Decide _____

_____

Estimate _____

_____

Carry Out _____

_____

Reread _____

3. **Read** At the beginning of the colony's history, the British sent a number of convicts to Australia. Each of the 11 ships that brought the first governor from Britain carried an average of 136 persons, half of whom were convicts. Many Australians claim descent from that original group of convicts. Before the practice stopped, a total of 160,000 convicts were sent to Australia by the British. What percentage of all the convicts were among the original settlers?

Decide _____

_____

Estimate _____

_____

Carry Out _____

_____

Reread _____

4. **Read** There was a gold rush in Australia in 1852. Huge nuggets were found near the surface of the earth. Among the biggest was the one called Welcome Stranger, which weighed 64 kilograms and was worth $50,000. Today, gold sells at about $13 a gram. How much more would the Welcome Stranger be worth today than when it was found? One kilogram equals 1,000 grams.

Decide _____

_____

Estimate _____

_____

Carry Out _____

_____

Reread _____

▶ **Real Life Connections** Name a problem that you are trying to solve at home or in school. Use the five steps in solving word problems to help you. Which step is the most helpful?

Syllables

When dividing words of three syllables, you use the same methods of deciding where to divide between syllables that you use with two-syllable words. The only difference is that you generally will have to use two different guides.

In dividing the word *suddenly,* for example, you use two different guides.

1. Divide between the double consonants: sud denly.
2. Divide between the root word and the suffix: sud den ly.

Following is a summary of some guides to help you divide words into syllables.

Guide 1. In a compound word, divide between the two smaller words.

Guide 2. In words with double consonants, divide between the double consonants.

Guide 3. In words with a prefix or suffix, divide between a root word and its prefix or suffix.

Guide 4. In words with two consonants between two sounded vowels, divide between the two consonants.

Guide 5a. In words with one consonant between two sounded vowels, with the first vowel long, you usually divide before the consonant.

Guide 5b. In words with one consonant between two sounded vowels, with the first vowel short, you usually divide after the consonant.

Guide 6. Do not divide between consonant blends or a consonant and *-le.* Consider a consonant blend as if it were one consonant.

Divide each of the words below into three syllables. Write the syllables separately on the line to the right of the word. Then write the numbers of the guides that you used on the line to the left of the word. The first answer is filled in for you.

1. __4, 5a__ estimate __es ti mate__
2. _____ triangle _____
3. _____ different _____
4. _____ arrangement _____
5. _____ dismantle _____
6. _____ fiberboard _____
7. _____ lumbering _____
8. _____ transparent _____
9. _____ diplomat _____
10. _____ candlelight _____
11. _____ bicycle _____
12. _____ brilliantly _____
13. _____ favorite _____

14. _____ liberty _____
15. _____ possessive _____
16. _____ dangerous _____
17. _____ hemorrhage _____
18. _____ inclusive _____
19. _____ calendar _____
20. _____ nectarine _____
21. _____ nonmember _____
22. _____ balloonist _____
23. _____ performance _____
24. _____ persimmon _____
25. _____ jewelry _____
26. _____ supervise _____

Prefixes

A **prefix** is a word part that is added to the beginning of a word to change its meaning. Eight prefixes and their meanings are given below.

Prefix	Meaning	Prefix	Meaning
de	undo	non	not
dis	away, apart	pre	before
mid	middle	sub	under, beneath
mis	wrong or badly	trans	over, across, or beyond

Read each word below and the meaning that follows it. Then write the correct prefix before each of the words.

1. _____interpret   to interpret wrongly

2. _____set   to set beforehand

3. _____placed   moved away from its place

4. _____atlantic   across the Atlantic

5. _____stop   not stopping

6. _____frost   to undo frost by thawing

7. _____marine   under the surface of the sea

8. _____behave   to behave badly

9. _____continental   across the continent

10. _____view   to view beforehand

11. _____resident   not a resident

12. _____air   middle of the air

13. _____code   to undo a code into understandable language

Use one of the words above to complete each sentence below.

1. _____ students at the state university pay higher fees.

2. Lindbergh made his _____ flight in *The Spirit of St. Louis*.

3. The storm _____ the telephone wires.

4. Mrs. Baron told Pat not to _____ while she was working.

5. Sponges are _____ animals.

6. It takes less time to cook a frozen chicken if you _____ it first.

7. The spy was able to _____ the secret message.

8. As long as the note is clear, Carol will not _____ it.

9. _____ the selection before you read it.

Lesson 15

Inferences

Sometimes you can **infer**, or figure out, information that is not stated directly in a selection. Read the following selection about tennis star Evonne Goolagong, using the facts to infer information.

Evonne Goolagong

1. On the day of the women's singles final match at Wimbledon, England, in 1971, something unusual happened. Evonne Goolagong, a 19-year-old part-Aboriginal tennis player from Australia, casually strolled onto the court. Spectators were amazed. In championship tennis matches, players are expected to look serious, nervous, and tense. Goolagong was smiling.

2. Evonne Goolagong upset her opponent, defending champion Margaret Court of Australia, in a match that lasted just over an hour. Goolagong's victory made her the youngest Wimbledon champion since 1962.

3. Goolagong was born and raised in the tiny, remote town of Barellan, in Australia's outback. The town's population in 1971 was 936 people, including the 10 members of the Goolagong family. The Goolagongs were the only family in Barellan with an Aboriginal heritage.

4. A month after her Wimbledon victory, Goolagong returned home to Barellan. Newspaper headlines declared, "Moochie Is Home!" The whole town came out to welcome her, and she led a parade through streets lined with banners proclaiming, "Welcome Evonne."

5. Goolagong's success at Wimbledon and other tennis championships in 1971 earned her top honors. The Associated Press named her the top woman athlete in the world that year, and her country named her Australian of the Year. In 1972, Goolagong lost her Wimbledon crown to Billie Jean King of the United States. But in 1980, Evonne Goolagong won the Wimbledon championship once again.

For each of the following paragraphs, put a check mark next to the statement that can be inferred from information in the paragraph. On the lines that follow, write the information given in the paragraph that has the clue that you found. Then explain how you inferred the information.

Paragraph 1 (check one)

_____ **a.** Evonne Goolagong had played at Wimbledon many times before.

_____ **b.** Spectators did not expect to see a 19-year-old part-Aboriginal tennis player.

_____ **c.** Evonne Goolagong was relaxed and at ease when she walked onto the court.

Clue _____

Explanation _____

Paragraph 4 (check one)

_____ **a.** Another person, named "Moochie," was also returning to Barellan that day.

_____ **b.** Evonne Goolagong's nickname at home was "Moochie."

_____ **c.** Barellan residents ignored Goolagong's Wimbledon victory.

Clue _____

Explanation _____

Main Idea and Supporting Details

Many paragraphs that you read are packed with information. Knowing how to find the main idea and the supporting details helps you understand the information in a paragraph. The **main idea** expresses the subject of a paragraph. A **major detail** is a supporting idea that is often an important example or a fact about the main idea. A paragraph usually contains more than one major detail.

Not all the details in a paragraph are major details. Paragraphs often contain details that are not important to the main idea. They are called **minor details**, and they explain or tell more about the major details.

The paragraph in the right column is about a group of animals found in Australia. The main idea and two major details in the paragraph are diagrammed to show how the major details support the main idea.

In the diagram, the sentences that explain the height and weight of kangaroos and the size of mice are not listed as major details. They are minor details that explain the major details.

Main Idea

> Marsupials are a varied group of mostly Australian mammals whose tiny young are nourished in a pouch on the mother's abdomen.

Major Details

> Kangaroos are the biggest marsupials.

> Marsupial "mice" are the smallest.

> Marsupials are a varied group of mostly Australian mammals whose tiny young are nourished in a pouch on the mother's abdomen. Kangaroos are the largest marsupials. Most stand about 6 feet (1.8 meters) tall and weigh about 100 pounds (45 kilograms). The so-called marsupial "mice" are the smallest marsupials. These marsupials grow to be the size of ordinary house mice.

As you read the following paragraphs, look for main ideas and major details.

Animals Indigenous to Australia

1. Antelope kangaroos roam the plains of northern Australia, while most wallaroos—kangaroos with stocky bodies and broad feet—live on dry, rocky hills. Eastern and western gray kangaroos inhabit mainly woodlands and forests. Red kangaroos make their homes in central Australia's deserts and dry grasslands. Scientists have studied red kangaroos more than any other species. Although called red, the males may be red or gray, and the females are blue-gray. These large species of kangaroos all live in the wild of Australia.

2. The koala is another marsupial. Because it looks like a teddy bear, it is sometimes called a koala bear. Koalas resemble teddy bears because they have soft, thick fur. They also have round ears and no tail. Like all marsupials, however, female koalas give birth to tiny, poorly developed

Mother and baby kangaroo

Mother and baby koala

offspring. The young koala spends its first six months growing in its mother's pouch and the next six months riding on her back.

3. A platypus is one of two mammals that lay eggs rather than give birth to live young. Along streams in Australia, the platypus digs a burrow, or a hole in the ground, and lives there alone. Some burrows are as long as 85 feet (26 meters). The furry brown platypus is sometimes called a duckbill because its wide, flat snout resembles the bill of a duck. Using this bill, the platypus scoops up shellfish, worms, and other small animals from the bottom of streams. Although platypuses were once endangered because they were hunted for their fur, laws have protected them since the 1920s.

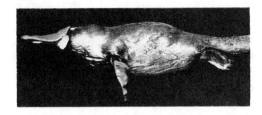

Platypus

Complete the diagram for each paragraph. In the box labeled "Main Idea," write the sentence that states the main idea as it appears in the paragraph. Use your own words for filling in the boxes labeled "Major Details."

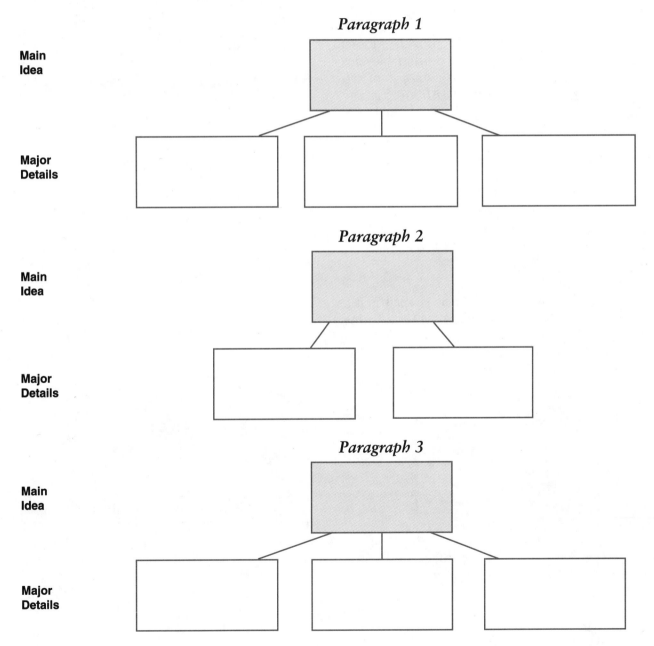

Paragraph 1

Main Idea

Major Details

Paragraph 2

Main Idea

Major Details

Paragraph 3

Main Idea

Major Details

Recognizing Street Signs

Street signs convey important messages quickly and clearly by using symbols, or pictures, and sometimes a few words. Many of these signs use symbols rather than words. These are known as international signs, because people of all languages throughout the world can understand them. In addition to a sign's symbols, its shape and color may help you recognize it.

The warning sign above probably looks familiar to you. It informs you that bicycles may be crossing the street. Warning signs tell you to be cautious, or careful. Although many warning signs are diamond shaped, an exception is the school-crossing sign.

The school-crossing sign is shaped like a pentagon, or five-sided figure. Most warning signs are yellow with black symbols. Some warning signs are orange. These signs alert you to road work.

Regulatory signs are black-and-white rectangles. The word *regulate* means "to control according to rules." Vertical regulatory signs give traffic laws, or rules. Compare the regulatory signs above.

Prohibitory signs tell you what you must not do. These square signs show a picture of what not to do, with a red circle around the picture and a red line drawn through it. The red line through the picture is the symbol for prohibiting, or forbidding, something. Can you figure out what the sign above means?

Some street signs give other messages, and therefore they have different shapes and colors. The familiar, red stop sign is an eight-sided figure, called an octagon. The round, yellow sign by railroad tracks is a railroad crossing sign. The X is a symbol for the word "crossing." Triangular signs are warnings for motorists.

A. Which sign conveys each of the messages listed below? Write the letter of the sign on the line next to the correct message.

1. _____ Handicapped Parking
2. _____ No Trucks Allowed
3. _____ Public Telephone
4. _____ Deer Crossing
5. _____ Hospital
6. _____ Slippery When Wet

a.

b.

c.

d.

e.

f.

B. Fill in the circle next to the phrase that correctly completes each sentence.

1. PED XING is a short way to write "pedestrian crossing." From looking at the sign, you can figure out that a pedestrian is a _____.
   ○ person in a car
   ○ person on foot
   ○ person in a wheelchair

2. This regulatory sign tells you that _____.
   ○ traffic must go this way only
   ○ two-way traffic ahead
   ○ all traffic must turn right

3. This regulatory sign indicates that _____.
   ○ only trucks are allowed on Baker Street
   ○ no trucks are allowed on Baker Street
   ○ trucks can go on Baker Street

4. This sign indicates a _____.
   ○ traffic signal ahead
   ○ stop
   ○ right turn on red, after stop

5. This prohibitory sign indicates _____.
   ○ a right turn lane
   ○ no right turn
   ○ a right turn on red, after stop

C. Complete each sentence by writing a word or phrase on the line provided.

1. Yellow, diamond-shaped street signs give _____.

2. The street sign that is a pentagon is a _____.

3. A sign to indicate that motorcycles are not allowed on a street has a picture of a

   _____ in a circle, with _____.

4. School-crossing signs at corners near schools warn _____ to slow down.

Reading a Literature Selection

▶ **Background Information**

In this story, a young man works very hard to equip himself for a hobby as a photographer, for which he then has very little time. To compensate, he works even harder to buy more equipment, hoping that it will make him a better photographer.

▶ **Skill Focus**

What the **main character** of a story is like as a person can be revealed in one or more of the following ways.

1. **Through the main character's actions and speech**
   For example: Catherine whirled on the dog following her and shouted, "I'm not at all scared of you! What do you think of that?"
2. **Through the main character's thoughts and feelings**
   For example: Catherine wondered how she would ever finish her homework in time. She knew that she wasn't good in French; she was sure that she would fail miserably.

3. **From the opinions and comments expressed about the main character by other characters**
   For example: Peter thought that Catherine was kind. "I'll never forget how thoughtful she was last year when I was in the hospital."

The following questions will help you understand the main character.

1. What does the main character do or say that reveals what he or she is like?
2. How do the main character's thoughts and feelings reveal his or her personality?
3. What do other characters say or feel about the main character?
4. What conclusions can you draw about the personality of the main character?

▶ **Word Clues**

Read the following sentences. Look for context clues that explain the underlined word.

To the casual observer or an <u>exasperated</u> father whose patience was being taxed to the limit, the room was a total wreck . . . . Angrily, he turned on his heel and disappeared down the stairs.

If you do not know the meaning of the word *exasperated*, the phrase, *whose patience was being taxed to the limit*, and the word *angrily* can help you. You can figure out the meaning of *exasperated* by reading the details in the same sentence. By doing so, you can infer that *exasperated* means "upset; annoyed; irritated; and irked."

Use **detail** context clues to find the meanings of the three underlined words in the selection.

▶ **Strategy Tip**

As you read "Getting Things in Focus," pay attention to clues about what the main character is like as a person. Ask yourself what his actions, speech, and thoughts reveal about his personality. Also, look for clues in the opinions and comments of the other characters in the story.

Getting Things in Focus

Mr. de Vega reached for the ringing wall phone. "Hello . . . well, I suppose this *is* the number for Carlos-Cleans-Up Home Maintenance. Just a moment, while I see if Carlos is in." Mr. de Vega grumbled as he climbed the stairs to his son's room. He pushed the door ajar and scanned the scene inside.

The room was extremely cluttered. Wrinkled clothes were piled on a chair. The desk was littered with cameras, cases, and lenses; photographs were strewn about the room. To the casual observer or to an exasperated father whose patience was being taxed to the limit, the room was a total wreck. It also looked unoccupied, but that impression was just an illusion. A closet door, labeled "Darkroom," opened, and a head emerged from the dim, red-lighted interior.

"Telephone call for Carlos-Cleans-Up! Obviously, the caller has never seen this room," shouted Mr. de Vega. Angrily, he turned on his heel and disappeared down the stairs.

Emerging from his darkroom, Carlos looked preoccupied and <u>disheveled</u>. He pushed a shock of hair off his forehead. One shoelace was untied, and his shirt tail hung out of his pants. He seemed tired, too. Staring after his father, he wondered if his dad would ever understand him. English professors don't make good business people, he thought. They have their heads in the clouds all the time. Carlos, on the other hand, knew the importance of a dollar and the work it took to earn one. Hadn't his businesses given him the money that he needed to buy his photographic equipment?

Impatiently, Carlos flew down the stairs. Maybe this was a new customer for his housecleaning service. He could fit this client in on Thursday afternoons, between babysitting for the Fosters and raking the Lloyds's leaves . . .

The next day, as Carlos was scanning the photography club's bulletin board, Teiko came by. Carlos liked Teiko, especially since she was also interested in photography. They had much in common.

"Carlos, are you going to the dance Friday night?" Teiko asked.

"Can't," said Carlos. "That's the night I work at the supermarket."

"Carlos! You're incredible! What are you doing to yourself? Every time I turn around, you have a new job."

"I need the money!" retorted Carlos.

"For what?" asked Teiko. "Besides, what good is all that money if you don't have any time for friends or fun?"

"I need the money for my photography." Carlos grew <u>animated</u>. His voice rose in pitch. He couldn't seem to stand still. "I saw a new zoom lens at Shapiro's Camera <u>Emporium</u> yesterday. That photo center is terrific. It has just about every kind of camera equipment available, including the lens I want. And it's on sale right now for only two hundred dollars."

"I thought you already had a zoom lens! As a matter of fact, I know you have one but you never use it," said Teiko.

"It's not as good as the new one," claimed Carlos. "This one works underwater!"

"Oh, Carlos," laughed Teiko. "You'd be hilariously funny if you weren't so serious. You never go swimming! You say you don't have the time! Why do you think you need so much fancy equipment anyway? You should listen to Mr. Shapiro. He's right, you know—it really is your own eye that has to focus on a good subject. As Mr. Shapiro says, 'The camera is just an instrument.' "

Carlos was growing irritated with Teiko. As a fellow photographer, she should know that the best photos are made with the best equipment. After all, the photo's subject isn't as important as what the equipment can do.

Carlos's eyes strayed to the bulletin board and fixed on a small announcement. A camera company was sponsoring a photo contest. First prize was $250. The prize money would be enough for the new lens, and it would also show Teiko.

"Are you entering the contest?" he asked Teiko, pretending just a casual interest.

"I will if I can take a good enough photo," replied Teiko. "I thought I'd stop by Shapiro's for an entry blank. Because you're so busy, shall I get one for you, too?" Teiko's smile had a bit of challenge in it.

"Of course." Carlos smiled.

Over the next week, Carlos took his cameras and equipment everywhere. He snapped away, busily interchanging lenses, switching light filters, trying close-ups and wide-angle shots. He wasn't always familiar with all the equipment. Teiko had been right.

> With all his special equipment, he knew he was bound to get a great shot.

A lot of it he didn't use much, but with all his special equipment, he knew he was bound to get a great shot.

Occasionally, he saw Teiko. She claimed that she hadn't yet taken a photo good enough to enter. "I haven't seen it yet," she told Carlos.

Carlos chuckled to himself over that remark. How could she expect to get a good shot? She didn't have a zoom lens or an electronic flash. She didn't even have a single-lens reflex camera.

Carlos finally selected his own entry—a rainy street scene taken with his new prism lens that broke the subject into repeating geometric images. He thought it was very artistic, even better than a similar scene on the cover of the instruction booklet for his prism lens.

Weeks went by after the contest closed. Carlos was almost run ragged with his many jobs. The more money he earned, the more he spent on equipment, which was beginning to crowd him out of his own room. Carlos's parents often threatened to have a competing cleaning service clean his room. "This place is a disaster area!" his mother said. "Why can't you take just a few minutes to clean it?"

"I just don't have the time, Mom," said Carlos.

One afternoon, the school PA system crackled to life: "Somerset High has two winners in the photo contest! The results are posted at Shapiro's Camera Emporium."

Ecstatic, Carlos almost floated into the camera store. Mr. Shapiro's gray head peered up from a slide case. "So, Carlos, you must have heard! You won third place in the contest. Quite an honor indeed!"

Carlos's heart sank. Only third place! The prize money might not be enough to buy the zoom lens, but it was still a prize.

"Where is Teiko?" asked Mr. Shapiro. "I assumed she came with you. That was quite a photo. The expression on that baby's face was priceless!"

Carlos's mind went blank. What was Mr. Shapiro talking about? What baby photo? Suddenly, the light dawned! Teiko was the winner, not he! He stammered something unintelligible and bolted out the door.

Outside, he stumbled into Teiko, the winner with her simple camera! He mumbled his congratulations.

Teiko placed a hand carefully on his arm and asked, "Do you have a minute?"

"I guess I've lots of time," sighed Carlos, resignedly.

"That's the first sensible thing you've said in eons," said Teiko. "For months, you haven't had time for your friends; you haven't even had time for yourself. You became a slave to your jobs and to that fancy equipment you kept purchasing."

"I know," answered Carlos. "I guess it took a photo contest and someone with an eye for the simple things to show me that I just didn't have my hobby in focus! The first thing I have to do is sell the equipment that I don't use. Then I'll . . ."

RECALLING FACTS

1. a. Is the narrator a character in the story?

   _____

   b. Does the narrator reveal the feelings and thoughts of the main character?

   _____

   c. Does the narrator reveal feelings and thoughts of other characters?

   _____

   d. Circle the point of view from which this story is told.

   first person   third person limited

2. How does Carlos's many jobs affect his life?

   _____

   _____

   _____

3. a. How are Carlos and Teiko alike?

   _____

   _____

   _____

   b. How are Carlos and Teiko different?

   _____

   _____

   _____

   _____

   _____

   _____

4. A story's climax marks the turning point in the plot. After the climax, the reader can predict the story's ending. Fill in the space between the lines next to the statement below that describes the climax in this story.

   || In Shapiro's Camera Emporium, Carlos learns that Teiko won first prize.

   || Carlos tells Teiko about the zoom lens that's on sale.

   || Carlos decides to sell his unused camera equipment.

5. Write the letter of the correct meaning on the line next to each word.

   _____ disheveled   a. lively

   _____ animated   b. a large store

   _____ emporium   c. messy

1. What effect does winning third place have on Carlos?

   _____

   _____

2. How does the contest change the relationship between Carlos and Teiko?

   _____

   _____

3. How do you think Carlos will pursue his hobby in the future?

   _____

   _____

4. Will Carlos continue to have so many jobs? Explain.

   _____

   _____

5. On the lines provided, complete the statement that Carlos is making at the end of the story.

   _____

   _____

6. Carlos and Teiko are both students with a similar hobby—photography. However, they use their time differently. What is the author saying about how one spends free time? What is the story's theme?

   _____

   _____

   _____

   _____

SKILL FOCUS

1. On the line next to each statement, write the letter of the technique that the author uses to reveal Carlos's personality. Then tell what the passage reveals about Carlos.

   a. through his actions and words

   b. through his thoughts and feelings

   c. through the opinions and comments of other characters

   _____ "Telephone call for Carlos-Cleans-Up! Obviously, the caller has never seen this room," shouted Mr. de Vega. Angrily, he turned on his heel and disappeared down the stairs.

_____ Carlos, on the other hand, knew the importance of a dollar and the work it took to earn one. Hadn't his businesses given him the money that he needed to buy his photographic equipment? . . . Maybe this was a new customer. . . . He could fit this client in on Thursday afternoons . . .

_____

_____

_____ Suddenly the light dawned! Teiko was the winner, not he! He stammered something unintelligible and bolted out the door. Outside, he stumbled into Teiko, the winner with her simple camera! He mumbled his congratulations.

_____

_____ "That's the first sensible thing you've said in eons," said Teiko. "For months, you haven't had time for your friends; you haven't even had time for yourself. You became a slave to your jobs . . ."

_____

_____

2. Write a paragraph of five sentences describing why and how Carlos changed by the end of the story.

_____

_____

_____

_____

_____

_____

_____

_____

_____

3. The reader knows the thoughts and feelings of only Carlos, the main character. The reader does not know what Teiko thinks or feels. Instead, the reader learns about Teiko only by what she says and does and by what Carlos thinks of her.
   a. What do Teiko's speech and actions tell you about her?

_____

_____

   b. What do Carlos's thoughts tell you about Teiko?

_____

_____

▶ Real Life Connections Do you agree or disagree with Carlos that the best photographs are made with the best equipment? Tell why.

Using Statistics

__ Reading a Social Studies Selection __

▶ Background Information

This selection gives statistics about changes in the U.S. labor force from the 1940s to 1990s.

▶ Skill Focus

Statistics are numerical facts, frequently presented on tables, graphs, and maps. Statistics help people study and understand **quantitative information**—that is, information about how many or how much. Because statistics can show an important trend, or pattern, people often use them to draw conclusions or make predictions.

When using statistics that accompany a text, it is important to know if the statistics are approximate or exact. When exact figures are not available, approximate numbers are used.

Statistics present only a partial picture of what happened or is happening. For example, statistics about the labor force cannot show all the reasons for an increase or a decrease in the number of people in blue-collar jobs. Additional information is often necessary for you to use and interpret statistics effectively.

Use the following steps when reading and interpreting statistics on graphs.

1. **Identify the type of statistical information given.**
   The graph's title and labels tell what type of information is provided.
2. **Practice reading the statistics.** Statistics often involve very large numbers. Often not all place values are shown. For example, the number 50 could stand for 50,000,000. Read the key to figure out the numerical value of each number.
3. **Look for relationships between numbers.** By comparing numbers that show similar kinds of information, you can infer relationships between different time periods and groups.
4. **Use the statistics and accompanying text to draw conclusions about the information.** You can use both statistics and information in the text to draw your own conclusions and to evaluate the author's conclusions.
5. **Use statistics to make projections or forecasts.** Interpret both the statistics and the information in the text to make predictions about future trends.

▶ Word Clues

Read the sentence below. Look for context clues that explain the underlined term.

> The labor force is the part of a nation's population that works for pay or that is looking for a paying job.

If you do not know the meaning of the term *labor force,* the rest of the sentence tells what it means. The meaning of a new word or phrase can often be found elsewhere in the text, before or after the new word or phrase.

Use **definition** context clues to find the meanings of the three underlined words or phrases in the selection.

▶ Strategy Tip

Before reading, preview the selection by studying the graphs. As you read, use the information in the text to interpret the statistics on the graphs and to draw conclusions about the changes that have occurred in the labor force.

Trends in the Labor Force: 1940s–1990s

The labor force is the part of a nation's population that works for pay or that is looking for a paying job. In 1800, the United States had about 2 million people in its labor force. Most of them worked on farms; most of them were men. In 1993, about 130 million Americans were in the labor force. The majority of these workers were found in large cities; 46 percent of them were women.

New Kinds of Jobs

In the twentieth century, the U.S. labor force has undergone many changes. One of the most significant of these changes is in the decline in the number of <u>blue-collar</u> jobs and the rise in the number of <u>white-collar</u> jobs.

A blue-collar job involves manual or outdoor labor. Blue-collar workers include factory assemblers, riveters, and welders; carpenters, plumbers, mechanics, and painters; construction workers, stevedores, and truck drivers. Although the number of blue-collar workers increased in the twentieth century, the future will see a declining need for such workers. Some of their jobs will be taken over by advanced automated and computerized machinery that can do certain blue-collar jobs more quickly and efficiently than people can.

In contrast, a white-collar job involves work that is not chiefly manual. For example, white-collar workers include accountants, engineers, teachers, lawyers, and sales personnel. In 1900, white-collar workers made up about 20 percent of the labor force; today, 67 percent of all American wage earners hold white-collar jobs. Advances in computer technology have created many new white-collar jobs, such as those in programming and information processing. These changes will continue to dramatically change the nature of existing jobs.

The Rise of Women in the Labor Force

Until 1940, the opportunities for women to hold jobs were limited. Prejudice and discrimination against women forced many of them to find employment as teachers, nurses, and secretaries. In 1940, women held only 25 percent of the jobs.

✗ World War II—1941 through 1945—brought about many changes in the labor force. Men were drafted to serve in the armed forces of the United States. At the same time, the country needed labor to keep factories running at full production to support the war effort. As a result, women were suddenly needed and hired even though they had been previously excluded from such jobs. Women not only repaired airplanes and land vehicles, but they also drove trucks, operated radios and machinery, and did clerical work.

Working Women in the Labor Force

Women as a Percent of Total Labor Force

1940	WWII	1950	1960	1970	1980	1990
25%	35%	30%	33%	38%	43%	45%

SOURCE U.S. Labor Department

During the war years, the percentage of women in the labor force rose from 25 percent to 35 percent. Married women, many of whose husbands were in the armed forces, made up the greatest number of new women workers. In 1940, fewer than half of working women were single, but by 1945 a majority of women workers were married. By the end of the war, one out of every three workers in industry and business was a woman.

The Postwar Years

After the war, the men who returned from the armed forces went back to the same jobs they had held prior to the war. As a result, many women lost their wartime jobs. However, not all the women who had held jobs for the first time returned to their former roles as homemakers. Women had proved they could do these jobs well. As a result, the traditional barriers against the employment of women in such industries as steel and shipbuilding started to disappear. As the postwar prosperity continued, new positions became available for the returning men and for the many women workers now in the labor force.

Many women found that they enjoyed not only employment outside their homes but also the benefits of paying jobs. Many women were beginning to see work as a permanent part of their lives. By earning their own income, they became less dependent and more self-sufficient. Their independence gave them new choices and made them aware of a wider range of roles available to them.

> In general, families in the 1970s, '80s, and '90s have had fewer children than families of earlier generations.

The economic prosperity that followed the war also enabled many young couples to purchase houses. Many began raising families. Some women chose to stay at home to raise their children, while their husbands went to work. As a result, the percentage of women workers declined after the war, but it never went as low as it was in 1940.

The 1960s to the 1990s

The 1960s saw the beginning of many social changes in the United States, some of which were brought about by the women's liberation movement. Many women became keenly aware that they were often paid less than men for doing the same kind of work and that they were not promoted as easily or quickly as men. They also found that discrimination in jobs and in education still existed.

As a result of women's protests, equal opportunity laws were passed that made discrimination against women in jobs and education illegal. This legislation opened up to women many business and professional positions that had previously been closed to them.

The 1970s were troubled by ongoing inflation. For many couples, the high standard of living, combined with the high cost of living, made it necessary for both the husband and wife to hold paying jobs. Out of necessity, many married women, college-educated in the 1960s, joined the labor force in the new and emerging white-collar jobs of the time. The two-income family became a way of life that continues today. Many divorced, separated, or widowed women also entered the labor force in the 1970s.

The 1980s brought more changes. Many businesses were not able to survive the recession of that period. The auto, steel, textile, and clothing industries, for example, suffered at the hands of increased competition from foreign countries. As a result, many plants and factories closed; the number of available jobs sharply declined. Because of the recession more mothers of young children entered the labor force.

✔ In general, families in the 1970s, '80s, and '90s have had fewer children than families of earlier generations did. There has therefore been less need for women to stay at home for many years to care for young children, and more married women have been free to join the job market.

Coupled with the trend toward two-income families, the labor force participation of married women with young children has risen dramatically since the 1960s. About 19 percent of mothers with children below age 6 were employed in 1960. In 1993, almost 60 percent were employed.

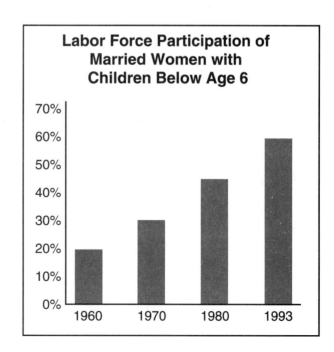

Labor Force Participation of Married Women with Children Below Age 6

A Changing Labor Force

Shifts from blue-collar to white-collar jobs and the increase in the number of working women continue to affect the labor force. These trends are altering the relationship between workers and their work, and people require new skills and training in all fields of employment. Nevertheless, today's workers—whether blue-collar or white-collar, male or female—earn higher wages, work shorter hours, and receive more fringe benefits than workers prior to the 1940s.

RECALLING FACTS

1. Decide if each statement is true or false. Write *true* or *false* on the line provided.

   _____ a. In 1800, most of the labor force worked on farms.

   _____ b. White-collar workers do manual labor in factories and on construction sites.

   _____ c. In World War II, married women made up the greatest number of new women workers.

   _____ d. In 1993, women held 46 percent of the jobs in the labor force.

2. How are blue-collar jobs different from white-collar jobs?

   _____

   _____

   _____

   _____

   _____

   _____

   _____

3. Reread the paragraph that has an X next to it. Underline the sentence that best states the main idea of the paragraph.

4. During World War II, why were women offered jobs formerly held by men?

   _____

   _____

   _____

   _____

   _____

   _____

5. Complete each statement with the correct word or phrase.

   white-collar   blue-collar   recession

   a. People who work with their hands may be happy in _____ jobs.

   b. The economy is in _____ when the number of jobs declines.

   c. Advances in office technology increase demand for _____ jobs.

INTERPRETING FACTS

1. Identify the following statements as fact or opinion. Write *F* or *O* next to each statement.

   ____ a. In 1993, about 130 million Americans were working at paying jobs.

   ____ b. White-color jobs are more rewarding than blue-collar jobs.

2. Reread the paragraph that has a check mark next to it. Write a sentence describing its main idea.

_____

_____

_____

3. World War II and the increased cost of living in the 1970s were two causes of women's entering the labor force.

   a. How are these causes similar?

_____

_____

_____

   b. How are these causes different?

_____

_____

_____

4. What do you think are the most important benefits of greater job opportunities for women?

_____

_____

_____

SKILL FOCUS

Use the selection and the graphs to answer the following questions. To use the graphs, first read the titles. For the first bar graph on page 73, read down the left column, which gives you the number of workers in millions. For the second bar graph on page 74, the left column gives percentages. Next, read across the bottom line to find the year for each bar. For the circle graphs on page 73, look at the time period that each circle represents. Then, in each circle, read the number that shows the percentage.

1. Identify the type of statistical information given in the graphs.

   a. What do the titles tell you about the graphs?

_____

   b. What years does each graph cover?

   First graph: _____   Second graph: _____

   c. For what two groups of people are statistics given?

_____

_____

2. Practice reading the statistics.

    a. In what year did women make up 33 percent of the total labor force? _____

    b. In what year did women make up 43 percent of the total labor force? _____

    c. Approximately how many working women were there in the United States in 1960?

    _____

3. Study the graphs to find relationships among numbers.

    a. When did the number of women in the labor force decrease? Explain why.

_____

_____

_____

    b. Did the number of women in the labor force increase or decrease between 1960 and 1970? Explain.

_____

_____

_____

    c. Did the percentage of married women in the labor force who had young children increase or decrease between 1980 and 1993? Explain.

_____

_____

_____

_____

4. Use statistics to make projections or forecasts.
What trend do you see emerging for working women in the United States?

_____

_____

_____

_____

5. Fill in the circle next to each of the following statements that is true.

    ◯ **a.** The first bar graph indicates the number of working women in the United States at ten-year intervals between 1940 and 1990.

    ◯ **b.** The bar graph figures are exact numbers.

    ◯ **c.** The circle graphs show the percentage of working women in the labor force.

    ◯ **d.** In some years, women have formed a majority of the working people in the United States.

▶ **Real Life Connections** Investigate the number of working women in your city or town. What percentage of the total work force in your community does this represent?

Diagrams

Reading a Science Selection

▶ Background Information

Although atoms cannot be seen, even with the most powerful microscopes, these particles of matter make up every known object. While scientists have never seen an atom, they have collected enough information to build a model of an atom. In this selection, you will work with diagrams of this scientific model to learn about the parts and the characteristics of atoms.

▶ Skill Focus

Books often contain **diagrams** to show what is being explained in the text. Diagrams can often be best understood if you read the text first. Then look at the diagrams. Be sure to read the **captions** and the **labels.** They usually contain important information about what is being explained in the diagram. Sometimes, if you have trouble completely understanding the pictures or symbols in a diagram, the captions and labels will make things clearer. Also, as you study the diagram, think about the text that you just read and how it relates to the diagram. Because the diagram

is there to help explain information in the text, there will be a strong connection between the text and the diagram. It may be helpful to go back to the text again and try to visualize the diagram. When you understand the diagram, read the text one more time. The information in both the text and the diagram should be clearer then.

Use the following steps for reading a selection with diagrams.

1. Read the paragraph or paragraphs before each diagram, and then study the diagram. Be sure to read the labels and caption. The paragraph below the diagram may also explain what is pictured. Read that paragraph, too.
2. Read the rest of the text. Look back at the diagrams whenever you think they will help you.
3. After you have finished reading the text and studying the diagrams, look away from the selection. Try to picture what you have read and the details in the diagrams. If you are not able to do so, read the material again.
4. Follow this method until you understand all the ideas in the selection.

▶ Word Clues

Read the sentences below. Look for context clues to the underlined word.

An atom has two major regions: The heavy, central core is called the underlined nucleus (NOO klee əs). The second region consists of one or more "cloudy" rings in which electrons (ə LEK trahns) orbit the nucleus.

The word *nucleus* is explained by details in the sentence.

Use **detail** context clues to find the meanings of the three underlined words in the selection.

▶ Strategy Tip

While you read this selection on atoms, study the diagrams carefully. It may be helpful to go back and forth from the selection to the diagrams to understand the information that is being presented. Use the four steps described in the Skill Focus.

The Atom

People have always been fascinated with matter, the material that makes up the earth and all the things on and around the earth. In ancient Greece, scientists pondered whether there is a limit to how small a particle of matter could be cut up and still retain its properties. The Greek scientist Democritus (di MAHK rə təs) thought there was such a limit, and he called the smallest units of matter **atoms.** The word *atom* comes from the Greek word *atomos,* meaning "not to be cut." Although Democritus's idea of atoms interested scientists for some time, it was eventually forgotten.

Not until the seventeenth century did the idea of atoms resurface. At that time, scientists were making observations that could be explained best if matter were composed of tiny units. In the nineteenth century, scientists discovered that, given the characteristics of atoms, they had to be made up of even smaller particles. Later, it was discovered that these particles contain even smaller parts. Today's ideas about atoms grew from this research.

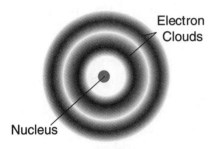

Figure 1. Atoms are composed of even smaller particles.

Atomic Structure

Figure 1 shows a model that reflects scientists' current ideas about the structure of atoms. An atom has two major regions: The heavy, central core is called the **nucleus** (NOO klee əs). The second region consists of one or more "cloudy" rings in which **electrons** (ə LEK trahns) orbit the nucleus. Compared with the nucleus, the area occupied by the electrons is enormous. If an atom were the size of a baseball stadium, the nucleus would be the size of a marble in the middle of the stadium.

The nucleus is the heavy, positively charged part of the atom. It is composed of smaller particles; two of these are the **proton** (PROH tahn) and the **neutron** (NOO trahn). The *nuclei* (NOO klee eye, the plural of nucleus) of all atoms have one or more protons and, except for those of hydrogen, one or more neutrons. Protons and neutrons have the same mass, and each is more than 1,800 times heavier than an electron. For this reason, most of an atom's mass is concentrated in its nucleus.

Atoms usually do not have an electrical charge; they are neutral. Two kinds of particles contained in atoms, however, do have charges. Each proton has a positive charge, and each electron has a negative charge, as shown in Figure 2. The positively charged nucleus attracts the negatively charged electrons and keeps them from escaping. For an atom to be neutral, the number of negatively charged electrons must equal the number of positively charged protons. The number of neutrons in an atom does not affect its charge. Neutrons, as their name suggests, have no charge and are neutral.

The number of protons in an atom's nucleus determines the kind of atom it is. The number of protons, called the **atomic number,** is used to identify the atom. A hydrogen atom, for example, has one proton in its nucleus, and its atomic number is 1. A carbon atom has 6 protons, an oxygen atom has 8 protons, and a uranium atom has 92 protons. Their atomic numbers are 6, 8, and 92, respectively.

A material containing only one kind of atom is called an **element.** Hydrogen, carbon, oxygen, copper, iron, and sodium are all

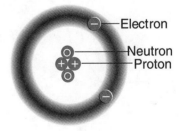

Figure 2. Two of the particles contained by atoms have a charge.

examples of elements. In all, there are 109 known elements. Of these, 90 occur naturally, and the rest have been produced in laboratories.

Although neutrons do not determine an atom's atomic number, they are included in its **atomic mass.** A neutron has about the same mass as a proton; each is considered to have a mass of one unit. Therefore, the sum of the protons and the neutrons in an atom's nucleus determines the atomic mass of the atom. Oxygen, with 8 protons and 8 neutrons, has an atomic mass of 16. Iron, with 26 protons and 29 neutrons, has an atomic mass of 55.

Nuclei of the atoms of certain elements can differ in the number of neutrons that they contain. For example, while most carbon atoms contain 6 neutrons, some have 8 neutrons. When atoms differ in this way from other atoms of the same element, they are called <u>isotopes</u> (EYE soh tohps) of that element. See Figure 3.

The isotopes of an element are distinguished by their atomic masses. Carbon atoms with 6 protons and 6 neutrons have an atomic mass of 12, and these atoms are called carbon-12. Carbon atoms with 6 protons and 8 neutrons have an atomic mass of 14, and these atoms are called carbon-14.

The atoms of different elements are able to join, or bond, to one another to form new substances, called **compounds.** Each group of bonded atoms is called a **molecule** (MAHL ə kyool), and molecules are the smallest units of compounds. For example, when the elements sodium and chlorine bond, they form the compound sodium chloride, or common table salt. The elements hydrogen and oxygen can bond to form water. See

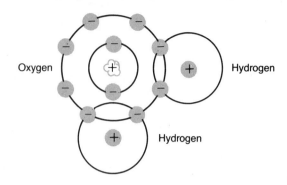

Figure 4. Two hydrogen atoms and one oxygen atom bond together to form a water molecule.

Figure 4. When calcium, carbon, and oxygen combine, they form the rock known as limestone. Because most kinds of atoms can bond with many other kinds of atoms, it is not surprising that the earth contains such a diversity of matter.

Radioactivity

Late in the nineteenth century, scientists discovered that certain atoms give off something that darkens photographic film. What these scientists discovered is a form of energy, called **radioactivity,** which scientists now know results from changes in the nucleus of an atom. Large atoms—those with high atomic numbers—are especially likely to be radioactive. For some reason, their nuclei can break apart with no outside cause. When they do, matter and energy are released, and a new atom, with a different atomic mass, results. Energy is released in the form of **gamma rays,** and matter is released in the form of <u>alpha particles</u> and <u>beta</u> (BAYT ə) <u>particles.</u> Each alpha particle is composed of two protons and two neutrons; each beta particle is composed of an electron. See Figure 5.

Elements that release radioactivity are said to undergo **radioactive decay,** a process that changes the radioactive element into a nonradioactive element. For instance, radioactive uranium-235 decays to form nonradioactive lead.

Radioactive Dating

One way in which scientists can use the natural process of radioactive decay is in **radioactive dating.** Radioactive dating is a method for determining the age of some things. Carbon-14 is a radioactive isotope

6 Protons   6 Neutrons

6 Protons   8 Neutrons

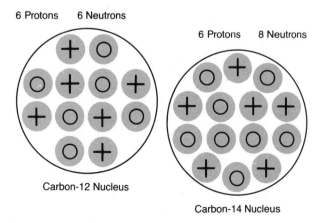

Figure 3. This diagram shows two isotopes of carbon.

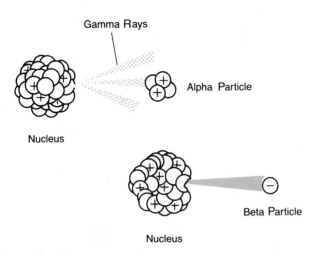

Gamma Rays

Alpha Particle

Nucleus

Beta Particle

Nucleus

Figure 5. Radioactive atoms release energy in the form of gamma rays and matter in the form of alpha and beta particles.

that gives off beta particles and gamma rays. This isotope is often used in the radioactive dating of items that were once alive or that were made from something once alive, such as wood. All living things contain both carbon-14 and carbon-12. The ratio of carbon-14 to carbon-12 remains unchanged as long as the organism is alive. When the organism dies, its carbon-14 begins to undergo radioactive decay. The decayed atoms are no longer carbon-14 atoms.

Scientists use the rate of carbon-14 decay to date the age of the organism. They have discovered that half of the radioactive carbon-14 atoms that an organism contains when it dies decay and become nonradioactive in 5,730 years. The span of 5,730 years is called the **half-life** of carbon-14. After 11,460 years, the number of remaining carbon-14 atoms is equal to one-quarter of the original number—or half of the carbon-14 atoms that remained after the first half-life. After 17,190 years, one eighth of the original number of carbon-14 atoms are left, and so on. In this way, scientists can determine the age of the item.

As time goes on, scientists are constantly adjusting their ideas about atoms. New discoveries about the behavior of atoms affect scientific theories. In the future, scientists will continue to find new ways to put their understanding of atoms to practical uses.

RECALLING FACTS

1. What are the two major regions of an atom?

   _____

   _____

2. Which particles form an atom's nucleus?

   _____

   _____

3. Why are atoms neutral in charge?

   _____

   _____

   _____

4. Which particle in a nucleus lacks a charge?

   _____

5. What characteristic distinguishes the atoms of one substance from the atoms of another substance?

   _____

   _____

6. What is an element?

   _____

   _____

7. What determines an atom's atomic mass?

   _____

   _____

8. What are isotopes?

   _____

9. What do you call the substances formed when the atoms of two or more elements bond to one another?

_____

_____

10. What process changes a radioactive atom to a nonradioactive atom?

_____

_____

11. What does a radioactive atom give off?

_____

_____

_____

_____

12. What does the term *half-life* mean?

_____

_____

_____

13. What is the half-life of carbon-14?

_____

14. Draw a line to match each word or phrase with its explanation.

alpha particle

isotopes

beta particle

a. forms of an atom that vary only in the number of neutrons in their nuclei

b. two protons and two neutrons

c. an electron

INTERPRETING FACTS

Fill in the space between the lines next to the correct answer.

1. An atom with 10 protons and 11 neutrons in its nucleus has _____ electrons around its nucleus.
   - || a. 10 || c. 20
   - || b. 11 || d. 21

2. One atom has 92 protons and 235 neutrons. Another atom has 92 protons and 238 neutrons. What can be said about these two atoms?
   - || a. They are atoms of different elements.
   - || b. They are both radioactive.
   - || c. They are isotopes of the same element.
   - || d. They are isotopes of different elements.

3. A substance was analyzed and found to contain carbon, hydrogen, and oxygen. This substance was _____.
   - || a. an element
   - || b. a compound
   - || c. an isotope
   - || d. an atom

4. An atom with 92 protons and 238 neutrons undergoes radioactive decay and gives off two alpha particles. What is the new structure of this atom?
   - || a. 90 protons and 234 neutrons
   - || b. 88 protons and 236 neutrons
   - || c. 88 protons and 234 neutrons
   - || d. 90 protons and 235 neutrons

5. When two or more elements form a compound, the compound will _____.
   - || a. have properties that are different from either element
   - || b. have a negative charge
   - || c. always be a solid
   - || d. have the properties of one of the elements

6. Scientists used carbon dating to determine the age of a mummy. Tests revealed that three quarters of its carbon-14 atoms had decayed (one quarter still remained). What is the age of the mummy?
   - || a. 25,000 years
   - || b. 5,000 years
   - || c. 11,460 years
   - || d. 10,000 years

1. In Figure 1, is the distance between the nucleus and the electrons in scale? In other words, if the nucleus were the size shown, are the electrons the proper distance from it? Explain.

_____

_____

2. Explain Figure 2 in your own words. _____

_____

_____

3. Use Figure 2 to answer the following questions.
   a. How do you know that this atom does not have a charge?

   _____

   b. What is the atomic number of this atom? _____

4. Explain Figure 3 in your own words. _____

_____

_____

5. In Figure 4, what elements make up water? _____

6. Explain Figure 5 in your own words. _____

_____

_____

7. Hydrogen has three isotopes: hydrogen-1, called protium; hydrogen-2, called deuterium; and hydrogen-3, called tritium. Each has an atomic number of 1. Their mass numbers are 1, 2, and 3, respectively. In the box below, draw a diagram similar to Figure 3 that illustrates these three isotopes.

▶ Real Life Connections Draw a diagram of something you are studying in school or something else that interests you. Use labels and captions to make the information clear.

Circles

Reading a Mathematics Selection

▶ Background Information

Circles are frequently found in nature, as in a slice of a tree trunk, the border of the eye of a daisy, or the apparent shapes of the sun and the moon. Circles were also an important part of the previous lesson, which discussed atoms and the circular paths that electrons have around the nuclei of atoms.

The ancient Greeks believed that the circle was the perfect shape. For that reason, they assumed that the paths of the planets around the sun must be circular, even when careful measurements done by scientists showed that planetary paths were not circular.

Today circles are all around us. They are a common part of man-made objects. Many objects are in the shape of a circle. Wheels of all kinds are circles, of course. Balls, coins, and tires are also in the shape of a circle. The circle is also an important element in architecture, determining the shape of many buildings, and it is often used in the design of sports stadiums. Look around your home, school, and community to see how many objects are in the shape of a circle.

Because circles are so common, knowing the mathematics of circles can be more helpful than one might at first think. For example, when we buy new tires for a car, the tire will be described, in part, by its diameter. When you buy a ring, the jeweler will know what size is best for you by measuring the circumference of your finger.

▶ Skill Focus

A **circle** is a figure that is contained all in one flat surface, or plane. Within the plane, the circle consists of all the points that are the same distance from a specific point, called the **center**. The center of a circle is not a point on the circle itself. Because of its special relationship to the circle, however, the center is used in defining lines, distances, and angles related to the circle.

▶ Word Clues

Many of the words used in geometry have their origins in the Greek language. The Greek word for circle is *kirkos*, which also means "ring." The distance across a circle, as measured through its center, is called the *diameter*. This word comes from the Greek words *dia*, meaning "across," and *metron*, meaning "measure."

Other words that are related to circles come from Latin. The distance around a circle, or its *circumference*, is from the Latin words that mean "to carry around." A line segment from the center to the circle itself is called a *radius*, which is the Latin word meaning "ray."

▶ Strategy Tip

As you read "Circles," study the diagrams and their labels carefully. Letters are used for geometric labels. A circle is labeled at its center; a line is labeled at its two end points. So a circle could be labeled O or P, while a line segment could be labeled OP or AB.

Circles

A **circle** is a figure that consists of all the points that are the same distance from a specific point, called the **center** of the circle. This distance is known as the **radius** of the circle. *Radius* is also the name of the line segment from the center of the circle to any point on the circle. In the figure below, the radius of circle O is the distance from the center O to point P on the circle; it is also the line segment OP.

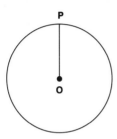

A line segment through the center of a circle that has both its end points on the circle is a **diameter**. Because the diameter can be thought of as two *radii* (RAY dee eye, the plural of radius), the length of the diameter is two times the length of the radius. The diameter is also the longest line segment that can be drawn in a circle; its length is the width of the circle.

In the figure that follows, segment AB is the diameter of the circle. Notice that AB passes through point O, the center of circle O.

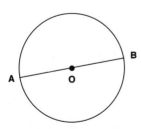

From early times, people noticed that the **circumference,** or the distance around any circle, was always the same multiple of its diameter. Before people had instruments for precise measurements, they thought that the distance around the circle was three times the diameter. As measurement techniques improved, however, people learned that the circumference was slightly more than three times the diameter. The exact number was named π, a Greek letter that is pronounced like the word *pie*.

For any circle, π is the ratio of the circumference to the diameter. Careful measurement showed that π was close to— but not exactly— $\frac{22}{7}$ or 3.14. You can use either of the two values for π, but the fraction $\frac{22}{7}$ is not exactly equal to the decimal 3.14. Both numbers are different approximations of π. The formula for the circumference (C) of a circle with a diameter of d is as follows:

$$C = \pi \times d \ \text{ or } \ C = \pi d$$

In mathematical formulas, either two letters or a number and a letter can be written together with no sign between them. In such cases, you are to multiply the values of the letters, or multiply the value of the letter by the number.

Because the diameter of a circle is easier to measure than its circumference, the formula for the diameter is usually used to find the circumference. For example, if a circle has a diameter of 100 centimeters, the formula shows that the circumference C is found as follows:

$$C = \pi \times 100$$

Using 3.14 for π, the answer is 3.14×100, or 314 centimeters.

Because the diameter is twice the radius, you can also find the circumference of a circle when you know the radius (r). In this case, the formula is as follows:

$$C = 2 \times \pi \times r \ \text{ or } \ C = 2\pi r$$

For example, the radius of a circle is 7 meters. To find the circumference, you would substitute 7 for r to get $C = 2 \times \pi \times 7$, or $C = 2 \times \frac{22}{7} \times 7$. You may find it easier to multiply if you write all the numbers as fractions:

$$C = \frac{2}{1} \times \frac{22}{7} \times \frac{7}{1}$$

Notice that you can cancel the 7 in the numerator and the 7 in the denominator. So the answer is just 2×22, or 44 meters.

1. What is the relationship of the circle to its center?

_____

_____

2. What are two meanings for the word *radius?*

_____

_____

_____

3. Where is a circle labeled?

_____

4. What do you call a line segment that has both end points on the circle and that passes through the middle of the circle?

_____

5. How would you describe the circumference of a circle?

_____

6. What is the symbol that stands for the exact ratio of the circumference of a circle to the circle's diameter? _____

7. What is a good approximation for the number that you must multiply the diameter by to get the circumference of a circle? _____

8. What is the formula used for finding the circumference of a circle when you know the radius?

_____

INTERPRETING FACTS

1. If you know the diameter of a circle, how can you find the radius?

_____

2. Suppose the distance around a circle were exactly three times the diameter. What would be the formula for finding the circumference of a circle given the diameter?

_____

3. In the formula $A = 2ab$, what operation must be used to find A if you know that $a = 3$ and $b = 5$?

_____

4. In the selection, 3.14 was used for π in one application, and $\frac{22}{7}$ was used in the other. Why was $\frac{22}{7}$ chosen in the second problem?

_____

_____

_____

_____

A. Find the missing value.

1. radius = 4 centimeters, diameter =

_____

2. diameter = 9 meters, radius =

_____

3. diameter = 10 centimeters,
   circumference (use 3.14 for π) =

_____

4. radius = 35 meters, circumference
   (use $\frac{22}{7}$ for π) =

_____

5. diameter = 14 meters, circumference
   (use $\frac{22}{7}$ for π) =

_____

6. radius = 6 centimeters, circumference
   (use 3.14 for π) =

_____

B. For each circle, find the circumference. Use either 3.14 or $\frac{22}{7}$ for p, whichever is easier.

1.

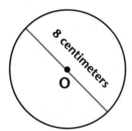

_____

3.

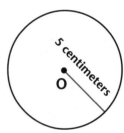

_____

2.

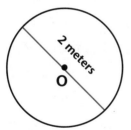

_____

4.

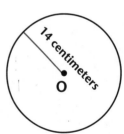

_____

C. Solve each problem. Use 3.14 for π.

1. A wheel has a radius of 35
   centimeters. What is the distance the
   wheel travels in one revolution?

_____

2. The diameter of a circular swimming
   pool is 25 meters. What is the distance
   around the edge of the pool?

_____

3. The distance around the circular trunk
   of a tree is 157 centimeters. How thick
   is a cross-section of the tree through
   the center?

_____

4. The diameter of a round table is 5
   meters. What is the distance around
   the edge of the table?

_____

▶ **Real Life Connections** Name an item that you use or see everyday that is the shape of a circle. Find its radius and circumference.

Suffixes

A **suffix** is a word part that is added to the end of a word to change its meaning. If the root word ends in *y* or *e*, its spelling may have to be changed.

When a word ends in *y* preceded by a consonant, you change the *y* to *i* before adding a suffix. When the *y* is preceded by a vowel, you make no spelling change.

lazy + ness = laziness

play + ful = playful

When a word ends in *e* and the suffix begins with a vowel, you drop the final *e* before adding the suffix. You do not make any spelling change if the suffix begins with a consonant.

value + able = valuable

grace + ful = graceful

Below are eight suffixes and their meanings. Study them carefully.

Suffix	Meaning	Suffix	Meaning
able	that can be	ful	full of
al	the process of	ly	like in manner
ance	the act of	ness	quality or state of
ant	that has or shows	ous	characterized by

Write the correct suffix after each word below. If the word requires a spelling change before the suffix can be added, cross out the final *e* or *y*. The first one is done for you.

1. compare __able__   that can be compared
2. hope _____   full of hope
3. fame _____   characterized by fame
4. perform_____   the act of performing
5. beauty_____   full of beauty

6. joy _____   characterized by joy
7. happy _____   the state of being happy
8. defy_____   that shows defiance
9. deny_____   the process of denying
10. harsh_____   in a harsh manner

Use one of the words above to complete each sentence below.

1. Bill told us in a bold and _____ manner that he was very much against our plans.

2. The driver wanted to test the car's _____ on rough roads.

3. Your encouragement makes me feel very _____.

4. Uncle Hank bought gifts of _____ value for the twins.

5. The judge listened to the defendant's _____ of the charges against him.

6. The marriage of Laura and Michael was a _____ occasion.

7. Graduating from high school gave her much _____.

8. When an author's book becomes a bestseller, he becomes _____ and wealthy.

9. The sun was shining, and the spring day was _____ and pleasant.

10. Kim scolded her dog _____ for running across the street.

Main Idea and Supporting Details

To understand a paragraph, it is important to know how the main idea of a paragraph is developed. The **main idea** is the most important idea in a paragraph. It states what the paragraph is about. The main idea is developed by the details in the rest of the paragraph. These details are called **supporting details** because they give more information about the main idea.

There are two kinds of supporting details. The more important details, called **major details**, tell important information about the main idea of a paragraph. Other details of less importance, called **minor details**, give more information about the major details.

As you read each of the following paragraphs about physician assistants, first look for the main idea. Then try to determine which of the details are major details and which are minor details.

Physician Assistants

1. As their job title suggests, physician assistants (PAs) provide support for medical doctors. PAs are trained to do many of the routine but time-consuming tasks that doctors usually perform. PAs examine patients, record their medical histories, treat minor injuries, order and interpret laboratory tests, make a preliminary diagnosis, and, in some states, prescribe medications. PAs may also have managerial duties. For example, some order medical supplies and equipment. Others supervise technicians and medical assistants.

2. Physician assistants always work under the supervision of a doctor. How closely a PA is supervised, however, depends on the location. For example, a PA who works in a rural or inner-city clinic, where a doctor may be available only one or two days a week, may provide most of the day-to-day health care for patients; the PA would consult with the supervising physician by telephone. Other PAs make house calls or hospital visits and then report back to the physician. The specific duties of a PA are determined by the supervising physician or by state regulations.

3. Admission to an educational program for physician assistants usually requires two years of college and some work experience in the health-care field. Many people who apply to PA programs have worked as emergency medical technicians, nurses, or other health professionals. The education program includes both classroom instruction and supervised training in a clinic or physician's office. PA programs generally last two years. Almost all states require new PAs to have completed an approved education program.

For each paragraph listed, complete the diagram on the next page. In the box labeled "Main Idea," write the sentence that states the main idea as it appears in the paragraph. In the boxes labeled "Major Details" and "Minor Details," use your own words. Use the completed boxes to guide you. Not all major details have minor details.

Paragraph 1

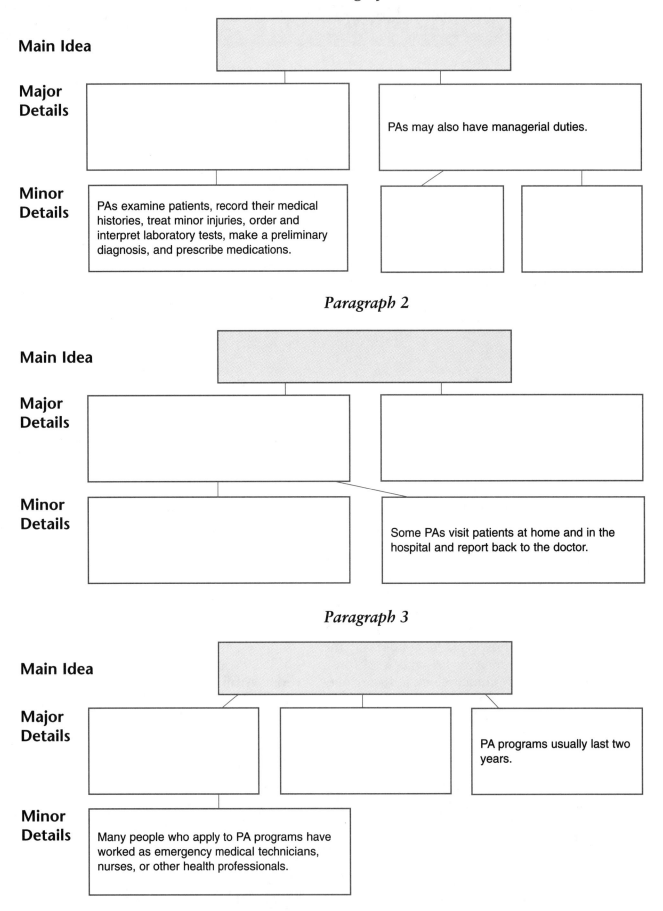

Main Idea

Major Details

PAs may also have managerial duties.

Minor Details

PAs examine patients, record their medical histories, treat minor injuries, order and interpret laboratory tests, make a preliminary diagnosis, and prescribe medications.

Paragraph 2

Main Idea

Major Details

Minor Details

Some PAs visit patients at home and in the hospital and report back to the doctor.

Paragraph 3

Main Idea

Major Details

PA programs usually last two years.

Minor Details

Many people who apply to PA programs have worked as emergency medical technicians, nurses, or other health professionals.

Word Parts

When you are trying to figure out the meaning of an unknown word, knowing the meanings of the word's parts can be helpful. Roots, prefixes, and suffixes are word parts. Many of the words that you know are made up of roots, with prefixes and suffixes added to them.

The word *precede* is formed by combining the prefix *pre* and the root *cede*. The prefix *pre* means "before" and the root *cede* means "to go." If you know these meanings, you can figure out that *precede* means "to go before."

Look at the following roots, prefixes, suffixes, and their meanings. Notice that one of the roots has more than one spelling.

Roots		*Prefixes*		*Suffixes*	
ced (ceed, cess)	to go, yield	con	with, together	able	that can be
form	shape, form	pre	before	ation, ion	the act of
port	to carry	pro	forward, forth	ity	condition or
		re	back, again		quality
		trans	over, across		

Read each word below. Use the meanings of the word parts above to decide which meaning is correct. Write the letter of the meaning next to the word it defines.

Word		Meaning
_____ transport	**a.**	the act of going back
_____ portable	**b.**	to carry across
_____ recede	**c.**	that can be carried
_____ conform	**d.**	the act of going forward
_____ recession	**e.**	the act of forming over
_____ conformity	**f.**	to carry back
_____ procession	**g.**	to go back
_____ report	**h.**	the condition of forming together (of making the same)
_____ cession	**i.**	the act of yielding
_____ transformation	**j.**	to form together (make the same)

Use one of the words above to complete each of the sentences below.

1. The _____ of Guam to the United States by Spain took place in 1898.

2. The treasurer will _____ on how much money we have in the bank.

3. The biology class studied the _____ of a caterpillar into a butterfly.

4. Bob carried the _____ fan from the den to his bedroom.

5. After the tides _____, we are going to dig for clams.

Outlining

A good way to understand and remember something you read is to make an **outline**. An outline can be written quickly and read easily. A good outline shows how the main idea and supporting details in a selection are organized.

Read the following paragraph. Then look at the outline next to it.

Federal Budget

The federal budget gives the overall spending levels of the government. The total budget for 1996 was about $1.6 trillion. Of that, 48 percent was budgeted for direct benefit payments to individuals, which includes social security, unemployment compensation, welfare, and health care. National defense expenses were 16 percent of the federal budget. Another 16 percent paid the interest —the charge for borrowed money— for the country's debt. That left 15 percent for grants to state and local governments and 5 percent for other programs and government operations.

Federal Budget

I. Spending levels
  A. Direct benefit payments (48%)
    1. Social security
    2. Unemployment compensation
    3. Welfare
    4. Health care
  B. National defense (16%)
  C. Debt interest (16%)
  D. Grants to state and local governments (15%)
  E. Other federal programs (5%)

Notice that "Spending levels," the main idea of the paragraph, is written next to Roman numeral I. "Direct benefit payments," written next to capital letter A, is the first major detail about the federal budget. "Social Security" is written next to number 1. These words tell a minor detail about direct benefit payments. Notice that the outline uses only words and phrases.

Several other things are important to know about outlining. Every outline should have a title. An outline should always include at least two main ideas, so that it will never have a Roman numeral I without a II. There should be at least two major details under each main idea and at least two minor details under each major detail.

Read the next two paragraphs about the federal budget. Use the information in them to complete the outline.

The U.S. government spends the largest part of its budget on direct benefit payments to individuals. The country's major direct benefit program is social security. Full social security payments go to workers who reach retirement age. The Social Security program also provides benefits for workers who become disabled and cannot work, and for the families of workers who die. The second largest direct benefit program funds health care, including Medicare for retired workers, Medicaid for needy people, and other medical payments. The third largest direct benefit program provides unemployment compensation for people who are willing and able to work but who are involuntarily unemployed. All workers covered by unemployment compensation receive monthly payments for as long as they qualify. This program does not cover agricultural workers, domestic workers, public employees, and self-employed workers. Finally, the federal government gives a broad range of income assistance to needy families and individuals.

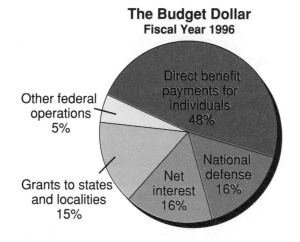

The Budget Dollar
Fiscal Year 1996

Direct benefit payments for individuals 48%

Other federal operations 5%

Grants to states and localities 15%

Net interest 16%

National defense 16%

Housing aid is given through low-income housing, public housing, and home ownership assistance. Several programs provide food and nutrition aid.

National defense, the second largest expense budgeted, includes activities having to do with the defense and safety of the United States. More than half of national defense spending is for conventional forces that stop or react to non-nuclear military threats. The money in this category pays the salaries of military personnel, as well as the expenses of buying, running, and maintaining ships and aircraft. A second category of national defense spending covers strategic forces. The money in this category is budgeted to develop the latest in weapon systems, particularly missiles. It also goes toward building bombers and submarines. A third national defense budget category involves outlays for supporting activities. Included in this category are research and development programs to devise new and better weapons for changing military needs. Training is also covered in this part of the budget.

II. Direct benefit payments to individuals _____

   A. Social Security _____

      1. _____

      2. Payments for disability _____

      3. _____

   B. _____

      1. Medicare for retired people _____

      2. _____

      3. _____

   C. _____

      1. Monthly payments _____

      2. _____

   D. _____

      1. Housing aid _____

      2. _____

III. _____

   A. Conventional forces _____

      1. To pay for military personnel _____

      2. _____

   B. _____

      1. _____

      2. To build bombers and submarines _____

   C. _____

      1. To devise new weapons _____

      2. _____

Car Insurance Application

Car insurance helps you pay the costs to repair or to replace your car if you have an accident or if your car gets stolen. Car insurance also helps you pay any medical expenses if you are injured in a car accident. In fact, most states require that every car owner have insurance before operating a vehicle.

A car insurance application asks for information about the owner and about others in the household who will drive the car. It also requires information about the applicant's driving record and the type of car being insured. When completing an application, you often need the help of an insurance agent to furnish the technical information.

Read the sample car insurance application on the next page.

A. Decide if each question can be answered by using information on the car insurance application. Write *yes* or *no* on the first line. On the second line, for each question answered *yes,* write the line number(s) or heading from the application that requires this information. Do not write the information itself.

1. How many drivers are in the applicant's household? _____ _____

2. What is the applicant's social security number? _____ _____

3. Where is the applicant employed? _____ _____

4. How old is the applicant's car? _____ _____

5. Does the applicant have a driver's license? _____ _____

6. How many miles does the applicant put on her car each year? _____ _____

7. What color is the applicant's car? _____ _____

8. Has the applicant's car ever been repainted? _____ _____

9. Has the applicant's car insurance ever been cancelled? _____ _____

10. Was the applicant in any car accidents five or more years ago? _____ _____

11. Does the applicant wear glasses or contact lenses when driving? _____ _____

12. Has the applicant's car been stolen during the past three years? _____ _____

B. Answer each question by using the information from the insurance application.
1. Which drivers drive the second car? _____
2. Who in the family drives the least? Explain why.

_____

3. Which driver probably drives the farthest to work? How do you know?

_____

4. Name the people involved in an accident in March 1994. Also describe the kind of accident, if anyone was hurt, and the cost of the damages.

_____

_____

| 110 | ☐ | NAME OF APPLICANT
35 Irene Kellogg Harris | | FROM (Mo.-Day-Yr.)
3 – 15 – 96 | TO (Mo.-Day-Yr.)
3 – 14 – 97 |

| 111 | ☐ | NUMBER AND STREET
30 1904 21st Street | |

| 112 | ☐ | CITY OR TOWN
30 Atlanta | COUNTY
DeKalb |

| 113 | STATE
2 GA | ZIP CODE
5 30338 | STATE
2 | CITY
2 | COUNTY
2 | RATE
2 | TAX DISTRICT
4 |

| 114 | ☐ | TELEPHONE NUMBER (INCL. AREA CODE)
12 404-821-7498 | SURCHARGE — COMPLETE
FOR CAR-RATE III ONLY | LIABILITY
3 | PHYS. DAM.
3 |

DRIVER INFORMATION: (Show all licensed operators in the household, whether separately insured or not.)

| TYPE
D-Driver
N-Non-Driver
S-Driver, but not rated | IMPAIR
Any driver who has any mental or physical impairments including heart or diabetic conditions (If yes, explain in detail in Remarks.) | YOUTHFUL DRIVERS
Stu. Away (If yes, give name of school in Remarks.)
Dr. Trng. (If yes, attach certification.) |

	ACT		DRIVER NAME (First, Middle Initial, Last)	BIRTH DATE	SEX M/F	MARRIED Y/N	IMPAIR. Y/N	*SOCIAL SECURITY NUMBER
120	☐	1	26 Irene K. Harris	1-23-48	F	N	N	11 612-40-8527

	TYPE	DRIVER LICENSE NUMBER	CAR PERCENTAGE OF USE	DATE LIC. (If less than 5 yrs.)	Stu. Away Y/N	Dr. Trng. Y/N
121	D	20 H-472-043-926-855	1 3 85 2 3 30 3 3	mo. — yr.	YOUTHFUL DRIVERS ► N	Y N

| 122 | ☐ | 2 | 26 Jonathan M. Harris | 4-8-73 | M | N | N | 11 075-43-1298 |

| 123 | D | 20 H-994-127-586-640 | 1 3 0   2 3 60   3 3 | mo. — yr. | YOUTHFUL DRIVERS ► N | Y N |

| 124 | ☐ | 3 | 26 Lauren K. Harris | 12-20-76 | F | N | N | 11 075-62-2049 |

| 125 | D | 20 H-874-290-138-772 | 1 3 5   2 3 30   3 3 | mo.1 – 82 yr. | YOUTHFUL DRIVERS ► Y | Y N |

| 126 | ☐ | 4 | 26 Robert S. Harris | 2-17-78 | M | N | N | 11 358-26-3812 |

| 127 | D | 20 H-160-622-431-998 | 1 3 10   2 3 40   3 3 | mo.9–83 yr. | YOUTHFUL DRIVERS ► N | Y Y |

GENERAL INFORMATION: (All of the following questions must be answered.)

| During the past 3 years has the applicant or any driver currently a resident of the household:
Had insurance* 1-Canceled?
2-Declined?
3-Renewal Refused?
4-None of above.
*If 1, 2, Or 3 Explain in Remarks | Had driver's license suspended or revoked?
Y N | Does the Applicant Own Any Trailers not to be insured?
Y N | If number of private passenger, farm or utility vehicles owned by the applicant or spouse is more than those described in Vehicle Information, indicate the number of vehicles.
CARRIER   NAME OF PREVIOUS CARRIER |

| 140 | ☐ | 4 | | N | | N | | 3 | |

STATEMENT OF ACCIDENTS: Has the applicant or any other driver currently a resident in the household been involved in an auto accident while operating any private pass. or utility auto, resulting in damage to any property, including his/her own, or in bodily injury or death during the 39 months preceding the month in which this policy is to become effective?   Yes ☑   No ☐

(If yes, complete appropriate blocks below.)

ACCIDENT CODES ▼
A-Auto legally parked.
B-Auto struck in rear and driver or household resident not convicted of a moving traffic violation.
C-Dr. or owner reimbursed by or on behalf of person responsible for acc. or has judgment against such person.
D-Other person in accident convicted of a moving traffic violation. Applicant or household resident not convicted.
E-Damages by "hit and run" driver, accident reported to police within 24 hours from time of accident.
F-Accident involved damages from contact by animals or fowl.
G-Accident involved physical damage limited to and caused by flying gravel, missiles, or falling objects.
Z-At fault.

	ACT	DRIVER	LOSS DATE	ACCI-DENT CODE	BODILY INJURY Y/N	PROPERTY DAMAGE AMOUNT OWN	OTHER
145	☐	1	5 – 12 – 93	Z	N	4 $400	4 $850
146	☐	2	3 – 6 – 94	B	N	4 $600	4

STATEMENT OF OTHER LOSSES:
Have you had any other auto losses or claims (Fire, Glass Breakage, Theft, Towing, Vandalism, etc.) in the past 3 years?   Yes ☑   No ☐   If yes, explain in REMARKS.

STATEMENT OF CONVICTIONS: Has the applicant or any driver currently resident in the household been convicted of a moving traffic violation during the 39 months preceding the month in which this policy is to become effective? (If yes, complete the appropriate blocks.)   Yes ☐   No ☑

	ACT	DRIVER	CONVICTION DATE	VIOLATION DESCRIPTION	ACT	DRIVER	CONVICTION DATE	VIOLATION DESCRIPTION
150	☐		— —	10	☐		— —	10

FINANCIAL RESPONSIBILITY: Is the applicant or any other driver currently a resident in the household required to make a financial responsibility filing?   Yes ☐   No ☑
(If yes, complete the appropriate blocks.)

DRIVER	INCIDENT	FILING DATE	DATE FILING EXPIRES	DRIVER	INCIDENT	DATE	FILING DATE	DATE FILING EXPIRES
		— —	— —			— —	— —	— —

VEHICLE INFORMATION: (Use codes for Body Type, Car Type, and Car Use.)

| BODY TYPE
1-Sedan 2 Door   4-Hardtop 4 Door   7-Other
2-Sedan 4 Door   5-Convertible   8-Non Customized
3-Hardtop 2 Door   6-Station Wagon   9-Customized | CAR TYPE
1-Compact   4-Pick-up   6-Antique
2-Mobile Home   5-Pick-up   7-Regular
3-Utility Trailer   w/Camper   8-Van | CAR USE
1-Used in Business or Occupation
2-Driven to Work Under 3 Miles One Way
3-Driven to Work More Than 3 Miles but Less Than 15 Miles One Way
4-Driven to Work 15 Miles or More One Way.
5-Farm   6-Pleasure (not regularly driven to work) |

LINE	ACT	CAR	YEAR	TRADE NAME	BODY TYPE	IDENTIFICATION NUMBER	MODEL	CAR TYPE	CAR USE	ANNUAL MILES	SYM-BOL	HORSE POWER	CUBIC INCHES	HIGH PERF	BUMP /DISC
160	1	2	93	6 Ford	6	17 A003089K	6 Taurus	7	3	5 10,000		3	3		2
161	2		90	Honda	1	JH25301	Civic	1	4	17,000					

Has any vehicle been modified and/or altered to increase performance or value, such as carburetors, cams, wide wheels, custom paint job, etc.? (If yes, indicate vehicle number, modifications, and total value in Remarks Section.)   Yes ☐   No ☑

Actual number of miles driven one-way to work, school or commuting point: 5 (Car 1)   15 (Car 2)   ___ (Car 3)

Lesson 27

Tone

Reading a Literature Selection

▶ **Background Information**

In most newspapers and magazines, readers can state their opinions about current issues in a column of letters to the editor. In this selection, you will read two letters about retraining workers to perform new jobs with new skills.

▶ **Skill Focus**

Tone is an author's attitude toward or feelings about a subject. A speaker can express feelings by the sound of his or her voice, but an author must rely on written words.

Read the sentences below.

You cannot be too careful when taking care of pets. They must be looked after, groomed properly, appropriately fed, and, most important, loved.

You can tell that the tone of the paragraph is serious because the author uses such words as *careful, must, looked after, properly,* and *appropriately.*

A lighthearted, playful tone might sound something like the following.

Don't forget! Your pet will wiggle with delight and give you lots of cuddles if you remember to keep that dinner dish full, that curly coat combed, and that shaggy tail wagging.

The meanings of the two paragraphs are the same, but the tone is quite different.

The following questions will help you identify tone.

1. What kinds of words does the author use?
2. What do the words tell you about the author's attitude toward or feelings about the subject?
3. How does your attitude or feelings compare with the author's?

▶ **Word Clues**

Read the sentence below. Look for context clues that explain the underlined word.

Why is a member of the business community supporting an <u>innovative</u> idea, such as reskilling—or retraining, if you prefer—instead of standing fast for some old-fashioned idea?

If you don't know the meaning of the word *innovative,* the phrase, *instead of standing fast for some old-fashioned idea,* can help you. It tells you that an innovative idea is not an old-fashioned one. *Innovative* means "new, recent, modern." *Innovative* and *old-fashioned* are antonyms, or words that are opposite in meaning.

Use **antonym** context clues to find the meanings of the three underlined words in the selection.

▶ **Strategy Tip**

As you read the following two letters, examine how tone is revealed. Look at the words used by the two letter writers. Think about how their words reflect their feelings. Compare your feelings about retraining with those expressed in the letters.

Just Good Business Sense

To the Editor:

As president of Bodwell Industries, I would like to comment on your recent editorial entitled "Helping Hand for Those Whose Skills Are Outdated."

I agree that it makes good business sense to replace skills no longer needed in the marketplace by retraining workers. Why is a member of the business community supporting an innovative idea, such as reskilling—or retraining, if you prefer—instead of standing fast for some old-fashioned idea?

It's good business to make sure that industry assumes some responsibility for developing the supply of skilled, well-trained workers. Most industries depend on selling goods to consumers. And what are consumers but people with jobs and with money to spend? Most businesses cannot survive without people to buy their products. Consumers without jobs have little money to spend. Reskilling programs that keep the labor force meaningfully employed make sense.

Let me add a word of caution, however. Let us ensure that the new skills that workers acquire are the skills they will need to secure long-term employment. Too many well-meaning retraining programs have taught skills that have little or no usefulness. This type of retraining program is shortsighted and reflects no interest in serving long-range goals. Although practical, these programs lack advance planning.

May I offer, as an example of advance planning, an experiment from my own firm, Bodwell Industries? It is an experiment of which I believe we can be justly proud.

Several years ago, our advance planners clearly saw that the demand for bobbins was decreasing. The choice was obvious: remain <u>solvent</u> or go bankrupt. To save Bodwell, we decided to change with the times. We invested in new electronic robot equipment, gave up bobbin making, and moved into microchip technology.

With that decision, however, came the realization that, in making the change, we would be displacing several hundred employees. A loss of that many jobs in one small town can be devastating. Witness the ruin that has come to towns where the local coal mines or steel mills have closed. The loss of jobs has a ripple effect. Soon other local businesses are badly affected. I wouldn't want to be looking at the profit-and-loss statements for businesses in some of those towns in recent years.

But I digress. Back to the Bodwell Industries experiment. Realizing that we had a problem in changing over to the new technology, we called in a special consultant. She pointed out that, even though our workers didn't know a thing about robots, they did have basic skills that could be upgraded. For example, a crew chief in charge of bobbin makers could be retrained to be head of robot repair. A quality checker could learn microchip quality control, and so on.

Of course, it took an investment of considerable resources on our part, but the Board of Directors agreed that it would be money well spent. We now have a skilled and loyal work force. At the same time, our community has been able to retain, rather than lose, its liveliness along with its workers' livelihoods.

Our experience with retraining has led me to some conclusions about the roles of industry and government planners in the years ahead. I would suggest that those in charge of retraining programs concentrate on skills in such areas as communications, video, computers, and space technology.

Economists tell us that we are undergoing a change much like the Industrial Revolution of the nineteenth century. Unlike that era, however, this revolution is eliminating, rather than creating, many jobs and is replacing human workers with electronic machinery. Economists also see a trend toward jobs in service industries—businesses that provide services rather than goods—such as communications, health care, and home entertainment.

As an employer, I suggest to employees of the future that they embark on their work lives prepared to learn new skills.

Sincerely,

Marguerite Horwath

Marguerite Horwath
President, Bodwell Industries

If Great-Grandpa Did It, So Can He

To the Editor:

Well, here we are again! Coming as I do from a long line of people whose skills have become obsolete or whose work became <u>archaic</u> because of modern technology, I am not surprised that I must now be reskilled.

My great-grandpa was a blacksmith until Henry Ford came along with the automobile. A weaker person might have been overcome with <u>despair,</u> but not Great-Grandpa. He just hitched up his overalls, studied those newfangled machines, changed the sign on his smithy, and became an auto mechanic. He said that he was tired of shoeing horses anyway.

Then there was Great-Granddad on my mother's side. He inherited a factory that made buttonhooks, just as high-button shoes went out of fashion. He survived for a while by making collar stays. You say you have no idea what buttonhooks or collar stays are for? That was Great-Granddad's problem, too. People forgot awfully fast—as soon as the items in question went out of style. Great-Granddad died a broken man, the only person in his neighborhood still wearing high-button shoes and shirts with stiff collars.

My Aunt Maxine was a society reporter for a big city newspaper. She wrote about the famous people who sailed back and forth between the United States and Europe on big ocean liners. Then came the airplane, and celebrities stopped making news by traveling on liners. Aunt Maxine developed a new specialty: crime reporting. Hours after a crime occurred, she was famous for publishing her scoops, but then came television. No matter how hard she tried, television cameras beat Maxine to the punch. Now she edits videotape clips for the six o'clock news. She says that she's happy, but co-workers say that she's always muttering, "Stop the presses," under her breath.

What about me? Well, I used to be the chief of the bobbin-making crews at Bodwell Industries. Unfortunately, bobbins aren't such a big seller these days. So Bodwell decided to be high-tech. Microchips made by robots are the Bodwell mainstay now.

Am I unemployed and depressed? No, thanks to some farsighted thinking by my employer. I must say, Bodwell had the welfare of its employees uppermost in its corporate mind. Similarly, Bodwell had the interests of those expensive robots in mind. Somebody in the front office realized that even a robot can have a breakdown if it doesn't get some care and consideration from human beings. So, rather than lay me off, Bodwell sent me to classes to learn how to repair those intricate little fellows.

All kidding aside, as a member of the U.S. labor force, I am grateful for the opportunity to learn new skills as my old ones become outdated. Life can be frightening these days. Just as you think you're in the vanguard of a modern industry, you're told that your skills are obsolete.

Workers value the chance to work; they take pride in holding jobs. Take away peoples' chance to earn a living, eliminate the need for their skills, and you rob them of their dignity. You replace dignity with fear.

But change—even massive economic change—need not be fearsome if we plan for it. I'm told that my children, for example, could have as many as three separate careers in their lifetimes. If my children grow up knowing that change is inevitable, they won't fear it. And if they know that there will be opportunities for retraining, they won't have the fears that some of my neighbors have every time they hear rumors of their plant closing down or of automation being introduced in factories.

Reskilling can pay off by fostering reliable, loyal employees and taxpaying citizens. They will have hope in the future rather than fear of change.

As Great-Grandpa said, there's good and bad coming from a change in technology. "You can't feed one of those newfangled automobiles a lump of sugar when you've changed a tire. On the other hand, it won't try to rear back and kick you, either."

Sincerely yours,

T. Alvah Becker

T. Alvah Becker

1. According to the first letter writer, what happens to business when consumers lose their jobs?

_____

_____

_____

2. Why did T. Alvah Becker's Great-Grandpa become an auto mechanic?

_____

_____

_____

3. According to the first writer, what is one difference between the nineteenth-century Industrial Revolution and today's major technological changes?

_____

_____

_____

4. Why, according to the second writer, are his children likely to have as many as three separate careers?

_____

_____

_____

5. The people running Bodwell Industries decided to change their product before the company went bankrupt. What led them to make this decision?

_____

_____

6. Draw a line between each word and its opposite meaning.

archaic   impoverished

despair   current

solvent   hope

INTERPRETING FACTS

1. Are the personalities of the first and second writer similar or different? Explain.

_____

_____

_____

2. a. Which letter writer is more concerned with the effect of unemployment on people?

_____

   b. Which letter writer is more concerned with unemployment's and retraining's effects on business, in general?

_____

3. What conclusions can you draw about the management and future of Bodwell Industries?

_____

_____

_____

4. What conclusions can you draw about the employment possibilities for displaced workers who, like T. Alvah Becker, are willing to be reskilled?

_____

_____

_____

5. T. Alvah Becker's relatives all had to change with the times to survive.

a. Of the three—Great-Grandpa, Great-Granddad, and Aunt Maxine—who do you think adapted to change most successfully?

_____

_____

_____

_____

b. Who do you think adapted least successfully?

_____

_____

SKILL FOCUS

1. What is the opinion of each letter writer about reskilling displaced workers?

_____

_____

2. Is the tone, or attitude, of each letter writer similar or different? _____

3. a. Underline the words below that best identify the tone of the first letter.

    sentimental   businesslike   proud   humorous   bitter   serious

  b. Go back to the first letter to the editor. Underline the words and phrases that reveal the writer's attitude.

4. a. Underline the words below that best identify the tone of the second letter.

    scholarly   humorous   realistic   appreciative   matter of fact   sentimental

  b. Go back to the second letter to the editor. Underline the words and phrases that reveal the writer's attitude.

5. In one of the letters, the writer changes the tone halfway through.

  a. In which letter does the tone change?

_____

  b. Put brackets around the phrase that signals this change of tone.

c. How does the tone change?

_____

_____

6. Write a letter to the editor of your local newspaper, expressing your feelings about having three different careers in your lifetime. The paragraph should reflect a tone that is either favorable or unfavorable.

_____

_____

_____

_____

_____

_____

_____

_____

_____

_____

_____

_____

_____

_____

_____

_____

_____

_____

_____

_____

▶ **Real Life Connections** Look in your local newspaper to find two letters to the editor expressing views on the same issue in different ways.

Cause and Effect

___ Reading a Social Studies Selection _____

▶ Background Information

People have always looked for ways to make work easier and life better. In the last 200 years especially, technology has changed the way that people live and work. Sometimes, change has brought unexpected problems.

▶ Skill Focus

A **cause** is an underlying reason, condition, or situation that makes an event happen. An **effect** is the result or outcome of a cause. Sometimes a cause brings about an effect that in turn becomes the cause of another effect. This chain of causes and effects occurs frequently.

Causes and effects are often directly stated. Look for a chain of cause and effect relationships in the following paragraph.

> The invention of the inexpensively priced automobile made it possible for many people to own and drive automobiles. Over the decades, the widespread use of automobiles has caused problems, such as air pollution. This environmental danger resulted in the passage of emission control laws.

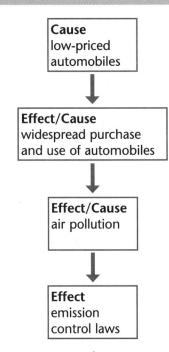

The diagram above shows the chain of causes and effects in this paragraph. Sometimes you have to infer, or figure out, a cause or an effect. As you read, try to understand how ideas are connected. When you think about the causes of particular actions, also think about the effects of those actions and how some of those effects become the causes of other effects.

▶ Word Clues

Read the following sentence. Look for context clues that explain the underlined word.

> Technology began with the first human being who <u>utilized</u>, or put to use, a stick or a rock as a tool.

If you don't know the meaning of the word *utilized*, the phrase following the word *or* can help you. *Utilized* means "put to use." The word *utilized* is explained in the appositive phrase set off by commas and the word *or*.

Use **appositive phrases** set off by commas, dashes, or the word *or* to find the meanings of the three underlined terms in the selection.

▶ Strategy Tip

Preview the following selection by reading the headings of its main sections. Then study the charts and graphs. As you read about new discoveries and their effects, look for a chain of causes and effects in which one effect becomes a cause of another effect.

Accelerated Technology Brings Constant Change

Technology began with the first human being who utilized, or put to use, a stick or a rock as a tool. For example, using a stick to knock a piece of fruit from a tree was immediately found to be more efficient than climbing the tree and picking the fruit. Since then, technology—the use of tools, machines, materials, and sources of power—has made our work more productive, our jobs easier, and our lives more pleasant. At the same time, it has also created a growing number of new problems.

Technology: Past and Present

Following the inventions of the first simple tools were such inventions as the wheel, the lever, and the pulley, all of which made moving and lifting heavy objects easier. For thousands of years, these devices, combined with human and animal power, remained very simple.

✔ In the early 1700s, an English inventor made a machine that could turn fibers into cloth. This was an example of <u>mechanization</u>, the use of a machine to do a task that people formerly performed. In the 1760s, James Watt found a way to drive a machine with steam,

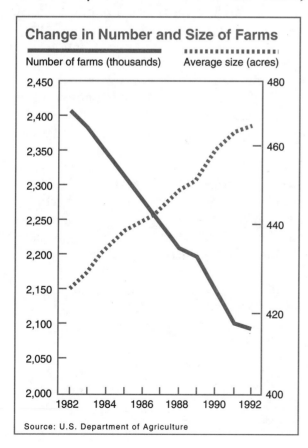

Change in Number and Size of Farms

Number of farms (thousands)   Average size (acres)

Source: U.S. Department of Agriculture

thus enabling machines to run at faster speeds than ever before. Soon electricity was used to turn a wheel, and the electric motor was born. Then natural resources, such as coal and oil, were burned to produce even greater amounts of power.

At the same time, machines were lightening the burden of work and performing the repetitious tasks that people formerly did by hand. The result was the beginning of an industrial society. Machines were transforming the nature of work, and industrial technology—the use of power-driven machines to mass-produce manufactured goods—was born. In 1840, manufactured goods accounted for less than a fifth of all United States production. By the late 1800s, the United States had become the largest industrial nation in the world.

In contrast, today's technological world is no longer a manufacturing, or goods-producing, society. It is a communication-oriented society. What counts is how information can be processed to most efficiently serve the needs of the consumer in such fields as health care, education, and entertainment. Today's employees are valued for their ability to analyze and use this information. The result is a "high-tech" society—a world in which industries and businesses use highly specialized and complex electronic computer systems to process information.

In yesterday's industrial society, the quantity of goods produced determined people's standard of living. In today's high-tech society, the quality of the services available determines the standard of living.

The Impact of Technology

As the nation shifts from an industrial structure to more of a service and high-tech orientation, modern technology continues to affect many aspects of daily life. This, in turn, has caused many changes—some beneficial, some not.

Increased Productivity

Technology has increased <u>productivity</u>, or the amount of goods and services that are created. Prior to the 1800s, a farmer, with the help of other workers and animals, could produce enough food to feed about four people. Today, the average American farmer, with a wide array of power-driven machinery, produces enough food to feed about 80 people. At the turn of the century, miners toiled all day with picks and shovels to produce a few tons of coal. With the aid of high-powered machinery, a coal-mining operator today can dig more than one short ton (.9 metric ton) of coal a minute. Today's computers can do in seconds what only 20 years ago would have taken clerks and mathematicians days to do.

The advances in computers and automation have created scores of new occupations.

The increased productivity that has resulted from technological advances has in turn caused environmental pollution. Hazardous wastes from factories contaminate the air, water, and soil. Power plants and factories that produce large quantities of goods pollute the air with smoke. Manufacturing plants produce waste products that are frequently dumped into nearby streams and unused land sites, ultimately threatening people's health. Fertilizers and insecticides, washed into rivers and lakes, kill fish and make the water undrinkable.

Increased productivity has also caused the depletion of natural resources, such as natural gas, coal, and oil. The earth's supply of these precious resources was once thought to be limitless. In recent years, however, shortages have developed.

Reduced Labor Force

✗ The accelerating pace of technology has reduced the size, as well as changed the nature, of the labor force. In the early 1800s, most factory work was done by hand. Many companies today have robots to perform the same jobs more quickly and accurately than people can. New factories that utilize high technology employ only half as many workers as conventional factories of the same size. Thinly populated production lines are proof that computerized robots have replaced many industrial workers.

The technology that enabled fewer people to do the work of many, and thus drastically reduced the size of the labor force, has in turn resulted in large-scale unemployment. Not only did production workers, such as the auto and steel workers in the 1980s, lose jobs, but their jobs became archaic and their skills became obsolete. Studies indicate that robots may eventually replace up to 75 percent of all factory workers.

New Occupations

High technology is also changing the nature of the labor force by creating new jobs. Advances in computers and automation have created scores of new occupations. Today's new employment fields include computer design and maintenance, robot and laser equipment repair, and industrial waste disposal. Future employment opportunities—considerably different from jobs available today—will require vastly different skills.

New occupations have resulted in the retraining of many workers who find themselves lacking the skills that today's employers need. These workers must adapt to the changing job market by being retrained for new occupations. For example, if a steelworker does not want to become a computer programmer, he or she might choose to retrain to service robots. Because a technologically literate labor force is critical for the new high-tech industries, retraining will

AMERICANS IN 2033 Based on Official Census Bureau Projections

Population	
1993	258,245,000
2033	305,778,000

Life Expectancy at Birth	
Men	
1993	72.5 years
2033	74.4 years
Women	
1993	79.3 years
2033	82.7 years

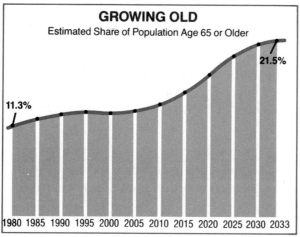

GROWING OLD
Estimated Share of Population Age 65 or Older

11.3%

21.5%

1980 1985 1990 1995 2000 2005 2010 2015 2020 2025 2030 2033

BASIC SOURCE U.S. Dept. of Commerce

be a lifelong process. Whether one chooses to become a data processor mechanic or a robot repair technician, rarely will a worker hold one job for life.

Higher Standard of Living

✗ The thrust of the new technology has also resulted in a higher standard of living, in both incomes and amenities. While thousands of assembly-line jobs have disappeared, hundreds of higher-paying technical positions have emerged. There is more job sharing and innovative work scheduling. For some, the workweek is shorter and the hours more flexible; many can even work at home. At the same time, however, many workers must not only update their knowledge and skills in their own specialities, but also be ready to change careers.

Medical technology has also enhanced the standard of living in a number of ways. For example, lasers make it possible for doctors to operate without making incisions, thus eliminating many surgical procedures. Laser procedures are short and painless and can often be provided on an outpatient basis, without anesthesia. Above all, medical technology has lowered the infant mortality rate and increased human life expectancy—the number of years a person can look forward to living. In 1900, the life expectancy of an average American was 47; today it is about 73 years for men and 79 years for women.

As a result of high-tech applications in the factory, office, and home, it is now possible to produce goods and to provide services that were impossible at the beginning of this century. Freed by technology from much of life's drudgery, people are now able to pursue more creative and rewarding interests. Education has become a lifelong pursuit, and work is more pleasant and rewarding.

RECALLING FACTS

1. Put the following events in the proper sequence.

   _____ invention of the electric motor

   _____ use of rocks and sticks as tools

   _____ discovery of the lever and pulley

   _____ use of robots and lasers

2. How was the productivity of a coal miner at the turn of the century different from that of a miner today?

   _____

   _____

   _____

   _____

3. Reread the two paragraphs that have Xs next to them. Underline the sentence that states the main idea in each paragraph.

4. Write the letter of the correct meaning on the line next to each term.

   _____ life expectancy

   _____ productivity

   _____ mechanization

   a. using machines to do tasks once done by hand

   b. the output of goods and services by workers

   c. projected number of years a person can expect to live

1. Some of the following statements are fact and some are opinion. Fill in the space between the lines next to each statement that expresses a fact.

   ‖ In the 1760s, James Watt invented a way to drive a machine with steam.

   ‖ Technology leads to a better life for everyone.

   ‖ In a technological society, education is a lifelong pursuit.

2. Use the chart on page 104 to answer the following questions. Fill in the circle next to the correct answer.

   a. In a 40-year period, the population of the United States will double.

      ○ true   ○ false

   b. The increase in life expectancy will be greater for women than for men.

      ○ true   ○ false

3. Use the graph on page 105 to answer the following questions.

   a. What is the projection for the growth of the population 65 years or older in 2033?

   b. Is the following statement true or false? By 2033, more than one out of every five Americans will be elderly.

   c. What do you think society needs to do to deal with this population increase?

4. Reread the paragraph with a check mark next to it. Write a sentence describing its main idea.

5. In your opinion, do the benefits of technology outweigh the problems it has caused? Explain.

1. Sometimes effects have to be inferred because they are not directly stated in a selection. Answer the following questions by inferring an effect.

   a. What may happen to unemployed workers in a technological society when they do not retrain for new jobs?

b. With new medical technology—especially the use of lasers—how might the role of the surgeon change?

_____

_____

c. How might the advances that reduce illness and physical disability affect older people?

_____

_____

d. Today's engineers are trying to develop new synthetic fuels. What effects might their discoveries have on Americans half a century from now?

_____

_____

e. A young person may need to continually learn new skills to carry him or her through a lifetime of work. What effect could this have on a person's career?

_____

_____

f. More and more communication is taking place through electronic means, rather than through newspapers and magazines. How might this affect the paper industry?

_____

_____

2. The development of high technology has resulted in four chains of causes and effects. Using the items listed in the box below, complete the cause-and-effect chain. You may go back to the selection, if necessary. Use the headings to help you.

large-scale unemployment	enviromental pollution
unsatisfying jobs	new occupations
increased productivity	changing patterns of work

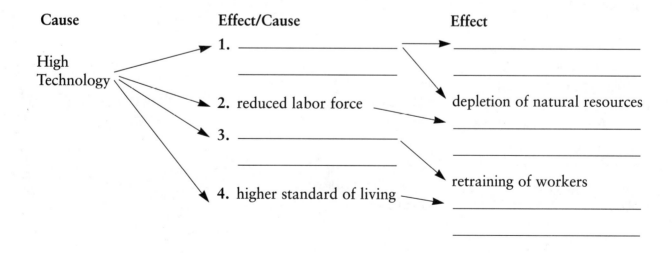

Cause

High Technology

Effect/Cause

1. _____
   _____

2. reduced labor force

3. _____
   _____

4. higher standard of living

Effect

_____
_____

depletion of natural resources
_____

_____
retraining of workers
_____

▶ **Real Life Connections** How does technology benefit your neighborhood or community? How does it hurt your neighborhood or community? Give examples.

Following Directions

Reading a Science Selection

► **Background Information**

The following selection discusses light waves, colors, mirrors, and lenses. It includes an experiment with directions that should be followed step by step. The experiment demonstrates how colored objects reflect different wavelengths of light.

► **Skill Focus**

Following directions is an important skill. For example, to carry out an experiment in a science textbook, you must follow directions.

Directions for an experiment are often set up in a certain way. Most sets of directions have five parts: Problem, Aim, Materials, Procedure, and Observations or Conclusions. Science experiments are always set up the same way, so that they can be repeated any number of times exactly as they were done the first time. This ensures that the results of the experiment are not affected by some slight variation in how the experiment is carried out. The following sections describe each part of the directions for an experiment.

Problem
The question that you should be able to answer at the end of the experiment

Aim
What will be done in the experiment

Materials
Objects or equipment needed for the experiment

Procedure
The steps that must be carried out in order to complete the experiment

Observations or Conclusions
Questions to answer or conclusions to draw about the outcome of the experiment

Use the following steps to help you read a science selection with directions for an experiment.

1. Read the paragraphs that explain the experiment. Be sure that you understand the ideas.

2. Read through the five parts of the directions: Problem, Aim, Materials, Procedure, and Observations or Conclusions.

3. Study the pictures or diagrams. Be sure to read the captions and labels.

4. Reread the Problem, Aim, Materials, Procedure, and Observations or Conclusions. Be sure that

you understand the steps in the procedure before you begin the experiment.

► **Word Clues**

Sometimes special terms are explained in a paragraph and also shown in a diagram. When this happens, study both the text and the diagram to help you understand the terms.

Use **diagram** clues as context clues to find the meanings of the underlined words in the selection.

► **Strategy Tip**

Before you read the selection, preview it. The headings and boldfaced words should help you to understand how the facts are organized. Look at the diagrams and captions. After you read the explanatory paragraphs, study the directions for the experiment.

Light

Light and sound are both forms of energy. Like sound, light energy travels as a wave. A wave is a means by which energy moves from one place to another. For example, the light waves that travel to Earth from the sun provide plants with the energy to grow.

There are many forms of light other than visible light. But all of these forms of light energy travel at the same speed. You know that light, like sound, can travel through the air. But light, unlike sound, can also travel through a vacuum. Light from the sun reaches the earth through the vacuum of space.

Light travels in a vacuum at the remarkable speed of 186,000 miles per second. This is approximately 300,000 kilometers per second. This speed is equivalent to about 7.3 trips around Earth's equator every second. At this speed, light leaving the sun reaches Earth in 8.3 minutes. However, if you could travel on a beam of light, it would take you about four years to reach the closest star.

In air, light travels almost as fast as it does in a vacuum, but its speed is slower when it travels through other media. The word *media* means "substances." When light travels from one medium (the singular of media) to another, it is bent, or **refracted,** by the new medium. This bending of light is why a soda straw in a liquid looks bent.

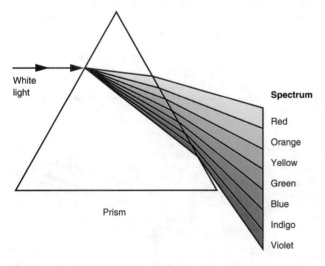

Figure 1. White light is actually composed of many colors.

Color

The light that we recognize as white light is actually composed of many colors. The makeup of light can be demonstrated by using a **prism** (PRIZ m), a triangular piece of glass. When light passes through a prism, it is refracted twice. It is refracted once when it enters the prism from the air and again when it moves from the prism back into the air. The result is a band of colors, called a **spectrum,** with red at the top and violet at the bottom.

A prism separates white light into its various colors because each color is made up of light waves of different frequencies. Of all the colors of the spectrum, red light has the lowest frequency and is refracted the least. Violet, with waves of the highest frequency, is refracted the most. Figure 1 shows what happens when white light passes through a prism.

The variety of colors that objects appear to be depends on the light that they reflect. Some objects, such as brick and wood, do not allow any light to pass through them. The color of opaque objects, which means objects that cannot be seen through, depends on the frequency of the light they reflect. For example, when white light is shined on an apple, the apple appears red. The reason is that the apple absorbs, or takes in, all the colors from white light except red. The red light is reflected, or bounced back, from the apple, and so we perceive it as red. The word *perceive* means "to be aware of." If an apple is placed in a green light, it will absorb all the green light waves but reflect nothing, since no red light would be present for reflection. Under these conditions, the apple would appear to be black, which is the absence of reflected light.

Mirrors

The way light is reflected and refracted can be put to use in mirrors and lenses. Mirrors reflect light from an object in such a way that we get an image, or picture, of that object. There are three types of mirrors: plane, convex, and concave.

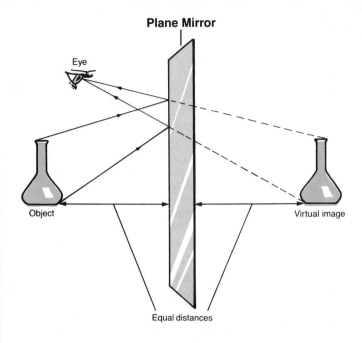

Plane Mirror

Eye

Object

Virtual image

Equal distances

Figure 2. A plane mirror produces a virtual image that appears to be behind the surface of the mirror.

A **plane mirror** is the type in a bathroom or dressing room. It produces an image that is the same size as the object that is reflected. This image, called a <u>virtual image</u>, appears to be behind the surface of the mirror. The apparent distance between the virtual image and the surface of the mirror is equal to the distance between the object reflected and the surface of the mirror. See Figure 2.

The arrows in Figures 4 and 5 represent light rays. The letter F in each diagram is the **focus**, or point either where the light rays cross or where they would cross if they could travel through the mirror.

A **convex mirror** is curved outward, like part of the surface of a sphere. Like a plane mirror, a convex mirror also produces a virtual image. The image, however, is smaller than the object reflected, making the object seem farther away than it really is. This type of mirror is often used in stores because it

---

Experiment

The following experiment demonstrates what happens when light of different colors shines on various objects.

Problem
What color do objects appear in colored light?

Aim
In this experiment, you will observe the reflected light of various opaque objects as you shine light of different colors on the objects.

Materials
You need a slide projector with a stand, colored filters (blue, red, yellow, and green), and a variety of colored objects (apple, banana, book with a blue cover, and a leaf).

Procedure
1. Set up the projector as shown in Figure 3.
2. Place the apple on a table.
3. Turn out the lights and pull down the shades.
4. Shine white light from the projector onto the apple, and record the color that the apple appears to be.
5. Now place the blue filter over the projector lens. Shine the blue light on the apple, and record the color that the apple appears to be.
6. Repeat step 5 using each of the other filters.
7. Repeat steps 3–6 using each of the other objects.

Observations or Conclusions
In white light, each object reflected the color that it is normally perceived to be. The same observation was made when light of the same color as the object was shined on the object. However, when the color of the shined light was different from the color of the object, the object absorbed all the colors and appeared to be black.

Figure 3. Shine the light from the projector onto the apple.

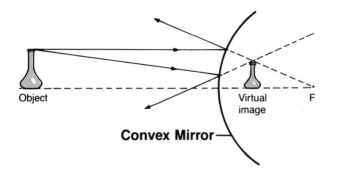

Figure 4. A convex mirror makes the reflected object look smaller.

Figure 5. A concave mirror produces an inverted image.

helps security people see a large area all at once. See Figure 4.

A **concave mirror** is curved inward, much like a cave. The image that it produces appears to be on the same side of the mirror as the object reflected; this is called a <u>real image</u>. The image appears smaller than the object, and it is <u>inverted</u>. The word *inverted* means "turned upside down." Figure 5 shows how images are produced by a concave mirror.

Lenses

A **lens** is a transparent material, usually glass or plastic, through which light can pass.

As light passes through a lens, it is refracted. There are two major types of lenses: convex and concave.

A **convex lens** has two focuses. One is on the side of the lens away from the object (the real focus), and the other is on the same side of the lens as the object (the virtual focus). The two diagrams in Figure 6 show the positions and types of images produced by distant and near objects through a convex lens. This type of lens is used in magnifying glasses. The image of an object at a great distance from such a lens is inverted and smaller. The image of an object

Convex Lens When Object Is Distant

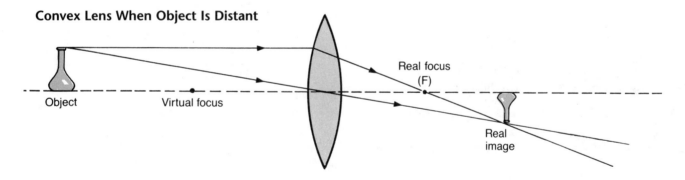

Convex Lens When Object Is Close

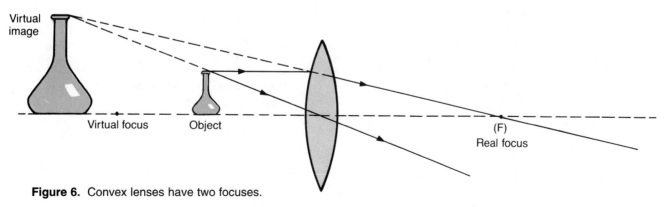

Figure 6. Convex lenses have two focuses.

close to the lens appears upright and larger.

A **concave lens** is thin in the center and thick at its edges. It spreads out light waves. A concave lens produces only virtual images that are upright and smaller than the object. The image produced is between the virtual focus and the lens. You can look through the lens to see the image. Figure 7 shows how a concave lens produces an image.

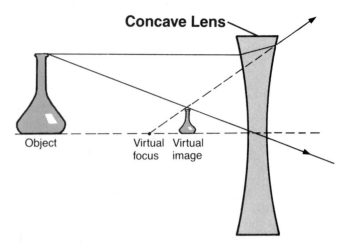

Concave Lens

Object Virtual focus Virtual image

Figure 7. Concave lenses produce only virtual images that are upright and smaller than the object.

RECALLING FACTS

1. How do scientists know that light is made up of colors?

_____

_____

2. What happens to light rays when they are refracted?

_____

3. What happens to the speed of light when it moves from air to glass or water?

_____

4. Why does an apple look red in white light?

_____

_____

_____

5. What kind of image does a plane mirror produce? Describe this image.

_____

_____

_____

_____

6. Describe the image produced by a concave mirror.

_____

_____

7. What kind of image does a convex lens form of a distant object?

_____

_____

8. What kind of image does a concave lens form of a close object?

_____

_____

9. Complete each statement with the correct term from the list below.

   virtual image   real image   inverted

   a. An image that is upside down is

   _____.

   b. A _____ appears to be on the same side of a concave mirror as the object reflected.

   c. A _____ appears to be behind a mirror.

Choose the word or phrase that completes each sentence. Then fill in the space between the lines next to the correct answer.

1. A convex lens makes a good magnifying glass because the image it produces is _____.
   || a. upright and smaller than the object
   || b. upright and larger than the object
   || c. a real image and larger than the object

2. A violet object in violet light would appear _____.
   || a. white
   || b. black
   || c. violet

3. The image that falls on the film of a camera is inverted. Cameras have _____ lenses.
   || a. convex
   || b. concave
   || c. plane

4. A convex mirror is used by security people in large stores because the image it produces is _____.
   || a. virtual and smaller than the object
   || b. virtual and larger than the object
   || c. on the same side of the mirror as the object

SKILL FOCUS

A. In your own words, write a summary of the experiment on page 110. When you finish, check your summary by rereading the experiment, and make any corrections that are necessary.

_____

_____

_____

_____

_____

_____

B. The experiment on the next page shows what color an object must be in order for it to appear the same color as the light shining on it. Use the same materials as in the experiment on page 110, but add an object that is white and an object that is black. Using the experiment on page 110 as a model, write the directions for this experiment on the lines provided. Be sure to number the steps in the Procedure part. Draw a chart for recording the information collected in the experiment.

Experiment

Problem

_____

Aim

_____

_____

_____

Materials

_____

_____

_____

_____

Procedure

_____

_____

_____

_____

_____

Observations or Conclusions

_____

_____

_____

_____

object / light	red	blue	green	yellow	black	white
red						
blue						
green						
yellow						

▶ **Real Life Connections** Describe one example that you have seen of colored light used to create a dramatic effect.

Exponential Notation

Reading a Mathematics Selection

▶ Background Information

Reading exponential notation is actually easier in some ways than reading numbers written in standard form. With exponential notation, you read fewer digits for very large or very small numbers. For example, the speed of light is 186,000 miles per second. The distance that light travels in one year, which is called a light year, is 5,880,000,000,000 miles. That's a huge number to read, write, or even say. But it's much easier to express it in exponential notation. Expressed that way, a light year can be writen as 5.88×10^{12}.

Similarly, it's easier to write very small numbers in exponential notation, too. For example, some computer operations take place in a very small amount of time, called a nanosecond. A nanosecond is one billionth of a second. If written out in its complete form, a nanosecond would be 1/1,000,000,000. But in exponential notation, a nanosecond is written as 1^{-9}.

▶ Skill Focus

A special method of writing very large or very small numbers in an abbreviated form is called **exponential notation**. This system of expressing numbers is sometimes called scientific notation. In the mathematical expression $10^2 = 10 \times 10 = 100$, 10 is the **base number**, or the number multiplied by itself. The **exponent** is the small numeral that tells how many times the base is used as a **factor**. Notice the position of the numerals.

When the base number is 10, the number of zeros after the 1 in the product is the same as the exponent.

When a number is expressed in exponential notation, it is written as a power of ten and a number between 1 and 10. For example, the number 3,572,000 is written as follows:

$$3.572 \times 10^6$$

Negative exponents are used to write decimal numbers, or numbers whose values are less than 1. Read the following expression.

$$10^{-2} = 0.01 = \tfrac{1}{100}$$

Negative exponents tell how many decimal places there are after the decimal point.

▶ Word Clues

When reading the following selection, look for these important words: *exponent, base number,* and *factor.* They will help you understand more about exponential notation.

▶ Strategy Tip

As you read each example of exponential notation in this selection, read the exponent carefully. Especially notice whether the exponent is negative.

Exponential Notation

In the number 10^2, the numeral 2 is the **exponent**. It is written above and to the right of the **base number**, which is 10. The exponent tells how many times the base number is multiplied by itself, or used as a **factor**. Factors are numbers that form a product when multiplied together. Therefore, the mathematical expression 10^2 means that ten is used as a factor twice, or 10×10. The expression 10^2 is read ten to the second power, or ten squared. The product for this number is 100.

$$10^2 = 10 \times 10 = 100$$

The mathematical expressions 10^3, 10^4, 10^5, and 10^6 are read ten to the third power, or ten cubed; ten to the fourth power; ten to the fifth power; and ten to the sixth power.

For each of the following examples, the exponent and the number of zeros in the product are the same. In other words, the exponent shows how many zeros are in the product. The dot between the tens is another sign for multiplication.

$$10^4 = 10 \cdot 10 \cdot 10 \cdot 10 = 10,000$$
$$10^6 = 10 \cdot 10 \cdot 10 \cdot 10 \cdot 10 \cdot 10 = 1,000,000$$

The number 10 is represented as 10^1.
The number 1 is represented as 10^0.
Other large numbers can be expressed as follows:

$$5,000,000,000 = 5 \cdot 10^9$$
$$557,000,000 = 557 \cdot 10^6$$

Scientists prefer to express the number before the multiplication sign as a value from 1 to 10. To change 557 to a number between 1 and 10, the decimal point is moved two places to the left, from 557. to 5.57. To make up for the two decimal places, the exponent is increased from 6 to 8. Both $557 \cdot 10^6$ and $5.57 \cdot 10^8$ equal 557,000,000.

Expanded Notation

Any large or small number can be written by using a method called **expanded notation**. Each digit of the number is written in terms of its place value. In the number 3,908, the 3 is in the thousands place and can be written as $3 \cdot 1,000$. The 9 is in the hundreds place and can be written as $9 \cdot 100$. The 0 is in the tens place and can be written as $0 \cdot 10$. The 8 is in the ones place and can be written as $8 \cdot 1$. The parentheses indicate that the mathematical expression inside them must be completed before the result can be used in another process.

$$3,908 = (3 \cdot 1,000) + (9 \cdot 100) + (0 \cdot 10) + (8 \cdot 1)$$

This can be simplified by using exponents.

$$3,908 = (3 \cdot 10^3) + (9 \cdot 10^2) + (0 \cdot 10^1) + (8 \cdot 10^0)$$

Negative Exponents

Negative exponents are used for representing values of less than one, or values to the right of the decimal point. The expression $10^{-1} = 0.1$, or $\frac{1}{10}$. The expression $10^{-2} = 0.01$, or $\frac{1}{100}$. Look at the following mathematical expressions.

$$10^{-4} = 0.0001 = \tfrac{1}{10,000}$$
$$10^{-5} = 0.00001 = \tfrac{1}{100,000}$$

For each example, the negative exponent is the same as the number of places to the right of the decimal point. It is also the same as the number of zeros in the denominator of the fraction.

With negative exponents, expanded notation can be used to write decimals. Look at the following expanded notation.

$$4.037 = (4 \cdot 1) + (0 \cdot .1) + (3 \cdot .01) + (7 \cdot .001)$$
$$= (4 \cdot 10^0) + (0 \cdot 10^{-1}) + (3 \cdot 10^{-2}) + (7 \cdot 10^{-3})$$

When numbers less than 1 are written with exponential notation, the exponent is always a negative number. For example, the number 0.0023 is written as $2.3 \cdot 10^{-3}$, and the number 0.000306 is written as $3.06 \cdot 10^{-4}$. A number with an exponent of -4 is always smaller than a number with an exponent of -3.

A negative exponent can be used to express a decimal that is less than 1. To do so, count the number of places to the right of the decimal point, up to and including the first numeral that has a value greater than zero. That number becomes the exponent. For example, in the number 0.0023, you would use 10^{-3} because there are three places to the right of the decimal point, up to and including the numeral 2.

Place the decimal point after that number. The number 23 is thus changed to 2.3. You now have a number between 1 and 10 to multiply by the power of 10, in this case 10^{-3}.

$$0.0023 = 2.3 \cdot 10^{-3}$$

In the decimal 0.000306, there are four places to the right of the decimal point, up to and including the numeral 3. So the expression 10^{-4} is used in the mathematical expression for 0.000306. To find the number between 1 and 10 that you must multiply by this power of 10, write the number that begins with the numeral 3. Place the decimal point after the first digit in that number. The number 306 is changed to 3.06 and then multiplied by 10^{-4}.

$$0.000306 = 3.06 \cdot 10^{-4}$$

To change a number in exponential notation with a negative exponent to a decimal, simply reverse the process. Use the following steps.

$$3.06 \cdot 10^{-4}$$

1. Write the number 3.06.
2. Count the numeral to the left of the decimal point in that number as 1. Then, from right to left, count the same number of places as the exponent.

$$3.06 \qquad \overset{\frown}{\cdot\,\,\,\,\,}3.06$$
$$\quad\qquad\quad 4\,3\,2\,1$$

3. Insert zeros for each place that you counted, and move the decimal point.

$$3.06 \cdot 10^{-4} = .000306$$

RECALLING FACTS

1. The mathematical expression 10^4 is read

   _____.

2. What is the name of the method in which the following expression is written?
   $(3 \cdot 10^1) + (5 \cdot 10^0) + (9 \cdot 10^{-1})$

   _____

3. What kind of exponents are used to represent numbers that have a value less than 1?

   _____

4. What place value does the zero have in 4,807?

   _____

INTERPRETING FACTS

1. What is the value of the expression 6^4?

   _____

2. In the expression 10^2, how many zeros are in the product? _____

3. How would you write the mathematical expression $4 \cdot 10^{-6}$ as a decimal numer? _____

4. In which two situations below would exponential notation be the most useful?
   a. to show the circumference of an ant's leg
   b. to show the speed of a plane
   c. to show the number of snowflakes in a field

   Write the letters on the line provided.

   _____

A. Write the following numbers by using exponential notation. The first one is done for you.

1. $947,000 = \underline{\ 9.47 \cdot 10^5\ }$

2. $2,500,000,000,000,000,000,000,000 = $ _____

3. $0.00000006 = $ _____

4. $0.0004 = $ _____

5. $4,002,000,000 = $ _____

B. In each of the following pairs of numbers, circle the one that has the greater value. Then write the value of that number on the line provided to the right of the pair.

1. $2.07 \cdot 10^{-2}$ $2.07 \cdot 10^{-4}$ _____

2. $6.3 \cdot 10^4$ $6.3 \cdot 10^6$ _____

3. $5 \cdot 10^{14}$ $5 \cdot 10^{-14}$ _____

C. Write the standard numbers for the following mathematical expressions. The first one is done for you.

1. $4.09 \cdot 10^{11} = \underline{\ 409,000,000,000\ }$

2. $5.093 \cdot 10^3 = $ _____

3. $3.3802 \cdot 10^0 = $ _____

4. $8 \cdot 10^{-6} = $ _____

5. $7.9374 \cdot 10^1 = $ _____

D. Write each of the following numbers in expanded notation by using exponents. The first one is done for you.

1. $305 = \underline{\ (3 \cdot 10^2) + (0 \cdot 10^1) + (5 \cdot 10^0)\ }$

2. $4,003 = $ _____

3. $3,098,124 = $ _____

4. $0.51 = $ _____

E. Write the following expressions in standard numbers.

1. $(7 \cdot 10^4) + (3 \cdot 10^3) + (0 \cdot 10^2) + (9 \cdot 10^1) + (1 \cdot 10^0) = $ _____

2. $(6 \cdot 10^{-1}) + (2 \cdot 10^{-2}) + (8 \cdot 10^{-3}) = $ _____

▶ **Real Life Connections** In what type of job would using exponential notation be beneficial?

Syllables

When dividing words of three or more syllables, you use the same methods of deciding where to divide between syllables that you use with two-syllable words. The only difference is that you will have to use two or more guides.

In dividing the word *recovery*, for example, you use three guides.

1. Divide between the prefix and the rest of the word: re covery.
2. Divide after the consonant in words with one consonant between two sounded vowels with the first vowel short: re cov ery.
3. Divide between the rest of the word and the suffix: re cov er y.

Following is a summary of some guides to help you divide words into syllables.

Guide 1. In a compound word, divide between the two smaller words.

Guide 2. In words with double consonants, divide between the double consonants.

Guide 3. In words with a prefix or suffix, divide between the root word and its prefix or suffix.

Guide 4. In words with two consonants between two sounded vowels, divide between the two consonants.

Guide 5a. In words with one consonant between two sounded vowels with the first vowel long, you usually divide before the consonant.

Guide 5b. In words with one consonant between two sounded vowels with the first vowel short, you usually divide after the consonant.

Guide 6. Do not divide between consonant blends or consonant and *-le*.

Divide each of the words below into syllables. Write the syllables separately on the line to the right of the word. Then write the numbers of the guides that you used on the line to the left of the word. The first word is done for you.

1. _1, 5a, 5b_ photocopy _pho to cop y_   13. _____ steeplechase _____
2. _____ belligerence _____   14. _____ nationalize _____
3. _____ miscellany _____   15. _____ environment _____
4. _____ decolorize _____   16. _____ leverage _____
5. _____ opportunist _____   17. _____ tinselly _____
6. _____ acceptance _____   18. _____ hibernate _____
7. _____ reactional _____   19. _____ surrenderer _____
8. _____ settlement _____   20. _____ marketplace _____
9. _____ bandanna _____   21. _____ saddlebag _____
10. _____ scholarship _____   22. _____ randomize _____
11. _____ caterpillar _____   23. _____ occasional _____
12. _____ immobile _____   24. _____ cucumber _____

Lesson 32

Accented Syllable and Schwa Sound

When words contain two syllables, one of the syllables is stressed, or accented, more than the other. In dictionaries, the **accent mark (')** is placed at the end of the syllable that is said with more stress. For example, the first syllable in the word *walrus* is said with more stress than the second syllable.

wal' rus

In words with three syllables, the accent is usually on one of the first two syllables. When you are trying to pronounce a word with three syllables, such as *important*, stress the first syllable. If the word does not sound right, say it again, stressing the second syllable.

im' por tant   im por' tant

Say each of the following words to yourself. Write an accent mark after the syllable that should be stressed.

1. dis cuss
2. sev er al
3. pro fes sor
4. oc cu py
5. con clu sion
6. sur prise
7. de scrib ing
8. doz en

Words of four or more syllables usually have two accented syllables. In the word *salamander*, the first syllable has the most stress. This syllable has the primary accent mark ('). The third syllable has more stress than the remaining two syllables but less than the first syllable. The lighter accent mark (') is placed after that syllable. This is called the secondary accent.

sal'a man' der

Say each of the following words to yourself. Write a primary accent mark after the syllable that has the most stress. Say the word again. Write a secondary accent mark after the syllable that has the second most stress.

1. hip po pot a mus
2. re ha bil i tate
3. ex am i na tion
4. Mas sa chu setts
5. ter ri to ry
6. ex plo ra tion
7. man u fac ture
8. O kla ho ma

The vowels *a, e, i, o,* and *u* can all have the same sound. This is a soft sound like a short *u* pronounced lightly. This short, soft *u* sound is called the **schwa** sound. In dictionary respellings, the symbol ə stands for the schwa sound. If you look up the word *canary* in the dictionary, you will find it respelled with the schwa sound.

kə ner' ē

Say each of the following words to yourself. Write a primary and secondary accent mark after the syllables that are stressed. Then circle the letter that stands for the schwa sound.

1. cap i tal ize
2. in stru men tal
3. pre lim i nar y
4. mat ri mo ny
5. trans at lan tic
6. ge o met ric
7. lo co mo tive
8. san i tar y

Look at the words in the list above. Notice that the schwa sound always falls in an unaccented syllable of a word.

Multiple Meanings

Some words have entirely different meanings when used in different subject areas. Examples of such words are listed below.

acute	capital	meter	period	solution
bank	graft	mill	revolution	volume
base	margin	order	ruler	

Read the two definitions for each word below. Write the word from the list that fits the two definitions on the line before the first definition.

1. _____
   Science: a stretch of rising land at the edge of a stream or river
   Social Studies: an establishment for receiving, lending, or sometimes issuing money

2. _____
   Science: a classification ranking above a family and below a class
   Social Studies: written instructions to pay money or hand over property

3. _____
   Literature: a collection of written or printed sheets bound together
   Mathematics: the amount of space occupied in three dimensions; cubic contents

4. _____
   Social Studies: a building with machinery for grinding grain into flour or meal
   Mathematics: one-tenth of a cent

5. _____
   Science: a shoot or bud of a plant or tree inserted into a stem or trunk of another so that it will grow there
   Social Studies: a dishonest use of one's position to get money, property, or power

6. _____
   Literature: rhythm in verse; regular arrangement of accented and unaccented syllables in each line
   Mathematics: the base unit of length in the metric system, equal to 39.37 inches

7. _____
   Science: movement of a body, as of a planet, in an orbit or circle
   Social Studies: overthrow of a government or social system, with another taking its place

8. _____
   Literature: the blank border of a printed or written page
   Social Studies: the difference between the cost and selling price of goods

9. _____
   Social Studies: a person who governs
   Mathematics: a thin strip of wood, metal, or plastic with a straight edge, used in drawing lines and measuring

10. _____
    Science: the time that goes by between happenings in a cycle involving a heavenly body, as between two full moons
    Literature: the pause in speaking or a mark of punctuation used at the end of a declarative sentence

11. _____
    Science: the dispersion of one or more substances in another, usually a liquid, so as to form a homogeneous mixture
    Mathematics: the solving of a problem

12. _____
    Mathematics: an angle less than 90 degrees
    Literature: keen or quick of mind; shrewd

Improving Reading Rate

A good reader is able to read at several speeds, depending on the material being read. When reading difficult or unfamiliar material, a good reader reads slowly. For example, social studies, science, mathematics, and poetry may be more difficult to read than most literature. So these materials are read more slowly. Sometimes, a reader needs to reread a paragraph to understand a complex idea. A good reader slows down when words or sentences are difficult. A good reader also stops to read diagrams and maps, which require increased attention, making it necessary to read at a slower rate.

The following selection can be used to check your reading rate. Use a watch or a clock with a second hand to time yourself. Start right on a minute, such as five minutes past ten o'clock. Write your starting time. Because it is a science selection, you should read it more slowly than you would read a story. Write your ending time at the end of the selection.

Starting time _____

Lasers: Making a Special Kind of Light

Science has uncovered the means to produce a thin beam of brilliant light. This beam, made by a laser, can compute distances, weld metals, and perform surgery on the human body. The word *laser* is an acronym for <u>l</u>ight <u>a</u>mplification by <u>s</u>timulated <u>e</u>mission of <u>r</u>adiation.

The light that a laser makes is very strong, powerful, and concentrated. A beam of laser light is different from the kind of light produced by a lightbulb or the sun. Light from the sun or a lightbulb is a mixture of waves that vibrate at a great number of frequencies. All the waves of a laser beam vibrate together at a single frequency. Laser light is also different in that it travels in only one direction. Light from other sources travels in all directions.

A description of the ruby rod laser can be used to show how lasers work. The ruby rod has two flat ends. One end, completely covered with silver, reflects like a mirror. The other end is partially covered with silver, but a small space is left for light to escape.

A lighted flash tube focuses a bright light on the rod. Electrons in the atoms of the rod gain energy. When atoms absorb energy, their electrons get "excited" and release energy in the form of red light waves. The waves reflect back and forth between the mirrored ends of the rod. These rapid reflections cause the light

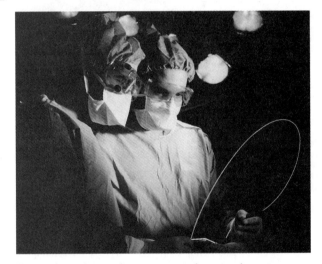

Doctors use lasers for surgery and research.

to increase in intensity so that the reflections are soon vibrating in a single wave. Finally, this wave bursts out of the small, uncovered space at one end of the rod. It escapes in the form of a powerful beam of laser light.

There are three main kinds of lasers: solid, gas, and liquid. Solid lasers are used most often. Crystal lasers (like the ruby rod), glass lasers, and injection lasers are all examples of solid lasers. Gas lasers use one gas or a mixture of gases to produce the powerful beam. Liquid lasers can create bursts of light or continuous light. Only a liquid laser can have its frequency changed.

Lasers are used in many ways. In communications, lasers can send television signals and voice messages. They can carry much more information than radio waves because they operate at a higher frequency. However, laser light cannot travel through rain, fog, or snow. For reliable communications, the laser beam is transmitted inside optical fibers made of glass. Using fiber optics, one laser beam can transmit many telephone calls at the same time. Lasers are also used to encode and "read" visual images and sound on laser discs and compact discs.

Lasers are as useful in industry as they are in communications. They can produce an intense heat for melting hard materials or for welding metal parts together. Because lasers produce an absolutely straight beam of light, they are also used for alignment in construction projects, such as drilling tunnels and laying pipelines.

In medicine, the intense heat of a laser is used in different kinds of surgery. Lasers can burn away diseased body tissue without harming healthy tissue. A laser can also be used to repair a detached retina in a patient's eye.

To find the total time that it took you to read the selection, do the following: (1) Subtract your starting time from your ending time. (2) Divide the number of words in the selection by the remainder expressed in seconds.

If it took you 3 minutes and 5 seconds (3 × 60 + 5 = 185 seconds) to read the selection, you would have read 3 words per second (555 ÷ 185 = 3). (3) To find the number of words per minute (WPM), multiply your rate per second by 60. Your answer would be 180 WPM.

Words in selection: 555

	Hr.	Min.	Sec.
Ending time:	_____	_____	_____
Starting time:	_____	_____	_____
Total time:	_____	_____	_____

$\dfrac{\text{No. words: } 555}{\text{No. seconds: } \rule{2cm}{0.4pt}}$ = ___ × 60 = ___ WPM

To check your understanding of the selection, underline the answer to each question.

1. What kind of light has waves that vibrate together in a single frequency?
   a. lightbulb   **b.** sunlight   **c.** laser light

2. How does laser light differ from other light?
   a. It travels in only one direction.
   b. It travels in two directions.
   c. It travels in all directions.

3. What happens when a bright light is focused on a ruby rod laser?
   a. Excited electrons become trapped in the rod.
   b. Excited electrons release energy in a powerful beam.
   c. Excited electrons escape in all directions.

4. Which kind of laser is used most often?
   a. gas   **b.** liquid   **c.** solid

5. What can the intense heat of a laser do?
   a. heat a house
   b. weld metal parts together
   c. cook a frozen dinner in seconds

6. Which one, two, or three of the following things can lasers do?
   a. send voice messages
   b. melt hard materials
   c. read information stored on discs

7. In what way are lasers more useful than radio waves?
   a. They can carry more information.
   b. They can carry messages over water.
   c. They can travel more quickly.

8. In which ways have lasers been used in medicine?
   a. to repair a detached retina in an eye
   b. to mend a broken bone
   c. to burn away diseased body tissue

Credit Card Application

People buy on credit either because they don't want to carry cash or because they don't have enough money to get what they want right away. With a **credit card,** people can buy now and pay later.

To obtain an extension of credit from a company, you must fill out and submit an application. Once the company receives your application, it checks your credit rating. The businesses with whom you already have credit regularly report the status of your accounts to the credit bureau. The credit bureau keeps a record of credit ratings. If you always pay your bills on time, you have a good credit rating. If you usually do not pay your bills, or if you do not pay them on time, your credit rating is not good.

When you buy on credit, you should remember to charge only what you will be able to pay for when you receive your bill. If you do not, you can overextend yourself, that is, charge more than you can afford. Once you are overextended, you can become a bad credit risk.

Study the front side of an application for a gasoline company credit card. With this card, the applicant will be able to buy now and pay later at the company's gas stations.

CALCO CREDIT CARD APPLICATION

Important instructions: Please use the pre-addressed envelope provided to return this application or mail it to CALCO, PO Box 2024, Santa Monica, California 90404. To insure prompt handling, print or type all information requested below. Be sure to read and sign the agreement on the reverse side. Applications submitted without your signature on the reverse side cannot be processed.

APPLICANT'S NAME - FIRST	INITIAL	LAST	AGE	SOCIAL SECURITY NUMBER
Gina	R.	Martinelli	23	614-38-2553

CURRENT ADDRESS

STREET ADDRESS AND APARTMENT NO., IF APPLICABLE (NO P.O. BOX PLEASE): 63 Fifer Lane
☐ OWN ☑ RENT — ☑ HOME ☐ APT. — OTHER — YRS. AT THIS ADDRESS 2½

CITY	STATE	ZIP	HOME PHONE NUMBER	NO. DEPENDENTS
Lexington	Massachusetts	02173	AREA CODE (617) 555-8129	1

PREVIOUS ADDRESS

IF AT PRESENT ADDRESS LESS THAN ONE YEAR, GIVE PREVIOUS ADDRESS

CITY	STATE	ZIP	YRS. AT THIS ADDRESS

EMPLOYMENT

PRESENT EMPLOYER	NATURE OF BUSINESS
Boston Museum of History	museum

STREET ADDRESS: 6000 Beacon Street — JOB TITLE (RANK, IF IN MILITARY SERVICE): tour guide — YEARS EMPLOYED 2½

CITY	STATE	ZIP	BUSINESS PHONE NUMBER
Boston	Massachusetts	02122	AREA CODE (617) 555-4400

PREVIOUS EMPLOYER & ADDRESS (IF WITH PRESENT EMPLOYER LESS THAN 5 YEARS): Camp Wiki   Naples, Maine 04055 — YEARS EMPLOYED 4 summers while student

CREDIT REFERENCES

If credit refernces are under a name other than the applicant's, please indicate name beside each credit reference.

FIRM NAME	ACCOUNT NUMBER
Gaylin's Department Store	225-02-876

ADDRESS: 7500 Beacon Street   Boston, MA

FIRM NAME	ACCOUNT NUMBER
Porter's	191-33-649

ADDRESS: 430 Roxbury Street   Lexington, MA

FIRM NAME	ACCOUNT NUMBER
Charg-it card (under Franco Martinelli)	4226-298-717

ADDRESS: 1499 Revere Avenue   Boston, MA

BANK

BANK NAME	ACCOUNT NUMBER
Lexington Bank and Trust Company	011840-184-2

ADDRESS: 641 Linwood Street   Lexington, MA — TYPE ACCOUNTS: ☑ CHECKINGS ☐ SAVINGS ☑ LOAN

SPOUSE INFORMATION

If a spouse will be permitted to use this account, please complete information below.

SPOUSE'S NAME - FIRST	INITIAL	LAST
Franco	P.	Martinelli

EMPLOYER AND ADDRESS: Newton High School 390 Main St., Newton, MA

NAME & ADDRESS OF NEAREST RELATIVE	HOME PHONE NUMBER
Mabel Russo 2 Cranberry Lane, Harrison, Maine 04040	AREA CODE (207) 555-0465

CARDS WILL BE USED FOR (NOTE: IF CREDIT CARD IS TO BE USED FOR BUSINESS, PLEASE WRITE TO ABOVE ADDRRESS FOR COMMERCIAL APPLICATION.)	☑ CAR ☐ BOAT ☐ TRUCK ☐ PLANE	ESTIMATED MONTHLY CALCO CREDIT CARD PURCHASES $100.00	NO. CARDS DESIRED 2	DRIVER'S LICENSE NO. AND STATE MA 614-38-2553

A. Read the statements about the gasoline credit card application. Write *T* or *F* on the lines provided.

_____ 1. A Calco credit card can be used to purchase gas for a car, truck, boat, or plane.

_____ 2. The applicant owns her home at 63 Fifer Lane.

_____ 3. The applicant has a credit card with Charg-it of Boston.

_____ 4. The applicant has a charge account at a Boston store named Gaylin's.

_____ 5. If the applicant charges gas at another gas station, that station could be used as a credit reference.

_____ 6. Mable Russo is probably the applicant's mother, grandmother, sister, or aunt.

_____ 7. The applicant's spouse can use the Calco credit card even if no information about him is filled in on the application.

_____ 8. The applicant's spouse works at Newton High School.

_____ 9. The applicant currently works at Porter's in Lexington, Massachusetts.

_____ 10. The applicant has a Massachusetts driver's license.

_____ 11. The applicant has checking and savings accounts at Lexington Bank and Trust Company.

_____ 12. The applicant has lived at her current address for less than one year.

B. Fill in the circle next to the phrase that correctly completes each sentence.

1. This application cannot be processed unless the applicant _____.
   ○ signs her name on the reverse side
   ○ fills in every space on the application
   ○ has a good credit rating

2. The reason that the applicant provided the information about her spouse—her husband—is that _____.
   ○ she is required to provide that information because she is married
   ○ she wants a separate Calco charge account from her husband
   ○ her husband may use her charge account with Calco

3. The applicant filled in $100 in the space for "Estimated Monthly Calco Credit Card Purchases" because she _____.
   ○ expects to charge a total of $100 worth of Calco gas each time she is at the gas station
   ○ and her husband expect to charge a total of $100 worth of Calco gas each month
   ○ and her husband expect to spend a total of $100 on auto repairs each month

4. From the way the applicant filled in the space for "Previous Employer & Address," you can tell that she _____.
   ○ has been with her present employer for more than five years
   ○ worked at Camp Wiki for four years
   ○ worked only summers at Camp Wiki while she was a student

5. The application asks for bank and credit references because _____.
   ○ Calco will check the applicant's credit rating before extending credit
   ○ Calco can confirm that the applicant is telling the truth about where he or she has accounts
   ○ only people who have a bank account and other charge accounts will apply for a credit card

Lesson 36

Figures of Speech

Reading a Literature Selection

▶ **Background Information**

Figures of speech describe one thing in terms of something else. They help readers see relationships as imaginatively as the writer sees them.

▶ **Skill Focus**

Writers use **figures of speech** to present ideas and objects in imaginative comparisons. Figures of speech use words in an unusual manner.

Sometimes a writer makes a clearly stated comparison between two different objects or ideas by using the word *like* or *as*. This comparison is a figure of speech called **simile**.

> A Persian cat is like a powder puff,
> a rounded, silken, bit of fluff.

Sometimes a writer only suggests a comparison between two different objects or ideas. This figure of speech is called **metaphor.**

> Crimson leaves flickered as they fell to the ground—

> Flames that set afire hills for miles around.

The words *flickered* and *set afire* show you that the writer is comparing autumn leaves to flames.

In **personification**, a writer assigns human traits to nonhuman things or invests an inanimate object with life.

> Skyscrapers stride the horizon, bedecking themselves in glittering jewels as twilight beckons them to a party.

A **symbol** is an object that stands for something else. For example, the bald eagle symbolizes America.

▶ **Word Clues**

When you read, you may encounter words that name a special person, place, or thing. If no nearby context clues explain the word, a clue may be elsewhere. Read the following lines.

> You are madmen, playing the hatter's[1] game . . .

The raised number after the word *hatter* is a signal to look at the bottom of the page for a footnote with the same number. The footnote gives a brief definition or explanation of the word.

> [1]hatter: a hatmaker; the reference is to the Mad Hatter in *Alice in Wonderland*. In the nineteenth century, hatters suffered from mercury poisoning, an occupational hazard related to making felt hats. One symptom was madness—hence the expression "mad as a hatter."

Use **footnote** context clues to find the meanings of the five other numbered words in the selection.

▶ **Strategy Tip**

In the poems that follow, the poets use figures of speech to describe the feelings and events that they experienced. Look for examples of metaphor, simile, personification, and symbolism in each poem.

Woodpeckers in Summer Frolic
David Nava Monreal

Dizzy red-headed
birds,
you make me laugh
with your babbling
and throaty gibberish.   5
Darting and dashing
between trees like
fickle children
in indecision.
You are madmen   10
playing the hatter's[1]
game,
pounding insanely at
the bark with your
yellow beaks as   15
though your
souls were enclosed
within.
Your noise is
shattering   20
and your antics[2]
are crazy,
but your brilliant
life adds
plumage[3] to the   25
drab
leaves.

Long Distance
Carole Gregory

That phone call, the one that you wait for
but never expect to come
was phoned today. And
that voice, the voice you ache for
but seldom expect to hear   5
spoke today. And that
loneliness, the loneliness you hurt from
but always held inside,
flies out like thin stones across water.

First Snow
Ted Kooser

The old black dog comes in one evening
with the first few snowflakes on his back
and falls asleep, throwing his bad leg out
at our excitement. This is the night
when one of us gets to say, as if it   5
   were news,
that no two snowflakes are ever alike;
the night when each of us remembers
   something
snowier. The kitchen is a kindergarten   10
steamy with stories. The dog gets stiffly up
and limps away, seeking a quiet spot
at the heart of the house. Outside,
in silence, with diamonds in his fur,
the winter night curls around the legs   15
   of the trees,
sleepily blinking snowflakes from his lashes.

In the beginning was the
Lillian Morrison

Kickoff.
The ball flew
spiralling true
into the end zone
where it was snagged,   5
neatly hugged
by a swivel-hipped back
who ran up the field
and was smeared.

The game has begun.   10
The game has been won.
The game goes on.
Long live the game.
Gather and lock
tackle and block   15
move, move,
around the arena
and always the beautiful
trajectories.[4]

---

[1] hatter: a hatmaker; the reference is to the Mad Hatter in *Alice in Wonderland*. In the nineteenth century, hatters suffered from mercury poisoning, an occupational hazard related to making felt hats. One symptom was madness—hence the expression "mad as a hatter."

[2] antics: high-spirited fun and frolics, jovial clowning, carefree merriment.

[3] plumage: feathers used ornamentally; elaborate dress; finery.

[4] trajectories: the curved paths of hurled objects, or missiles.

For a Hopi Silversmith
Joy Harjo

he has gathered the windstrength
from the third mesa[5]
into his hand
and cast it into silver

i have wanted to see   5
the motion of wind
for a long time

thank you
for showing me

[5] mesa: a large land formation, usually rising in
   a desert, with a broad flat top. From the
   Spanish word meaning table.

RECALLING FACTS

1. Describe the setting of the poem "First Snow."

_____

_____

2. What has the Hopi silversmith cast into silver?

_____

3. What does the poet of "Long Distance" say about loneliness?

_____

_____

4. Complete each sentence with the correct word below.

plumage   trajectories   antics   mesa

a. At last, the explorers reached the top

of the _____ and stared
down at the vast desert.

b. We are tracking the probable

_____ of the two satellites
as they re-enter the atmosphere.

c. The _____ of circus clowns
make everyone laugh.

INTERPRETING FACTS

1. a. In the poem "In the beginning was the," why does the poet use football imagery?

_____

_____

_____

b. Underline words and phrases in the poem that suggest football imagery.

2. a. In "For a Hopi Silversmith," what do you think the poet was looking at or thinking about that inspired this poem?

_____

_____

_____

_____

_____

128 Lesson 36 *Identifying figures of speech*

b. In "For a Hopi Silversmith," whom does the speaker thank? Why?

_____

_____

_____

c. What do you think the wind symbolizes?

_____

_____

_____

3. Reread "Long Distance."
   a. Who do you think the caller is? Explain.

_____

_____

   b. What is the mood of the speaker before the phone call in "Long Distance"?

_____

   c. Will the speaker's mood change after the phone call? Explain.

_____

_____

_____

4. How is the first snow of the year different from other snows?

_____

_____

_____

_____

_____

5. Reread "Woodpeckers in Summer Frolic."
   a. What is the poet's attitude toward the woodpeckers in lines 1–22?

_____

_____

_____

   b. Circle the word in the poem after line 21 that signals a change in tone.

   c. How does the tone change? Why?

_____

_____

_____

_____

_____

SKILL FOCUS

1. For each poem, reread the lines as indicated below. Then identify and explain the figure of speech used by the poet in those lines.
   a. "Woodpeckers in Summer Frolic"

Lines 7–9 _____ _____

_____

_____

Lines 10–12 _____ _____

_____

_____

   b. "Long Distance"
Lines 7–9 _____ _____

_____

_____

Lesson 36 *Identifying figures of speech* **129**

c. "First Snow"

Line 10 _____ _____

_____

_____

Line 14 _____ _____

_____

2. The poet who wrote "In the beginning was the" is concerned with more than a mere game of football.

    a. The game—the kickoff, the ball's flying into the end zone, a player's being smeared— stands for the game of life. Explain this metaphor.

_____

_____

_____

_____

    b. Reread lines 14–19, paying special attention to the word *trajectories*. What is the symbolic meaning of this word?

_____

_____

_____

_____

3. The last lines of "Woodpeckers in Summer Frolic" suggest a meaning that is larger than the scene they describe. What do the expressions "brilliant life," "plumage," and "drab leaves" symbolize?

_____

_____

_____

_____

4. In "First Snow," there is a real dog and a figurative one.

    a. Which lines are about the real dog? _____ The figurative dog? _____

    b. Which figure of speech does the poet use to describe the figurative dog? Explain.

_____

_____

_____

_____

▶ **Real Life Connections** Describe the weather outside. Use a simile, metaphor, or personification in your description.

Making Generalizations

___ Reading a Social Studies Selection ___

▶ **Background Information**

For thousands of years, people have lived in the area around the Mediterranean Sea. They have found the land and climate along its coastline suitable for settlement. The people and places of the Mediterranean region have played an important role in the history of humankind. In fact, some of the earliest civilizations, including ancient Greece and Rome, flourished in this region. The Mediterranean Sea is centrally located. Three different continents—Europe, Africa, and Asia—surround it. In biblical times, people thought that the far side of the Mediterranean Sea was the end of the world. People living at the eastern end of the sea didn't believe there was any place to go once they reached the western end of the Mediterranean, which today is called the Strait of Gibraltar.

▶ **Skill Focus**

Facts are an important part of geography, but facts alone do not provide a complete understanding of geographical regions. You must be able to make **generalizations,** or draw conclusions from a sampling of facts. A generalization is a broad statement that goes beyond the facts. To be reasonable, a generalization must be based on two or more facts. Often more than one generalization can be made from a given set of facts.

Examine the following facts.

> Factory towns are not common in the dry summer subtropics.
>
> Coal and iron are scarce in the dry summer subtropics.
>
> Shortages of fibers limit textile production in the dry summer subtropics.

Based on these three facts, the following generalization can be made.

> Little heavy industry and manufacturing go on in the dry summer subtropics.

All reasonable generalizations must be based on information that is true and can be proven. Generalizations supported by opinions rather than facts are weak, unsound, and often untrue.

▶ **Word Clues**

Read the paragraph that follows. Look for context clues that explain the underlined word.

> The Latin word *mediterranean* means "in the middle of land," and the Mediterranean Sea is, in fact, surrounded by the land of three continents. Europe is <u>adjacent</u> to its northern shores, North Africa is next to the sea's southern rim, and the western part of Asia borders the sea to the east.

If you don't know the meaning of the word *adjacent,* the phrase *next to* in the second part of the sentence can help you. The word *adjacent* and the phrase *next to* are synonyms. *Adjacent* means "next to, alongside, bordering."

Use **synonym** context clues to find the meanings of the three underlined words in the selection.

▶ **Strategy Tip**

Before reading "In the Middle of Land," preview it. Look at the illustrations and maps. Read the section headings. As you read, pay attention to the facts. You will use many of the facts to make generalizations about the Mediterranean area.

In the Middle of Land

The Latin word *mediterranean* means "in the middle of land," and the Mediterranean Sea is, in fact, surrounded by the land of three continents. Europe is adjacent to its northern shores, North Africa is next to the sea's southern rim, and the western part of Asia borders the sea to the east.

Compared with the great oceans of the world, the Mediterranean Sea is small. It covers about 969,100 square miles (2,519,660 square kilometers). From the Strait of Gibraltar, the sea's westernmost point, to Turkey on the sea's eastern shore, the distance is about 2,200 miles (3,520 kilometers). At its widest extent, from Albania in the north to Libya in the south, the sea is about 600 miles (960 kilometers) wide. The Mediterranean is more than three times as long as it is wide.

Despite its relatively small size, the Mediterranean <u>nurtured</u> many of the world's oldest and most influential civilizations. In turn, these cultures sustained for centuries the greatest water route in the world.

Climate and Land

The Mediterranean's large volume of water helps to give the surrounding lands a warm subtropical climate. These conditions provide what has become known as a "Mediterranean climate," even when they occur in other parts of the world.

✗ The climate of the Mediterranean offers some of the most favorable living conditions in the world. In this ideal climate, summers are dry and sunny, with daytime temperatures of 70° to 80°F (21° to 27°C) and night temperatures of 40° to 50°F (4° to 10°C). The winters are mild and rainy, with low temperatures around 40°F (4°C). Long periods of sunshine are typical of the Mediterranean area, making this region a very healthful and wholesome place to live. Summer skies are clear and blue, and there is some sunny weather even in the rainy seasons.

✔ A hot, parching wind called the *sirocco* (sə RAH koh) blows northward across the sea from Africa. From the opposite direction, a cold, dry wind called the *mistral* (MIS trel) blows south from France. A similar cold, dry wind called the *bora* blows south from Yugoslavia.

✗ ✗ The lands surrounding the Mediterranean have similar physical features. Mountains and rugged hills, often rising steeply from the shore, <u>abut</u> the coastal areas, except for the desert that borders the sea in North Africa. Streams from the mountains carry water into the valleys by the sea. As the map shows, all the Mediterranean nations face the sea; typically, their coastlines have a great number of bays, inlets, and natural harbors.

Agriculture and Other Industries

Agriculture is the most important industry in the Mediterranean region. The long growing season, many hours of sunshine, high

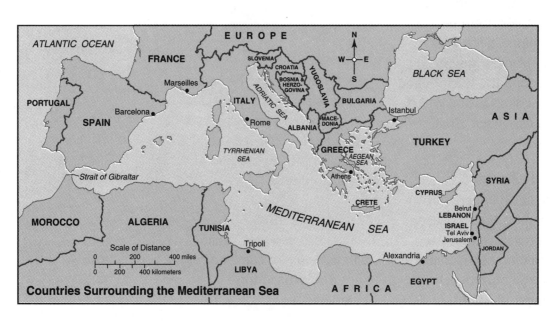

Countries Surrounding the Mediterranean Sea

Terracing has made the slopes and meager soil resources of this Mediterranean village fit for agriculture.

Level land is scarce along the Mediterranean coast. As a result, settlement has been forced up the slopes.

temperatures, and fertile soil all favor agriculture. The crops grown are those that do well in the rocky, shallow soil and warm climate found in most Mediterranean areas.

Similar kinds of crops are grown throughout the Mediterranean lands. Grains, such as wheat and barley, are planted in the fall to make use of the cool rainy season. In the summer, the Mediterranean farmers cultivate drought resistant, tree-borne crops, such as olives, nuts, and citrus fruits. The steep and rocky hillsides have been terraced to make agriculture possible, and grape vines thrive on the slopes facing the sun. Where irrigation is possible, multiple crops of vegetables are grown.

The Mediterranean people have also harvested the sea since ancient times. The Mediterranean provides an abundance of sea animals and fish, including sponges and sardines, the chief commercial catch. All along the coasts are small fishing villages with rows of <u>quays</u>. From these docks and wharves, fleets of boats venture forth every day. Fishing is of local significance in almost all Mediterranean economies.

Agriculture and fishing also provide the basis for the small number of factories near the coast. Canneries and other light industrial plants process fish and agricultural products. Because of the scarcity of coal and iron, heavy industry and manufacturing are not common.

The beautiful shoreline, moderate climate, and sandy beaches along the Mediterranean attract many tourists. The Riviera in France and the islands off the coast of Greece are famous

Much of the cultural heritage of the West began in the lands surrounding the Mediterranean.

vacation spots that attract the tourist and resort trade. In many coastal towns, hotels and restaurants cater to the tourism that supports the local economy.

Urban Centers

From early times, many people of the Mediterranean region have lived in concentrated settlements. From towns and villages grew cities. Among these were many great centers of learning, art, and culture. Istanbul, Athens, Rome, Alexandria, Marseilles, Barcelona, Jerusalem, and Beirut are only some of the great metropolitan centers of the Mediterranean. Today, modern buildings rise next to ancient structures that reflect the history of Western civilization. These cities remain vital centers of business and culture. In addition, Tel Aviv and Haifa have grown into major ports and commercial centers.

Cultures of the Mediterranean

Much of the cultural heritage of the West began in the lands surrounding the Mediterranean. Ancient Egypt and the city-states in the eastern Mediterranean were among the earliest sites of civilization. In these places, such skills as writing, mathematics, astronomy, and navigation developed thousands of years ago. Trading ships sailed the Mediterranean from Spain to countries as far away as Lebanon and Syria, and sailors traveled through the Straits of Gibraltar into the Atlantic Ocean.

The civilization of Greece produced many

great works of art, literature, and science. The Greeks excelled in architecture; their simple, elegant buildings reflected their love of balance and beauty. The achievements of the Greeks influenced artistic styles in Rome and in the rest of the Western world.

Roman law became the foundation for legal codes that later developed in Europe and that were carried to other parts of the world. Roman roads left a transportation system that future civilizations would use and improve. During the time that they ruled virtually all of the Mediterranean, the Romans called the Mediterranean *Mare Nostrum,* meaning "Our Sea."

Three of the world's major religions—Judaism, Christianity, and Islam—arose in the Mediterranean region. Their influence has helped to shape the ideas and philosophies of the modern Western world.

RECALLING FACTS

1. Next to each statement write either *cause* or *effect*.

   _____ Tourism is an important industry in the Mediterranean region.

   _____ The Mediterranean has numerous beaches, beautiful scenery, and a mild climate.

2. Reread the paragraph that has an X next to it. Underline the sentence that states the main idea of the paragraph.

3. Reread the paragraph with an XX next to it and underline the sentence that states its main idea. Circle the details that support the main idea.

4. Write the letter of the correct meaning on the line next to each word.

   ____ nurtured   a. piers

   ____ abut   b. supported

   ____ quays   c. adjoin

INTERPRETING FACTS

1. Why does summer rainfall provide less moisture?

   _____

   _____

2. Which will be less important in the Mediterranean in the near future: agriculture or heavy industry? Explain.

   _____

   _____

   _____

3. What kind of business would be more likely to succeed in a Mediterranean costal town: a factory or a hotel.

   _____

4. Do you think it's important to Mediterranean countries to preserve their ancient ruins? Why?

   _____

   _____

   _____

5. Fill in the space between the lines next to each statement of fact.

   ‖ a. The coastal Mediterranean lands have similar physical features.

   ‖ b. The French Riviera and the Greek islands will always be popular resorts.

   ‖ c. Much of the cultural heritage of the West arose in the Mediterranean region.

6. Reread the paragraph with a check mark next to it. Then circle the letter of the statement below that best states the main idea of the paragraph.
   a. A hot wind called the *sirocco* blows northward from Africa.
   b. Two cold winds, the *mistral* and *bora*, blow southward from Europe.
   c. Three major wind systems affect the climate of the Mediterranean region.

SKILL FOCUS

1. The box below contains three generalizations based on the selection. Following the box are two groups of facts based on information in the selection. Read each group of facts carefully. Then, for each group of facts, choose the generalization that is the most reasonable. Write the letter of the statement on the line provided.

> **Generalizations**
> a. The Mediterranean region has a favorable climate.
> b. The Mediterranean lands have similar geographical features.
> c. The Mediterranean region has many of the world's great cities.

Facts Most of the Mediterranean's coast is backed by mountains.
The Mediterranean coast is dotted with bays and harbors.
The countries of the Mediterranean all face the sea.

Generalization _____

Facts The Mediterranean has a sunny climate.
Summers in the Mediterranean are warm and dry.
Winters in the Mediterranean are cool and rainy.

Generalization _____

2. For each generalization stated below, write three facts from the text to support it.

Generalization Agriculture is more important than heavy industry in the Mediterranean economy.

Facts a. _____
_____
_____

b. _____
_____
_____

c. _____
_____
_____

Generalization Similar types of crops grow throughout the Mediterranean region.

Facts a. _____

       _____

      b. _____

       _____

      c. _____

       _____

3. For each of the following groups of facts, write a generalization. Remember that some facts can suggest more than one generalization.

Facts a. Writing, mathematics, astronomy, and navigation skills were developed in the Mediterranean region in ancient times.

      b. Ancient Greece contributed many classic works of art, literature, and science to civilization.

      c. Three major religions arose in the Mediterranean area.

Generalization _____

_____

Facts a. Even in ancient times, Mediterranean people tended to congregate in small, densely populated areas.

      b. Ancient cities—including Alexandria, Athens, and Jerusalem—were founded in the Mediterranean area.

      c. Modern cities, such as Tel Aviv and Haifa, are part of the Mediterranean world.

Generalization _____

_____

Facts a. Sardines and sponges are important Mediterranean products.

      b. Fishing is an important light industry in the Mediterranean.

      c. Fishing villages dot the Mediterranean coasts.

Generalization _____

_____

4. Read the following statements. Underline the statement that is a generalization. Then circle the letters of the statements that support the generalization.

    a. Mountain slopes provide a picturesque background for many towns and villages along the Mediterranean coast.

    b. The Mediterranean area has an ideal climate.

    c. The geography of the Mediterranean region makes it a flourishing resort area attractive to tourists and vacationers.

    d. The Mediterranean has a long growing season for agriculture.

    e. Bordering the Mediterranean are numerous beaches, bays, and inlets.

▶ **Real Life Connections** In your opinion, what would be most fascinating about visiting the area around the Mediterranean Sea?

Main Idea and Supporting Details

___ Reading a Science Selection ___

▶ Background Information

Biomes are naturally occurring regions of the earth that can be identified by their climate, type of vegetation, and typical wildlife. This selection describes the six major land biomes.

▶ Skill Focus

To understand how ideas in a paragraph are related and which ideas are more important, look for the main idea and supporting details.

The sentence with the **main idea** expresses the subject of the paragraph. The **major details** give more information about the main idea. They help to develop or support the main idea. A paragraph may also include **minor details**, which provide information of less importance than the major details.

Sometimes you need to read more than one paragraph to understand how ideas are related. For example, chapters in many textbooks are divided into sections. Each section usually begins with a heading in boldfaced type. Think of this heading as a main idea. It tells you the subject of the paragraphs in that section.

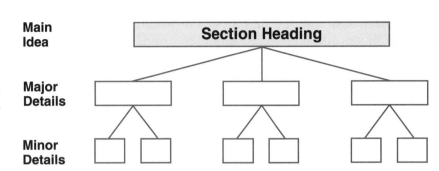

You can find the major details and minor details about that subject by reading all the paragraphs in the section.

When you read a textbook, use the following steps.

1. Use the heading of each section as the main idea.
2. Within each section, find at least two major details that develop or support the main idea.
3. Look for minor details that give more information about the major details.
4. Arrange the major and minor details to show how they are related. A diagram is one way to organize information. The diagram above shows how the key ideas in a section are related.

▶ Word Clues

Read the sentence that follows. Look for context clues that explain the underlined word.

In general, biomes are named for their predominant, or most frequently occurring, vegetation.

If you don't know the meaning of the word *predominant,* the appositive phrase *most frequently occurring* will help you. An appositive phrase explains a word coming before it and is set off by commas or dashes.

Use **appositive phrases** to find the meanings of the three underlined words in the selection.

▶ Strategy Tip

Each section of the selection describes three major characteristics of the biome: climate, plant life, and animal life. As you read, look for the major details that support the main ideas and the minor details that support the major details.

Land Biomes

1. Years ago, scientists traveling throughout the world noticed that many natural areas look surprisingly similar, even though they are separated by thousands of kilometers. These areas share many characteristics: similar climates and often similar plants and wildlife. From observations such as these and research, scientists now recognize six major types of land areas, called **biomes** (BY ohmz).

2. In general, biomes are named for their predominant, or most frequently occurring, vegetation. In turn, the vegetation in an area is determined by the climate, specifically by the amount of precipitation and the temperature. What follows is an overview of the six major land biomes, including their characteristics and climates.

Tundra

3. The **tundra** includes all the cold, icebound areas of the Far North and the tops of high mountain peaks throughout the world. The climate of the tundra is cold and dry, with the temperatures remaining below freezing for about nine months of the year. During the remaining three months, the climate is milder, but the growing season for plants is only about 80 days long. During the summer, the ground thaws, but rarely to a depth of more than 20 centimeters. Below this depth, the ground is permanently frozen. The thin soil layer on top of this frozen soil, called **permafrost,** becomes soggy with melted snow during summer, forming bogs and ponds.

4. In spite of its <u>desolateness</u>, or emptiness, the tundra has many plants and animals. Shrubs, grasses, mosses, and lichens are the predominant vegetation. Trees are not found in the tundra because the climate is too harsh, and deep tree roots cannot survive in the permafrost. While very few animals live in the tundra all year long, the short summer attracts many animals. The arctic tundra is a major breeding ground for many species of birds, especially ducks. Herds of large grazing animals, such as reindeer, moose, and caribou, feed here during summer and migrate to more hospitable areas as winter approaches.

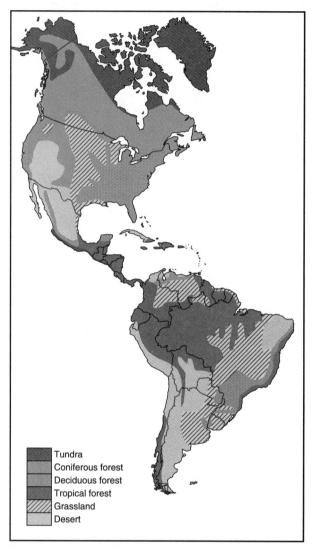

Tundra
Coniferous forest
Deciduous forest
Tropical forest
Grassland
Desert

This map shows the six major land biomes in the Western Hemisphere.

Coniferous Forests

5. South of the tundra are great expanses of **coniferous** (ke NIF er əs) **forest,** a biome whose predominant plants are coniferous, or cone-bearing, trees. Coniferous trees include firs, pines, spruces, and redwoods. The climate of the coniferous forest biome is not as harsh as that of the tundra. Precipitation ranges from about 40 to 100 centimeters per year. Winters are long, and summers may be cool. Yet, the growing season is generally much longer than it is in the tundra, ranging from 120 to 300 frost-free days.

6. Trees in a coniferous forest grow close together, preventing sunlight from reaching

Lizards, such as this shovel-snouted lizard, are common to the desert biome.

The jaguar's natural habitat is the rain forest biome in South and Central America.

the forest floor. The result is that few plants grow beneath the trees. The shrubs and herbs that do grow here are found almost exclusively at the forest edge, where there is more sunlight.

7. Foxes, wolves, squirrels, porcupines, mice, and hares are some of the mammals that live in the coniferous forest. Moose and caribou spend their winters in the forest but often migrate to the tundra during summer. Birds of this biome include ducks, eagles, owls, spruce grouse, and red crossbills. Spruce grouse and red crossbills are especially suited to this environment. Spruce grouse can live on a diet of spruce needles, and red crossbills have large, strong beaks that can easily split open pine cone seeds.

The availability of water also determines which organisms can survive in the desert.

Deciduous Forest

8. The **deciduous** (di SIJ oo wǝs) **forest** biome is characterized by trees—such as oak, hickory, maple, beech, and birch—that drop their leaves each autumn. This biome receives more precipitation and has more moderate temperatures than the coniferous forest does. Precipitation, ranging from 75 to 125 centimeters per year, is distributed fairly evenly throughout the year. This biome has four distinct seasons, with cold winters and warm summers.

9. Deciduous forests are vertically stratified, or layered. The tops of the tallest trees form the **canopy,** or upper layer. Because the canopy is not very dense, sunlight can filter through it to the forest floor. Below the canopy is the **understory,** a layer made up of shorter trees. Beneath the understory is the **shrub layer.** Below the shrubs is an **herb layer,** made up of small, soft-stemmed plants.

10. Like the vegetation in the deciduous forest, different animals are found in the various layers. Squirrels, woodpeckers, and crows are found primarily in the canopy. Tree frogs and opossums live in the short trees that make up the understory. Deer feed on the shrub layers. Many insects are found in the herb layer, and some insects are found in all the layers—except, of course, in winter.

Grassland

11. The **grassland** biome, as its name implies, is characterized by various kinds of grasses. Its climate is similar to that of the deciduous forest, except that it receives less rainfall and summer can be quite hot. The most important feature of this biome is that grasslands experience **droughts,** or periods without precipitation. Grasses can survive periodic drought, but trees cannot. As a result, the only trees in grasslands grow along the rivers and streams.

12. Like all other biomes, grasslands have typical animal residents. Most of the large animals in grasslands are grazing mammals: buffalo, pronghorn antelope, and elk. The smaller grazers include gophers, prairie dogs, and hares. The predators include foxes, coyotes, and wolves. Quail, hawks, and meadowlarks are some of the grassland birds, and grasshoppers are very common insects.

Desert

13. The **desert** biome, like the tundra, is an extremely harsh environment. Precipitation is low—less than 25 centimeters per year on the average—and in some years a desert may receive no precipitation at all. Because precipitation is so low, the air is dry and cannot hold heat very well. The result is that although daytime desert temperatures may be very hot, nighttime temperatures are cold. The growing season of a desert is limited more by the availability of water than by temperature. In only a few weeks after a spring rainfall, plants sprout, grow, flower, produce seeds, and die.

14. The availability of water also determines which organisms can survive in the desert. Desert plants conserve water in a number of ways. The stems and leaves of most plants have a waxy covering that reduces the loss of water through evaporation. Some plants grow leaves only after a rainfall, shedding them when water again becomes scarce. Many desert plants have only small leaves, and cacti have no leaves at all. Cacti store significant quantities of water inside their fleshy stems. Desert animals must also cope with the scarcity of water. Most desert animals reduce evaporation by staying out of the sun during the day. Mice and rats remain in underground burrows, while lizards and snakes stay in the shade of rocks and plants. In addition, some animals, like the kangaroo rat, have low water requirements because they excrete very little water in their wastes.

Tropical Rain Forest

15. The **tropical rain forest** biome, characterized by a wide variety of broad-leaved trees, straddles the equator. This biome receives 200–225 centimeters of rain a year and has a warm temperature all year long. These climactic conditions make the tropical rain forest a very <u>lush</u>, or rich, environment with a greater variety of plants than any other biome on earth. It contains more than 150 different species of trees alone, and most trees support numerous vines and **epiphytes** (EP ə fyts), such as orchids. Epiphytes are plants that do not root in soil but grow high in the branches of a host tree.

16. The animals in tropical rain forests are almost as varied as the plants. Flying squirrels, monkeys, toucans, and parrots live in the tops of the trees. In fact, some of these animals never go down to the forest floor. Sloths and numerous types of snakes live in the trees nearer to the forest floor. The forest floor itself is home to jaguars, armadillos, and many kinds of insects, including ants and termites.

RECALLING FACTS

1. What are the six major land biomes?

_____

_____

_____

2. Which biome has the greatest variety of plants? _____

3. Which biomes have few, if any, trees?

_____

4. Which biome is the coldest?

_____

5. What is permafrost?

_____

_____

6. Why are there few plants on the floor of a coniferous forest?

_____

_____

_____

7. Which biome receives the greatest amount of precipitation?

_____

8. What makes cacti well suited to live in deserts?

_____

_____

_____

9. What determines the length of the growing season in the desert?

_____

_____

10. Complete each statement with the correct word.

desolateness   stratified   lush

a. The _____ nature of the atmosphere can be understood by studying its different layers.

b. The plant growth in a jungle is usually very _____.

c. The _____ of the abandoned building made him feel uncomfortable.

INTERPRETING FACTS

Choose the phrase that completes each sentence. Then fill in the space between the lines next to the correct phrase.

1. An area that has frequent precipitation could be ———.

‖ **a.** grassland or tundra

‖ **b.** grassland or desert

‖ **c.** tropical rain forest or deciduous forest

‖ **d.** coniferous forest or desert

2. An area with layers of herbs, shrubs, and trees would probably be a ———.

‖ **a.** desert

‖ **b.** coniferous forest

‖ **c.** grassland

‖ **d.** deciduous forest

3. The biome that has the fewest rivers of all is the ———.

‖ **a.** coniferous forest

‖ **b.** desert

‖ **c.** deciduous forest

‖ **d.** grassland

4. The biome that is essentially without seasons is the ———.

‖ **a.** desert

‖ **b.** deciduous forest

‖ **c.** tropical rain forest

‖ **d.** tundra

SKILL FOCUS

The partially completed diagram on the next page shows how the major and minor details in the section on the tundra are related to the main idea. Make up the same type of diagram for each of any two other sections. For each diagram, write the heading in the main idea box. Then reread the paragraphs in each section. Write a sentence in each of the three Major Details boxes. One sentence should describe the climate of the biome, one sentence the plant life, and one sentence the animal life. To complete the diagram for each section, write at least two minor details by using phrases instead of sentences. One is done for you.

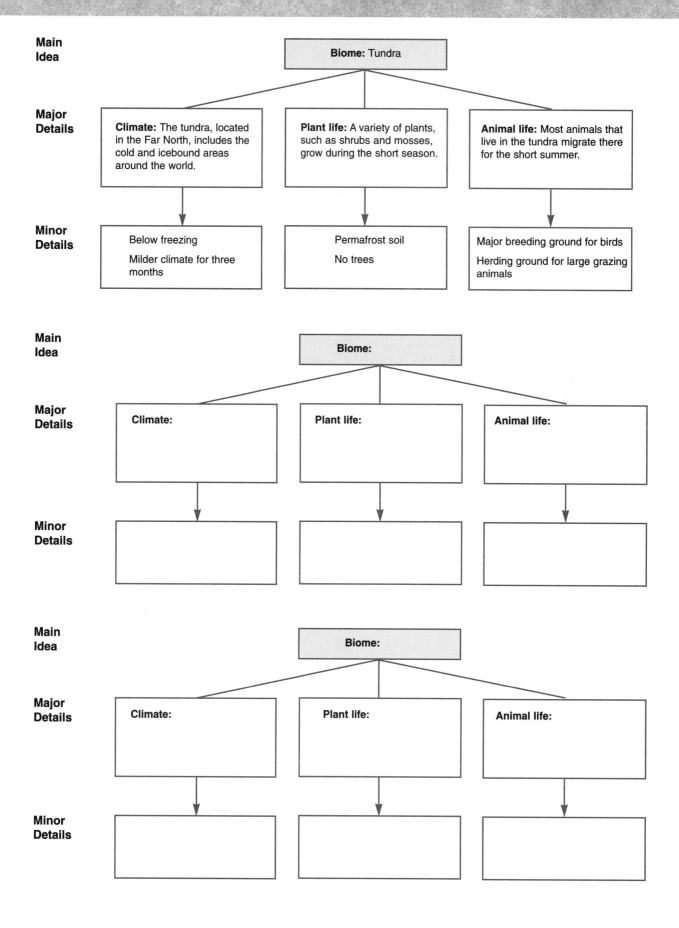

Main Idea

Biome: Tundra

Major Details

Climate: The tundra, located in the Far North, includes the cold and icebound areas around the world.

Plant life: A variety of plants, such as shrubs and mosses, grow during the short season.

Animal life: Most animals that live in the tundra migrate there for the short summer.

Minor Details

Below freezing

Milder climate for three months

Permafrost soil

No trees

Major breeding ground for birds

Herding ground for large grazing animals

Main Idea

Biome:

Major Details

Climate:

Plant life:

Animal life:

Minor Details

Main Idea

Biome:

Major Details

Climate:

Plant life:

Animal life:

Minor Details

▶ Real Life Connections Which biome or biomes occur in your geographic region?

Equations

___ Reading a Mathematics Selection ___

▶ Background Information

This selection deals with one of the basic skills in algebra, solving equations. As its name suggests, an equation is a statement that something is equal to something else. For example, 4 times 5 equals 20. Equations use symbols, so if "4 times 5 equals 20" were written as an equation, it would look like this

$$4 \times 5 = 20.$$

Equations are used to solve problems when we don't know what something is or when we don't know how much of something we have.

In an equation, the number or thing that we don't know is represented by a letter. The letter is usually x or a y, but it can be any letter at all. The purpose of solving the equation is to find out how much of the unknown thing we have.

Suppose you spend a certain amount of money each day, and you want to know how much money you spend in one week. You could keep counting the money as you spend it, of course. Or you could quickly determine how much money you spend in a week by writing and solving an equation that will give you this information. In this equation, the money you spend might be represented by an x. When you solve the equation you'll know, in only a few minutes, exactly how much money you spent for that week.

▶ Skill Focus

When you solve word problems in mathematics, your plan is stated in the form of a a mathematical sentence, or **equation**. The equations used in problem solving involve unknown numbers, which are represented by letters, called **variables,** such as $n, x, A,$ or $t.$ To solve the equation, you must find a number.

You can solve most simple equations by using the operations opposite to the ones shown in the equation. For example: If an equation uses addition, you find the answer by subtracting. If an equation uses subtraction, you add. For example,

$$x + 1 = 3$$
$$x + 1 - 1 = 3 - 1$$
$$x = 2$$

The same is true of multiplication and division.

▶ Word Clues

The word *equation* comes from the word *equal.* An equation is a statement that two numbers or quantities are equal. When you solve an equation, you change or restore the equation to a simple form. In this simple form, a variable is on one side of the equal sign, and a simple number is on the other side.

▶ Strategy Tip

As you read "Reading Equations," pay attention to the signs of operation in each equation: addition, subtraction, multiplication, and division. The signs will help you determine the operation that is necessary to solve the equation.

Reading Equations

You can solve many word problems by writing a mathematical sentence, called an **equation.** The branch of mathematics that includes solving equations is called **algebra.**

An equation is a statement that two numbers or quantities are equal. One of the two numbers is usually shown as an expression involving a **variable,** such as n, a, x, or T. A solution to an equation is found when the equation shows a variable alone on one side, such as x = 5. Read the following problem.

> Summer temperatures in Jacksonville, Florida, are about 15 degrees Celsius higher than winter temperatures. If the average summer temperature is 25 degrees Celsius, what is the average winter temperature?

For this problem, the two numbers are 25 (the number of degrees in summer) and another number that is equal to the winter temperature T plus 15 degrees. The following equation states that these two numbers are equal:

$$T + 15 = 25$$

The solution of this equation requires that T be isolated, or set apart, on one side of the equation. One way to isolate T is to subtract the same number from both sides of the equation. The addition sign in the equation is a clue to perform the opposite operation. Subtracting the same number from both sides of the equation gives you two new expressions that are still equal. In this case, you must subtract 15 from both sides of the equation.

$$T + 15 - 15 = 25 - 15$$

When "+ 15" and "– 15" are cancelled, the variable T is isolated.

$$T + 0 = 10$$
$$T = 10$$

The equation $T = 10$ is the solution to the original equation. The average winter temperature in Jacksonville is 10 degrees Celsius.

Read the following problem.

> The amount of rainfall in Jacksonville in the summer is $\frac{12}{5}$ of the rain that falls in Jacksonville in the winter. If the average amount of rain in the summer is 12 centimeters, what amount falls in the winter?

In this problem, the two numbers that are equal are 12 and $\frac{12}{5} r$, where r is the unknown amount of winter rainfall. The equation is therefore as follows:

$$\tfrac{12}{5}r = 12$$

Just as you can subtract a number from both sides of an equation, you can also divide both sides by a number other than zero. On the left side of the equation, there is no sign between the number and the variable. The operation on this side is therefore multiplication. To isolate the variable r, you need to perform the opposite operation, division.

$$\tfrac{12}{5}r \div \tfrac{12}{5} = 12 \div \tfrac{12}{5}$$
$$r = 5$$

The solution is that the average amount of rainfall in Jacksonville in the winter is 5 centimeters.

In some equations, the same variable occurs twice on one side of the equation. Look at the following equation:

$$3x + x - 4 = 8$$

First, you must add the two expressions with variables. Because $3x$ means 3 times x, or $x + x + x$, the sum of $3x$ and x is $x + x + x + x$, or $4x$. Another way to think of this is $3x + 1x$ is $4x$.

$$4x - 4 = 8$$

To isolate the variable $4x$, add 4 to each side of the equation.

$$4x - 4 + 4 = 8 + 4$$
$$4x + 0 = 12$$
$$4x = 12$$

Now divide each side of the equation by 4 to isolate the variable x.

$$4x \div 4 = 12 \div 4$$
$$x = 3$$

Sometimes the same variable occurs on both sides of an equation. The variables can be brought together by adding the proper multiple of the variable to each side. Look at the following equation.

$$3x + 8 = 2x - 15$$

In this case, a good plan is to begin by subtracting $2x$ from each side.

$$3x + 8 - 2x = 2x + 15 - 2x$$
$$x + 8 = 15$$

You can complete the solution by subtracting 8 from each side.

$$x + 8 - 8 = 15 - 8$$
$$x = 7$$

RECALLING FACTS

1. What is an equation?

_____

_____

2. How do you know when you have solved an equation?

_____

_____

_____

3. What is a varible?

_____

_____

4. Two expressions with the same variable occur on both sides of an equation. What should be your first step in solving the equation?

_____

_____

_____

INTERPRETING FACTS

1. To solve the equation $\frac{1}{8}n = 13$, by what number would you divide both sides of

the equation? _____

2. To solve the equation $4x = 30$, by what number would you divide both sides of

the equation? _____

3. If you add a different number to each side of a mathematical sentence, what do you do to it?

_____

4. To solve the equation $\frac{1}{3}x = 9$, by what number would you multiply both sides of

the equation? _____

SKILL FOCUS

Solve each equation. Use the space to the right of each equation to work it out.

1. $x + 9 = 17$

   $x =$ _____

2. $x - 4 = 11$

   $x =$ _____

3. $7x = 63$

   $x =$ _____

4. $\frac{1}{5}x = 11$

   $x =$ _____

5. $x - 4 = 16$

$x =$ _____

6. $x - 3 = 8$

$x =$ _____

7. $9 + x = 12$

$x =$ _____

8. $8 + x = 14$

$x =$ _____

9. $2x + 4 = 26$

$x =$ _____

10. $\frac{2}{3}x = 12$

$x =$ _____

11. $2x + 3x = 35$

$x =$ _____

12. $5x - 2x = 24$

$x =$ _____

13. $7x - x = 18$

$x =$ _____

14. $4x - x = 21$

$x =$ _____

15. $2x - x = 19$

$x =$ _____

16. $3x + 2 + 2x = 27$

$x =$ _____

17. $4x - 17 = 7$

$x =$ _____

18. $5x + 5 = 30$

$x =$ _____

19. $3x + 2 = 2x + 3$

$x =$ _____

20. $2x - 5 = x + 5$

$x =$ _____

21. $8x = 64$

$x =$ _____

22. $3x - x = 50$

$x =$ _____

23. $4x + 1 = 2x + 9$

$x =$ _____

24. $11x + x = 144$

$x =$ _____

25. $5x + x = 36$

$x =$ _____

26. $2x - 10 = x + 10$

$x =$ _____

27. $x - 8 = 12$

$x =$ _____

28. $3x - 4 = 2x + 10$

$x =$ _____

29. $\frac{3}{4}x = 12$

$x =$ _____

30. $5x + 20 = 45$

$x =$ _____

▶ **Real Life Connections** Name an instance in your daily life in which knowing how to set up an equation would help you solve a word problem.

Choosing the Correct Meaning

When you look up the meaning of an unfamiliar word in a dictionary, you often find several definitions. Always read all the definitions of a word before you decide on the correct meaning. Then find the meaning that fits the context of what you are reading.

Read each entry word and its definition below. Note that each definition is numbered. Then complete each of the sentences that follow by writing an entry word that fits the context of the sentence. In some of the sentences, you need to add an *s* to the word. Write the number of the meaning above the word. The first sentence has been completed for you.

bond 1 anything that binds, fastens **2** a binding agreement **3** the means by which atoms or groups of atoms are combined in molecules **4** a certificate issued by a government or corporation in return for a loan of money **5** an amount paid as surety or bail

cell 1 a small room or cubicle **2** a very small, hollow cavity, or enclosed space **3** a small unit of protoplasm **4** a container holding electrodes and an electrolyte

court 1 an uncovered space wholly or partly surrounded by buildings or walls **2** a short street, often closed at one end **3** an area for playing any of several ball games **4** attention paid to someone in order to get something **5** a place where trials are held, investigations made, etc.

head 1 the top part of the body in people **2** mind; intelligence **3** the membrane stretched across the end of a drum, tambourine, etc. **4** the source of a river, stream, etc. **5** the person in charge; leader

press 1 to act on with steady force or weight **2** to squeeze (juice, etc.) from (grapes, etc.) **3** to iron with a heavy iron or a steam machine **4** to keep on asking or urging **5** to lay stress on; emphasize

1. The city is going to issue ___4 bonds___ to pay for the new highways.

2. The movie producer plans to _____ the famous star.

3. All plants and animals are made up of many _____.

4. Bob will _____ his shirt for the dance tomorrow.

5. Your _____ contains your brain, eyes, ears, nose, and mouth.

6. Handcuffs or shackles are called _____.

7. _____ the elevator button for the ninth floor.

8. The case against Pat Thompson will be heard in _____ next week.

9. A battery is made up of dry _____.

10. Bees store honey in the _____ of a honeycomb.

11. The _____ of the Mississippi River is in Minnesota.

The Dictionary

Each word, abbreviation, prefix, suffix, or group of words that your dictionary explains is called an **entry word.** The entry word and all the information about it is called an **entry.** Most dictionaries that you use include from 50,000 to 80,000 separate entries. These entries are arranged in alphabetical order, with biographical entries alphabetized by surnames, or family names. To use a dictionary effectively, you need to know the function of each part of an entry.

Study the following descriptions.

guide words: Printed in boldfaced type at the top of the page, the left guide word shows the first full entry, and the right guide word shows the last.

syllables: Centered dots in the entry word show where to divide a word when you cannot write it all on one line.

respelling: This appears in parentheses following the entry word to help you pronounce the word.

etymology: The origin and history of the word are shown within brackets [ ], by means of symbols and abbreviations. For example, the symbol < means "derived from," and *OE* means "Old English."

definitions: Meanings for the entry word are listed together, according to their parts of speech.

idioms: Included at the end of the entry for the key word; an idiom is a group of words that has a different meaning from the meaning of the words by themselves.

Study the part of a dictionary page on page 149, and use it to answer the questions that follow.

1. What are the guide words for this page?

_____

2. Write the respelling of *black*.

_____

3. What is the fifth entry word on this page?

_____

4. What is the third adjective meaning of *bitter*?

_____

5. How big does a bittern grow to be?

_____

6. What three idioms are given for the word *bit²*? _____

_____

7. What key word is given in the pronunciation key for the long *i* sound?

_____

8. What is the noun form of the word *bitter*?

_____

9. Two entry words are homographs, words with the same spelling as another but with a different meaning. Write one of them.

_____

bi·son (bī′s'n, -z'n) *n., pl.* **bi′sons** [Fr. < L. < Gmc. *wisunt:* for IE. base see VIRUS] any of several mammals of the ox family, with a shaggy mane, short, curved horns, and a humped back, as the American buffalo

bisque¹ (bisk) *n.* [Fr.] **1.** a rich, thick, creamy soup made from shellfish or from rabbit, fowl, etc. **2.** a thick, strained, creamy vegetable soup

bisque² (bisk) *n.* [< BISCUIT] **1.** biscuit ceramic ware left unglazed in the finished state **2.** a red-yellow color

bis·ter, bis·tre (bis′tər) *n.* [Fr. *bistre*] **1.** a yellowish-brown to dark-brown pigment made from the soot of burned wood **2.** a color in this range

bis·tro (bis′trō, bēs′-) *n., pl.* **-tros** [Fr.] a small nightclub or bar

bi·sul·fate (bī sul′fāt) *n.* an acid sulfate; compound containing the monovalent HSO_4– radical

bi·sul·fide (bī sul′fīd) *n.* same as DISULFIDE

bit¹ (bit) *n.* [< OE. *bite*, a bite < *bitan*, to BITE] **1.** the metal mouthpiece on a bridle, used for controlling the horse **2.** anything that curbs or controls **3.** the part of a key that actually turns the lock **4.** the cutting part of any tool **5.** a drilling or boring tool for use in a brace, drill press, etc.: see illustration at BRACE AND BIT —*vt.* **bit′ted, bit′ting** to put a bit into the mouth of (a horse)

bit² (bit) *n.* [< OE. *bita,* a piece < *bitan,* to BITE] **1.** *a)* a small piece or quantity *[a bit* of candy*] b)* a limited degree: used as though it were an adverb meaning "somewhat" *[a bit* bored*] c)* a short time; moment *[wait a bit* longer*]* ☆**2.** [Colloq.] an amount equal to 12½ cents *[a quarter is two bits]* ☆**3.** a small part, as in a play —*adj.* very small *[a bit* role*]* —**bit by bit** little by little; gradually —**do one's bit** to do one's share —**every bit** altogether; entirely

bit·ing (bīt′iŋ) *adj.* **1.** cutting; sharp *[a biting* frost*]* **2.** sarcastic *[a biting* comment*]* —**bit′ing·ly** *adv.*

bitt (bit) *n.* [< ?] *Naut.* any of the deck posts, usually in pairs, around which ropes or cables are fastened —*vt.* to wind around a bitt

bit·ten (bit′'n) *alt. pp. of* BITE

bit·ter (bit′ər) *adj.* [< OE. < base of *bitan,* to BITE] **1.** having a sharp, often unpleasant taste; acrid *[bitter* medicine*]* **2.** causing or showing sorrow, pain, etc. *[bitter* memories*]* **3.** sharp; harsh; piercing *[a bitter* wind*]* **4.** characterized by hatred, resentment, etc. *[bitter* enemies*]* —*adv.* in a bitter way *[the night was bitter* cold*]* —*n.* **1.** something bitter *[take the bitter* with the sweet*]* **2.** [Brit.] bitter, strongly hopped ale: see also BITTERS —**bit′ter·ly** *adv.* —**bit′ter·ness** *n.*

bit·tern (bit′ərn) *n., pl.* **-terns, -tern:** see PLURAL, II, D, 1 [< OFr. *butor,* prob. < L. *butio*] a wading bird of the heron family, the male of which has a loud, deep, thumping call

bit·ter·root (bit′ər rōōt′, -root′) *n.* a plant of western N. America having fleshy, edible roots and white or pink flowers

bit·ters (bit′ərz) *n.pl.* a liquor containing bitter herbs, roots, etc. and usually alcohol, used as a tonic and for flavoring in some cocktails

bit·ter·sweet (bit′ər swēt′) *n.* **1.** a N. American woody vine bearing clusters of small, orange fruits which open to expose the red seeds **2.** an old-world climbing vine of the nightshade family, with purple flowers and poisonous, red berries — *adj.* **1.** both bitter and sweet **2.** pleasant but with some sadness

bit·ty (bit′ē) *adj.* **-ti·er, -ti·est** [< BIT² + -Y¹] ☆tiny: a playful term *[a little bitty* baby*]*

bi·tu·men (bi tōō′mən, bī-; -tyōō′-) *n.* [L. < Celt. < IE. base *gwet-,* resin, from which also comes CUD] any of several substances obtained in the process of distilling coal tar, petroleum, etc., or found naturally as asphalt —**bi·tu′mi·nous** *adj.*

bituminous coal coal that yields pitch or tar and produces much smoke when it burns; soft coal

bi·va·lent (bī vā′lənt, biv′ə-) *adj.* **1.** having two valences **2.** having a valence of two —**bi·va′lence, bi·va′len·cy** *n.*

bi·valve (bī′valv′) *n.* any mollusk having a shell of two parts, or valves, hinged together, as a mussel, clam, etc. —*adj.* having such a shell: also **bi′valved′**

BISON
(5½–6 ft. high at shoulder)

BITTERN
(to 31 in., including bill)

black (blak) *adj.* [OE. *blæc* < IE. base *bhleg-* < *bhel-,* to burn, gleam: orig. sense of black was "covered with soot from flame"] **1.** opposite to white; of the color of coal: see COLOR **2.** having dark-colored skin and hair; esp., Negro **3.** without light; in complete darkness *[lost in the black* cave*]* **4.** without cream, milk, etc.: said of coffee **5.** soiled; dirty **6.** wearing black clothing **7.** evil; wicked *[black* deeds*]* **8.** disgraceful **9.** sad; dismal; gloomy *[thinking black* thoughts*]* **10.** sullen or angry *[she gave him a black* look*]* **11.** without hope *[a black* future*]* **12.** humorous or satirical in a despairing or cynical way *[black* comedy*]* —*n.* **1.** *a)* black color *b)* a black pigment, dye, etc.

fat, āpe, cär; ten, ēven; is, bīte; gō, hôrn, tōol, look; oil, out; up, fur; get; joy; yet; chin; she; thin, then; zh, leisure; ŋ, ring; ə for *a* in *ago, e* in *agent, i* in *sanity, o* in *comply, u* in *focus;* ' as in *able* (ā′b'l); Fr. bäl; ë, Fr. coeur; ö, Fr. feu; Fr. mon; ȏ, Fr. coq; ü, Fr. duc; *r,* Fr. cri; H, G. ich; kh, G. doch; ‡foreign; ☆ Americanism; < derived from. See inside front cover.

---

10. How would you divide the word *bisulfate* into syllables? _____

11. How do you spell the plural of the word *bistro?* _____

12. Which two entry words are compound words? _____

13. How do you spell the past tense of *bit¹?* _____

14. How high is a bison at its shoulders? _____

15. What is the adverb form of the word *biting?* _____

16. What explanatory phrase is given for the third adjective meaning of *bitter?* _____

17. What is the origin of the word *bitter?* _____

18. What key word is given in the pronunciation key for the short *e* sound? _____

19. How many adjective meanings are given for the word *black?* _____

20. What is the origin of the word *bister?* _____

Recognizing Road Signs

When driving, particularly in an unfamiliar area, pay close attention to the **road signs** posted along the highways. These signs provide traffic rules, useful information about the road's condition, and help in getting you where you want to go. Road signs quickly and clearly convey important messages by using symbols, or pictures, and as few words as possible. In addition to the symbols and words, the shapes and colors of road signs also convey meanings.

On interstate highways, drivers find their way by means of red, white, and blue signs with coded route numbers on them. Even-numbered routes with two digits are east-west routes, and odd-numbered routes are north-south routes. A three-digit route number beginning with an odd number indicates a route into a city. A three-digit route number beginning with an even number indicates a route that goes through or around a city. The sign below indicates that Interstate 495 is to the right.

To enter or exit a highway, you go on a ramp, where you drive more slowly than you do on the highway. Traffic goes only one way on entrance and exit ramps, and often a white sign tells you how fast you can drive on the ramp. The sign below states that the fastest you may drive is 25 miles per hour.

Other road signs, called guide signs, give information to help you to get where you want to go. Green, rectangular guide signs tell

direction. For example, the guide sign below tells you to exit to the right if you want to get off the highway at exit 21.

Find the sign below that tells the number of miles ahead to a town. Which of the signs below identifies what you are passing on the road? Blue guide signs give information about services that are available to you on the road. Other guide signs tell the locations of parks or other places of interest.

Some highway signs show more than one direction. The sign below tells that if you exit left, you will be heading toward Barrister. Where will you be heading if you exit right?

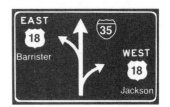

A. For each sign below, underline the correct message.

1. **Richmond NEXT 3 EXITS**
   a. You must get off the highway at one of the next three exits.
   b. You can get off the highway for Richmond at the next three exits.
   c. You can get off the highway for Richmond after three more exits.

2. ☎ ½ MILE
   a. There can be no talking for the next half mile.
   b. Drive one-half mile more, and then stop to telephone friends and relatives to let them know where you are.
   c. A public telephone is one-half mile ahead.

3.
   a. Two lanes merge to form one lane ahead.
   b. The road goes from three lanes to two lanes.
   c. The road curves to the left.

4. **THRU TRAFFIC ↓**
   a. All traffic must go straight through the sign.
   b. All traffic should be in the lane where the arrow is pointing.
   c. Traffic going straight ahead should be in the lane where the arrow is pointing.

5. **MINIMUM SPEED 30**
   a. You must drive no more than 30 miles per hour.
   b. You must drive at least 30 miles per hour.
   c. You must drive at exactly 30 miles per hour.

6. **TO INTERSTATE 75 ↑**
   a. A north-south route is straight ahead.
   b. An east-west route is straight ahead.
   c. A route that goes around the city is straight ahead.

B. Decide on the message that each of the signs below conveys. On the lines provided, explain the meaning of each sign in a complete sentence.

1. _____
   _____
   _____

3. _____
   _____
   _____

2.  _____
   _____
   _____

4.  _____
   _____
   _____

Lesson 43

Conflict and Resolution

Reading a Literature Selection

▶ Background Information

When two people talk, they do not always communicate. True communication is a skill that takes practice to master and requires skill to do well. In this story two friends do a lot of talking but very little communicating.

▶ Skill Focus

Often the characters in a short story have a goal to achieve or a problem to solve. The struggle to achieve the goal or solve the problem is called **conflict.**

A character can face three main types of conflict.

Conflict with Self

A character may struggle with emotions or feelings within himself or herself. This struggle is an internal conflict.

Conflict with Another Character

A character may struggle against another person. This struggle is an external, or outside, conflict.

Conflict with an Outside Force

A character may struggle against nature, society, technology, or a force over which he or she has little or no control. This struggle is also an external conflict.

By the end of the story, the character facing a conflict succeeds or fails in achieving the goal or solving the problem. The way a conflict is settled is called the **resolution.** Conflict and resolution are parts of a story's plot.

When there is more than one conflict, the major conflict is the more important one; the minor conflict is the less important one.

▶ Word Clues

When you read a word that you do not know, look for context clues to help you. Read the sentences that follow.

The only <u>obstacle</u> that I'm facing is my parents. They say that I'm too much of an urban kid and that I'm likely to get lost in the wilderness.

Sometimes there are no context clues to help you clearly understand the meaning of a new word. When that happens, you will need a dictionary to help you. You may find it more convenient to finish what you are reading first and then look up the word.

Use a **dictionary** to find the meanings of the three underlined words in the selection.

▶ Strategy Tip

Preview the selection; notice how the communication changes from letters to telephone conversations. Each letter is enclosed in a box; each phone conversation is written like the dialogue in a play. As you read, look for clues to the developing conflict.

Long-Distance Words

> January 15
>
> Dear Carla,
>
> It's certifiably weird not having you around here anymore after we lived on the same block for ten years. How are things at your new school? It must be tough getting acquainted with a new area and new people. How are you coping?
>
> Things are okay here. I'm in three classes with Margo Fitzsimmons, who's on the karate squad. She makes karate sound so fascinating that I think I may take it this semester. I absolutely can't wait to see you this summer. Don't forget—we're going camping!
>
> Love,
> *Rhonda*

> January 25
>
> Dear Rhonda,
>
> Hi, thanks for your note. Now that I'm used to this place, I really like it. But it was pretty strange entering in the beginning of the second semester the way I did. Imagine: You go into this enormous school, and 3,000 faces are staring at you, and you don't know a soul! You cannot help thinking, "What am I doing here?" The first weeks were really difficult. I didn't have any friends; everything was strange, but rather than wait for everyone to check me out, I decided to join the dance group. Now I'm also involved in a science club project. You know me—never happy unless I'm impossibly overworked. Hope things are going okay for you. Don't let the karate throw you! Just kidding.
>
> Love,
> *Carla*

February 10

Rhonda: Hi, Carla. It's me, Rhonda. Bet you didn't expect me to phone you long distance.

Carla: Rhonda, how great to hear from you! Why are you calling?

Rhonda: Oh, I just sort of felt like it. How's the dancing going?

Carla: Fantastic! I tried out for a part in *West Side Story,* and I'm waiting now to see if I get it. That's what I thought this phone call was going to be about.

Rhonda: Sorry.

Carla: Oh, that's all right. How's the karate going?

Rhonda: Great! I love it; it was hard getting used to all the moves and the balance at first. I *am* only a beginner, but I like the feeling of knowing I could defend myself if I had to. Margo says I should try out for the team next year.

Carla: I'll bet you're good at it. Do you wear those ridiculous pajama things?

Rhonda (*after a pause*): Ah, gee, yes. Well, it's been terrific talking to you, Carla. Just like old times, but I guess I'd better hang up before my money runs out. Listen, I'm really looking forward to camping this summer.

Carla: To what? Oh, the camping trip. (*politely*) Sure, so am I, Rhonda. Well, glad you called.

March 2

Dear Carla,

It's about time we started getting our camping trip organized. How about going to Yosemite National Park? It's halfway between me here in California and you in Oregon. The only obstacle that I'm facing is my parents. They say that I'm too much of an urban kid and that I'm likely to get lost in the wilderness. Can you fathom that? Somehow I'll persuade them. I can't wait to hike around the valley and see all those waterfalls.

Love,
Rhonda

March 24

Hi, Carla,

Haven't heard from you since I wrote about going to Yosemite. I wrote to the ranger station there for campsite reservations. These days it's difficult to get a site unless you sign up in advance. I made tentative reservations for the week of June 22. Okay?

Rhonda

April 8

Carla: Hello? Oh, Rhonda. Hi. How are you?

Rhonda: Fine. Say, didn't you get my last two postcards?

Carla: Yes, I got them.

Rhonda: Well, what about it? Is Yosemite okay with you? The hiking is supposed to be strenuous, but you'll feel like you're endless miles from anywhere, all alone at the summit of the world!

Carla (under her breath): Just where I always wanted to be. (louder) Okay.

Rhonda: Say, Carla, you don't sound too enthusiastic. Is there another place you'd rather go?

Carla (after a pause): No. If we're going camping, then it might as well be Yosemite as anywhere else.

Rhonda (astonished): What do you mean, if?

Carla: Well, naturally, if you want to go . . . .

Rhonda: Sure I want to go; it'll be great. So what have you been doing? Did you get the part you wanted in West Side Story?

Carla: Yes. I'm playing Anita. We're in rehearsal now. Listen, Rhonda, I have to go, but I just wondered how you can make camping plans when your parents don't want you to go?

Rhonda: Don't worry about that. They'll come around. This morning my mother said "if you go camping." That's better than yesterday's straight refusal. If I keep talking about how important it is that we see each other, by next week she'll be saying "when you go camping."

Carla: Okay, well, I have to hang up now.

Rhonda: Good talking to you, Carla.

April 14

Dear Carla,

Our campsite reservations are confirmed for the week of June 22. The people at the ranger station say the weather should be getting warm, but it may be wet. We may have to watch out for mudslides and swollen rivers. I told them a little mud wouldn't bother us! Margo says she's jealous. She's kidding, of course; you'd love her. She does a lot of hiking and camping.

Of course, karate is her specialty, and she's really been teaching me a lot. I learned to do katate tori the other day; that's where you put a flex and twist on your opponent's arm. I'll show you how to do it when I see you.

Love,
Rhonda

May 12

Dear Rhonda,

I'm sorry but I won't be able to make it in June. We're putting on *West Side Story* at the Downtown Civic Theater right after school lets out. We were incredibly lucky to have the theater rent-free, and there's no way I would or could back out now. I just wish you'd informed me before you made the reservations.

Carla

May 29

Dear Rhonda,

I'm sorry about our misunderstanding. I've been doing a lot of thinking about what happened. It seems that we really weren't communicating. I never told you how I felt, and maybe you didn't listen too well, either. Phone me collect when you get this, and we'll discuss it. Okay?

Love,
Carla

May 16

Rhonda: Carla? Is that you? Listen, what do you mean you can't make it?

Carla: I told you. That's when we're putting on *West Side Story.*

Rhonda *(angrily):* But that's when we agreed we were going camping! Now what do I do? My parents gave in just before I got your letter and said I could go, but only because you were going!

Carla: I never said I was going for sure, if you'll recall.

Rhonda *(outraged):* If you didn't want to go, why didn't you say so?

Carla: Anybody could see I didn't want to go. If you weren't so insensitive . . . !

Rhonda: You *said* you wanted to go.

Carla: I thought you wanted to go so desperately that I didn't want to disappoint you, and I never thought your parents would give their permission! I figured I could cooperate with you without having to make a commitment.

Rhonda: Cooperate! *(angrily)* Ha!

Carla *(yelling):* Listen, if you want to plod around in the mud and learn to break arms, that's fine with me. It just so happens that I have better things to do with my time!

Rhonda *(shouting):* Well then, do them! Be my guest! *(She slams down the receiver.)* Who needs her cooperation!

June 5

Carla: . . . So, Rhonda, let me tell you what I learned about communication. You can't just hint at something and hope the other person gets your message. You have to say exactly what you mean, and say it clearly, so that the other person understands. And the person listening really has to listen. Sometimes it helps to have the other person repeat what you said, so that you can tell if he or she understands. *(after a pause)* So, first I would say to you that I really don't want to go camping, but I still want to be friends. And you would say . . .

Rhonda: Wait. Then I say, "I understand you don't want to go camping but you want to be friends." Right? That's okay with me, Carla. Listen, I'll tell you what. I'm going camping and traveling with Margo instead. My parents realized that she'd be a good companion for a camping trip because she has a good deal of expertise. Plus, her uncle lives near the park. He's volunteered to drop us off there and pick us up after we hike out. But the amazing part is that he's due to travel to Oregon! He offered to drive us to see you afterward. I'd adore for you to meet Margo, and maybe we could see your performance!

Carla: Fantastic. I'd like that, Rhonda. Then you can demonstrate some karate, and I'll watch from a distance!

RECALLING FACTS

1. In what time span does this story take place?

_____

2. Why do Rhonda's parents think that Margo would be a good companion for Rhonda on her camping trip?

_____

_____

3. Why does Rhonda like karate?

_____

_____

4. Why can't Carla go camping the week of June 22?

_____

_____

5. Draw a line joining each word with its meaning.

tentative   **a.** understand

fathom   **b.** the knowledge of a highly trained specialist

expertise   **c.** conditional

INTERPRETING FACTS

1. **a.** Describe Carla's personality.

_____

_____

_____

    b. Describe Rhonda's personality.

_____

_____

    c. How do Rhonda and Carla change?

_____

_____

_____

2. Why is the camping trip so important to Rhonda?

_____

_____

3. Why didn't Carla come right out and tell Rhonda she didn't want to go camping?

_____

_____

_____

4. Who was more responsible for the failure in communication? Explain.

_____

_____

_____

5. Put a check next to each statement that expresses the story's theme.

_____ Distance can make communicating difficult.

_____ Karate is a fun sport.

_____ Communicating is more than just talking.

_____ Dancing is more artistic than karate.

Think about the major and minor conflicts in this story and how they are solved. Then, on the lines provided, answer the questions below.

1. Carla and Rhonda are good friends.
   a. What does each character do or not do that causes the major conflict in this story?

   _____

   _____

   _____

   b. Is the conflict internal or external? _____
   c. How is the conflict resolved?

   _____

   _____

2. Rhonda also faces a minor conflict.
   a. What is it?

   _____

   _____

   b. Is the conflict internal or external? _____
   c. How is it resolved?

   _____

   _____

3. Carla also faces a minor conflict. Circle the statement below that best describes it. Then tell how it is resolved.
   Should Carla try out for a part in *West Side Story?*
   Should Carla take the initiative to meet new people?
   Should Carla take up karate?

   _____

   _____

4. Although Carla and Rhonda resolve the major conflict, do you think their friendship will last for a long time? Explain your answer in terms of the external conflict(s) that may get in the way of their friendship.

   _____

   _____

   _____

▶ **Real Life Connections** How do you prefer to communicate—by letter or by telephone? Explain why.

Using a Primary Source

Reading a Social Studies Selection

▶ **Background Information**

The United States was the first country in the world to create a national park system. Our national parks contain some of the most spectacular natural scenery in America. Today, however, serious problems threaten the future of the parks. The following selection describes the national park system and the controversies surrounding it.

▶ **Skill Focus**

One way to learn about a current or past event is to read a **primary source**, or firsthand account. A primary source gives important facts about an issue or a particular society. It also shows how people of a certain time think, feel, and speak.

One kind of primary source is an editorial cartoon, which generally presents a point of view about a public matter. When reading an editorial cartoon, use the steps below.

1. **Learn all you can about the source.**
   a. Where did the cartoon first appear?
   b. When was the cartoon drawn?
   c. What issue does the cartoon deal with?

d. Who drew the cartoon?
   e. What is the person's background?

2. **Identify the cartoon's opinion.**
   a. What is the cartoonist's opinion about the subject?
   b. How does the cartoonist reveal his or her opinion in the drawing?
   c. What symbols does the cartoonist use?
   d. How do the words in the cartoon reveal the cartoonist's opinion?
   e. How would the cartoonist like to change the situation shown?

3. **Evaluate the cartoon's effect on you.**
   a. What was your opinion of the subject before looking at the cartoon?
   b. What was your opinion of the subject after looking at the cartoon?
   c. Did the cartoon influence your attitude toward the subject?

▶ **Word Clues**

When you read, you may come across a word that names a special person, place, or thing. If the paragraph has no context clues to explain the word, there may be a clue elsewhere.

Read the following sentences.

The source of this pollution is outside the parks— power plants, smelters,[1] mining industries, and other commercial plants.

Notice that there is a raised number after the word *smelters*. This raised number is called a footnote and is a signal to look at the bottom of the page for a footnote with the same number. A footnote gives a brief definition or explanation of a word. The footnote for *smelter* tells you what it is.

[1]smelter: an industrial device for melting ores to extract the metals that they contain

Use **footnote** context clues to find the meanings of the four other numbered words in the selection.

▶ **Strategy Tip**

Preview the editorial cartoons and the headings in the selection. As you read, think about how the cartoons relate to the information in the text.

The Plight of Our National Parks

Our national parks have been described as the crown jewels of the country. These preserved areas of natural beauty and historic importance belong to all Americans. They have been protected from land developers for present and future generations. Unfortunately, however, the parks share the problems and dangers of the modern world. Their air, water, wildlife, and solitude are becoming increasingly threatened.

Pockets of Beauty

In 1872, the U.S. government set aside Yellowstone Park as a pocket of natural beauty to be preserved forever. It was the first national park in the country and in the world. By 1916, the National Park System was born. Over the years, the Grand Canyon, the Grand Tetons, Yosemite, the Everglades, and the Great Smoky Mountains were made national parks. Historic places, such as the Lincoln Memorial, and recreational areas, such as Lake Mead, also became public property. Then, in 1978, 56 million acres of Alaskan land were added to the park system. National parks encompass over 76 million acres today.

✔ At first, the system favored areas with scenic and historic importance. Later, recreational areas were chosen for fishing, boating, skiing, and canoeing. In recent years, park officials have attempted to create and improve parks that are located near large, urban centers, to serve as large a part of the population as possible. And the people have been coming in greater and greater numbers.

In 1990, 260 million visitors entered the park system—137 percent more than in 1980.

Too Many People?

Sadly, the parks' popularity has been one of their biggest problems. At the height of the summer, many parks are the scenes of traffic jams and long waiting lines. The system is threatened by a conflict between the enjoyment of the public and the preservation of nature.

✗ Overcrowding defeats the most basic goals of the national parks. In some popular spots, the view of nature is obscured by crowds of people. The sounds of birds and other wildlife are drowned out by car engines and motorboats. The solitude of a woodland trail is disturbed by an army of backpackers. A family wishing to camp in the wilderness finds that the campgrounds are packed full.

Although the parks exist to serve the public, careless visitors create problems. When tourists lure the bears to their cars or campsites, they endanger both themselves and the animals. More everyday problems include littering, vandalism, and reckless driving.

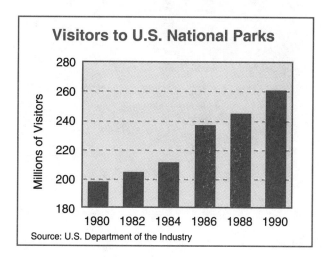

Visitors to U.S. National Parks

Millions of Visitors: 280, 260, 240, 220, 200, 180

1980 1982 1984 1986 1988 1990

Source: U.S. Department of the Industry

SOURCE: Langley in *The Christian Science Monitor* © 1981

"The line forms promptly at 8:06 A.M. to see the bears—chipmunks by appointment only."

The concession stands that cater to tourists in the parks are also considered a sore point. People who enjoy the natural beauty of parks think that the stands are blemishes. They commercialize the natural scenery. The tourists' attention is turned away from nature, toward postcards and souvenirs.

Various suggestions have been made regarding the problem of overcrowding in the parks. The system could put a daily limit on the number of people allowed in a park. Quiet zones, which would be free of cars and all other motorized vehicles, could be established. Commercial motels could be replaced with simple cabins. While these suggestions would help preserve nature, they might be unpopular because they would not serve all the public.

Too Much Pollution

According to the National Park Service, the lowering of air quality is the number one problem of the parks. In a recent survey, 45 percent of the park areas reported unsatisfactory levels of air pollution. This is true for parks not only near New York City, but also in remote places like the Grand Canyon.

The source of this pollution is outside the parks—power plants, smelters,[1] mining industries, and other commercial plants. In Arches National Park, for example, a sea of smog from a nearby uranium mill envelops the park for about one-quarter of the summer season. In the Grand Canyon, visibility is lowered for about one hundred days of the year by pollution that drifts from industries hundreds of miles away. The parks of the eastern United States share that area's generally low standards of air quality and visibility.

During recent years, scientists have become more aware of another type of airborne pollutant[2]—acid rain. This dangerous phenomenon is created by the release of the chemical sulfur dioxide into the air during the burning of fossil fuels.[3] When sulfur dioxide mixes with precipitation, the result is acid rain. The National Park Service has observed damage to wildlife, streams, plants, and soil from the poisoning effect of acid rain. The use of pesticides[4] and the dumping of toxic wastes[5] have also threatened the well-being of the parks' ecosystems.

The Controversy over Development

The national parks encompass not only some of the nation's most beautiful land but also some of its richest areas. The government has estimated that federal lands contain up to 37 percent of the nation's undiscovered crude oil, 43 percent of its undiscovered natural gas, 40 percent of its coal reserves, and large percentages of other minerals. A debate is now under way between those in favor of developing these natural resources and those in favor of preserving the natural state of the parks. There seems to be no way that both sides can win.

The focus of the controversy is on the southwestern states of Arizona, New Mexico, Utah, and Colorado. The deposits of natural resources are greatest there, and the grandeur

SOURCE: Courtesy in National Parks, September/October, 1981

[1]smelter: an industrial device for melting ores to extract the metals that they contain

[2]pollutant: a waste material that makes an environment less healthful for living things

[3]fossil fuels: fuels, such as coal, that contain the remains of plants or animals that lived long ago.

[4]pesticides: chemicals used to kill unwanted animals, such as insects

[5]toxic wastes: waste materials that are highly poisonous

of the scenery is at its height. Developers argue that the nation would benefit greatly by developing these resources. Conservationists argue that development would permanently damage the national parks of the area. They worry that local industry would further lower air quality and visibility. They also believe that smokestacks and strip mines within view of the parks would ruin the sense of natural isolation and beauty.

Our national parks are the natural heritage of the American people. While they are a source of enjoyment for the public, they are also a responsibility. The many problems facing the parks today are likely to increase in the coming decades. How these problems are solved will determine the types of parks that future generations will inherit.

RECALLING FACTS

1. Draw a line from each item in the left column to its correct description in the right column.

   Lincoln Memorial   scenic park

   Grand Canyon   recreational park

   Lake Mead   historic park

2. Write the effect of the following cause.

   Cause Sulfur dioxide, released into the air by the burning of fossil fuels, mixes with precipitation.

   Effect _____

3. What attitudes do the following two groups have about the use of natural resources in federal lands?

Conservationists _____

_____

Developers _____

_____

_____

_____

4. Read the paragraph marked with an X. Underline the sentence that states its main idea. Circle the details in the paragraph that support the main idea.

5. Match the words on the left with the definitions on the right.

   ____ pollutant

   ____ pesticides

   ____ toxic wastes

   a. poisonous refuse

   b. substances used for killing insects

   c. harmful chemical or waste material

INTERPRETING FACTS

1. Suppose the National Park Service put a limit on the number of people allowed into a park at one time. List two effects of that limit.

   a. _____

   b. _____

2. Why did some land developers in Alaska disapprove of the federal government's claiming 56 million acres of the state as national park land?

_____

3. a. What might be two advantages to the nation of using the fuel resources on federal lands?

_____

_____

b. What might be one disadvantage?

_____

4. Reread the paragraph with a check mark next to it. Write a sentence stating the main idea of the paragraph.

_____

5. Write a generalization based on the three facts below.

Facts **a.** Park campsites are overcrowded.

    b. Traffic jams occur in summer.

    c. There are long waiting lines for big park attractions.

Generalization _____

_____

6. Write an appropriate caption for the cartoon on page 160.

_____

_____

7. Use the graph on page 159 to answer the questions below.

a. How many people visited national parks in 1986? _____

b. How many more people visited national parks in 1990 than in 1986? _____

c. In which year did about 243 million people visit national parks? _____

SKILL FOCUS

Refer to the two editorial cartoons accompanying the selection to answer the following questions.

1. Learn all you can about the source.

a. Where did the cartoon first appear?

Cartoon 1 _____ Cartoon 2 _____

b. Who drew the cartoon?

Cartoon 1 _____ Cartoon 2 _____

c. When was the cartoon drawn?

Cartoon 1 _____ Cartoon 2 _____

d. What issue does the cartoon treat?

Cartoon 1 _____

Cartoon 2 _____

2. Identify the cartoon's opinion.

   a. What is the cartoonist's opinion about the subject?

Cartoon 1 _____

Cartoon 2 _____

   b. How does the cartoonist reveal his or her opinion in the drawing?

Cartoon 1 _____

_____

Cartoon 2 _____

_____

   c. What symbols does the cartoonist use in the cartoon?

Cartoon 1 _____

_____

Cartoon 2 _____

_____

   d. How do the words in the cartoon reveal the cartoonist's opinion?

Cartoon 1 _____

Cartoon 2 _____

_____

3. Evaluate the cartoon's effect on you.

   a. How would the cartoonist like to change the situation shown?

Cartoon 1 _____

_____

Cartoon 2 _____

_____

   b. How does the cartoon influence your attitude toward the subject?

Cartoon 1 _____

_____

Cartoon 2 _____

_____

▶ **Real Life Connections** Describe two problems found in a public park in your area. What solutions would you suggest?

Cause and Effect

___ Reading a Science Selection ___

▶ Background Information

Climate varies from one part of the world to another. The type of vegetation that grows in a place is usually the result of the climate. This selection deals with the northern forests.

▶ Skill Focus

A **cause** is a reason, condition, or situation that makes an event happen. An **effect** is the result of a cause. For example, a plant blooms when it has adequate sunlight. Sunlight is the cause, and the blooming is the effect of the cause. Sometimes one effect may be the result of many causes, or one cause may have many effects.

Sometimes one effect can be the cause of another effect. In this way, a chain of causes and effects is formed. Read the following paragraph.

Exceptionally dry winters can have a dramatic effect on all kinds of organisms. Small plants can die outright, and the buds of larger plants may dry up. Without small plants and buds for food, many small animals, such as mice,

Cause dry winter	→	Effect/Cause death of plants	→	Effect death or departure of smaller animals

either die or go elsewhere in search of food.

The first cause, dry winters, results in the first effect, the death or drying up of plants and parts of plants. The scarcity of plants is the cause of the second effect, small animals dying or leaving.

The diagram above shows the chain of causes and effects.

Causes and effects are often directly stated in textbooks. Sometimes, however, you have to infer, or figure out, an effect.

▶ Word Clues

Read the sentences below, and look for context clues to help you understand the underlined word.

Another name given to this area is the northern coniferous forest, to underline{distinguish} it from the coniferous forest to the south, which has different characteristics. To distinguish is to separate by differences.

If you do not know the meaning of the word *distinguish* in the first sentence, read on. The second sentence states what the word *distinguish* means. A word meaning that is stated directly can often be found before or after a new word.

Use **definition** context clues to find the meanings of the three underlined words in the selection.

▶ Strategy Tip

As you read "Taiga," use your knowledge of cause and effect to understand why the northern forests grow where they do. Think about how chains of causes and effects are formed.

Taiga

In the Northern Hemisphere, a band of forests stretches around the world. These forests are composed of cone-bearing trees, or **conifers** (KAHN ə fərz)—spruce, fir, hemlock, and pine. The Russian word for this forest is *taiga* (TY gə), which means "swamp forest." The name refers to the wetness of the forest in spring when the snow melts. Another name given to this area is the northern coniferous forest, to distinguish it from the coniferous forest to the south, which has different characteristics. To distinguish is to separate by differences.

The taiga has long, severe winters. The coldest months may have temperatures of -50 degrees Celsius or lower. The snow that falls stays on the ground for months. Summers are short—generally only about four months long—but temperatures may be high in summer, reaching 27 degrees Celsius. The amount of yearly precipitation ranges from scant (25 centimeters) to moderate (100 centimeters), and most of the precipitation comes as summer rains. In winter, the air is so cold that it can hold little moisture. Hence, the cold winters are very dry.

Coniferous Trees

Coniferous trees are well suited to the taiga. Their pyramidal, or inverted-cone, shape and flexible branches help them to shed winter snow. Their small, waxy needles help them to conserve water, especially during dry seasons. Conifers grow close together, shading the forest floor. Few plants can grow with so little sunlight, but the seedlings of many conifers can. The result is that, as mature conifers age and die, they are replaced by their offspring.

The floor of the taiga is usually covered by a thick mat of decaying needles. In this cold environment, however, decay is so slow that nutrients are not quickly released back to the soil. In addition, the fungi (FUN jy) that break down the needles form an acid as they work, making the soil very acidic. Fungi are decomposers, organisms that break down organic material. When it rains, the rainwater leaches nutrients deep into the soil, where the plants cannot use them for growth. To leach is to filter through. The result is a poor soil that is gray and ashy in appearance. Consequently, only certain plants and animals can survive in this environment.

Other Vegetation

There is more to the taiga than coniferous forests. This region also has many rivers, lakes, ponds, and bogs. Deciduous trees—trees that shed their leaves each autumn, such as willow, aspen, and birch—grow along the rivers and lakes. Shrubs, including blueberries and cranberries, grow in the bogs, which are soggy, meadowlike areas surrounding pools of brown, acidic water. The water takes its color and acidity from the peat that makes up the bog. Peat is the partially decayed remains of the dead plant material that has accumulated over the years.

Some very unusual plants are found in the bogs and ponds. The carnivorous, or meat-eating, plants include the sundew, Venus flytrap, pitcher plant, and bladderwort. All these plants can make their own food, but they must catch and digest insects to obtain nitrogen and phosphorus. These minerals exist only in small quantities in the taiga soil.

Animals

The taiga supports a variety of animal populations. Large animals, such as moose and mule deer, browse on shrubs and tree branches. Although porcupines normally feed on young trees, they may kill mature trees in winter, when food is scarce, by eating the

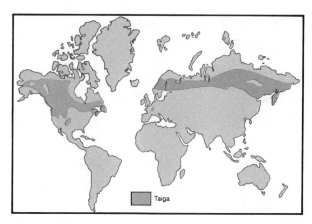

Taiga regions of the world

bark and growth tissue. Black bears and grizzlies live here as well, feeding on berries, insects, and fish. Mice and hares flourish, eating leaves and tree bark. Bobcats, wolves, foxes, and owls feed on the mice and hares.

Many birds are summer visitors to the taiga. Ducks and loons inhabit the lakes and ponds during summer. Insects are plentiful, but soil organisms, which are common in grasslands and deciduous forests, are found in smaller numbers in the poor taiga soil.

Areas Bordering the Taiga

The southern limit of the taiga is determined by the number of days without frost and the amount of precipitation. Deciduous trees need at least 14 weeks of summer to regrow their leaves and to produce the food that they must have to survive the next winter. Because they lack the conifers' adaptations to dry spells, these trees require precipitation that is distributed throughout the year. Where these conditions for frost-free days and precipitation are met, the deciduous trees win the competition with the conifers for growing space. At that point, the northern coniferous forest, or taiga, ends.

The northern limit of the taiga is also determined by climate. Where it is too cold and dry for trees to survive, the taiga ends and arctic tundra begins. Yet the <u>transition</u> from tall forest to open tundra is gradual, not abrupt. The word *transition* means "change." Closest to the tall forest, the trees are erect, or upright, but dwarfed. The limit of erect trees is called the **timberline.** Beyond this point, as conditions become more severe, the trees can no longer grow upright. Their trunks grow parallel to the ground, with only their branches extending upward. This area of contorted tree growth is called **Krummholz** (KRUM holtz), a German word meaning "twisted growth." Another name sometimes used is elfin wood. Both terms aptly describe this band of <u>bizarre</u> growth. The word *bizarre* means "very odd." Beyond this region, climatic conditions are so severe that trees cannot grow at all. At this point, the tundra begins.

Taiga, timberline, and Krummholz are not only found as one travels to northern latitudes. A climb up high mountains in the Northern Hemisphere, such as the Rockies, shows the same change of vegetation and increasing severity of climate. In fact, the taiga of these mountains is simply a fingerlike extension of the taiga occurring in the northern latitudes.

> *Where it is too cold and dry for trees to survive, the taiga ends and the arctic tundra begins.*

RECALLING FACTS

1. Why are dying conifers in the taiga replaced by more conifers?

   _____

   _____

   _____

2. What is the name given to the area of contorted tree growth that separates the taiga and tundra?

   _____

3. What unusual plants are found in the taiga?

   _____

   _____

4. How are conifers suited to their environment?

   _____

   _____

   _____

5. Complete each sentence by filling in the correct word from below.

    leaches   transition   bizarre

  a. Moving from Florida to Alaska can be

  a difficult _____.

b. Heavy rainfall _____
nutrients from the soil.

c. The characters in the horror movie

looked _____.

INTERPRETING FACTS

Fill in the space between the lines next to the correct answer.

1. During which season is the water-conserving ability of conifers in the taiga most important?
  || **a.** summer || **b.** fall || **c.** winter

2. In some areas below the timberline in the Rocky Mountains, the trees have the gnarled appearance of Krummholz. The best explanation for this is that
  || **a.** the climate in these areas is harsh.
  || **b.** the trees have some unusual disease.
  || **c.** the soil is so poor that the trees cannot get enough nutrients to grow erect.

3. Compared with those of the taiga, the conifers along the northern Pacific coast are giants. The best explanation for this is that
  || **a.** the West Coast trees are closer to the ocean.
  || **b.** the growing conditions along the northern Pacific coast are more favorable than those in the taiga.
  || **c.** there is too much precipitation in the taiga for conifers to grow well.

SKILL FOCUS

A. The effects given below have more than one cause. Write the causes on the lines provided.

  1. Effect   Few plants grow on the floor of the taiga.

  Causes _____

  _____

  _____

  _____

  2. Effect   The climate of the taiga is harsh.

  Causes _____

  _____

  _____

  _____

3. Effect   The taiga is replaced by tundra.

   Causes   _____

   _____

   _____

4. Effect   Coniferous trees can easily shed winter snow.

   Causes   _____

   _____

   _____

5. Effect   Deciduous trees do not grow in most parts of the taiga.

   Causes   _____

   _____

   _____

B. Complete the chains of causes and effects below. Write your answers in full sentences on the lines provided. The last effect for each chain has been done for you.

Cause	Effect/Cause	Effect
1. _____ _____ _____ _____	_____ _____ _____ _____	Taiga winters are dry.
2. _____ _____ _____ _____	_____ _____ _____ _____	Carnivorous plants are healthy even though they live in soil that lacks all the minerals they
3. _____ _____ _____ _____	_____ _____ _____ _____	The floor of the taiga forest gets little sunlight.
4. _____ _____ _____ _____	_____ _____ _____ _____	Porcupines kill mature trees.

▶ **Real Life Connections**   Does your geographical area include taiga? If not, where is the closest taiga area?

Reading Graphs

Reading a Mathematics Selection

▶ Background Information

Reading a graph involves more than just reading the equation that describes the graph. A graph is a diagram that is used to represent numbers or values. Graphs can represent both positive and negative numbers, but in this lesson you will learn how to plot points on a graph with only positive numbers. You will also learn how to graph an algebraic equation.

Graphs have many uses in many different areas. They can show very large numbers by using a simple line, and they can help you understand complicated information quickly because they show it in a simple form.

In algebra, a graph can help you find the value of an unknown number, or variable, by enabling you to solve an equation by representing it on a graph. This process can also work in reverse. Sometimes you are given a graph and have to figure out the numerical value of the variable. By correctly reading and interpreting the graph, you can determine the numerical value of the variable and solve the equation.

▶ Skill Focus

Graphs are used to show **data,** or information, in a form that is easy to read. The original numbers on which the graph is based may be in a table or they may be in an equation. Whether the numbers come from a table or an equation, the graph is prepared and used in the same ways.

In the equation $x + 4 = y$, there are two **variables,** or unknowns. By substituting a value for one of the variables, you can determine the value of the other. The following are some of the possible values for x or y:

x	y
1	5
2	6
3	7
4	8
5	9

When you know a number of values for each variable, you can plot the values on a graph. The graph of an equation with two variables is a way of showing the solution to the equation.

▶ Word Clues

In this selection, the word *graph* is used as both a noun and a verb. For example, *graph* refers both to the line that is the solution to an equation (a noun) and to the procedure for drawing that line (a verb). Other words that are also nouns and verbs, such as *point,* may have only one meaning in mathematics. A point in mathematics is a dot that is used to mark an exact location. It is always a noun. *Axis, horizontal,* and *vertical* are other important words in the selection.

▶ Strategy Tip

As you read the selection, keep in mind that some words in English can be both nouns and verbs. You can determine how the word is being used by looking at the context, or the rest of the sentence or paragraph, in which the word is used.

Reading Graphs

In algebra, **graphs** are shown on the **coordinate plane**, a plane indicated by a pair of lines that cross at right angles. These lines, called the **axes** (AK seez; singular, *axis*) of the plane, divide the plane into four regions. Points can be located in any of the four regions or on the axes themselves. This selection, however, deals only with coordinates that have positive values. You will therefore work with only one of the four regions.

The place where the axes cross is the point (0,0). The set of numbers in the parentheses is called the coordinates of the point. Each number has a special meaning. The first number is the value on the horizontal line. The second number is the value on the vertical line. From the place where the axes cross, the lines are labeled with positive numbers to the right and up. The lines to the left of and below the place where the axes cross are labeled with negative numbers. Below is the coordinate plane with the axes labeled x and y.

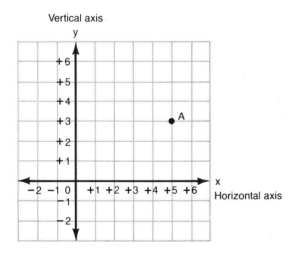

Every point on a plane is identified by two coordinates. On the next graph, to locate point A, whose coordinates are (+5,+3), you start where the two axes meet (0,0) and count 5 units to the right on the x axis. This point is +5. Then count up 3 units on the y axis. This point is +3. You have found the place where the x axis at +5 crosses the y axis at +3. This is point A, whose coordinates are (+5,+3).

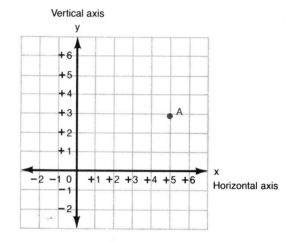

Sometimes you know the point on a graph and need to find the coordinates of that point. Simply look for the values on the x and y axes that are closest to the point.

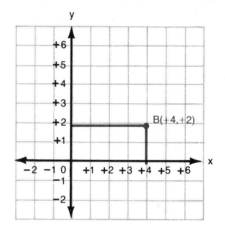

Start by looking along the x axis. In the graph above, point B is closest to and in line with the point on the x axis labeled +4. Then look along the y axis. Point B is in line with the point labeled +2. Therefore, point B is located at (+4,+2). Coordinates are often shown by writing B(+4,+2), or simply B(4,2).

In a pair of coordinates, the first number is the x value, and the second number is the y value. Thus, for an equation, such as $y = 4x$, the coordinates (3,12) or (5,20) are both solutions to the equation. The coordinates (3,12) are a solution because if $x = 3$ and $y = 12$, then the equation $y = 4x$ is true. Substituting the numbers in the equation gives $12 = 4(3)$, which is a true sentence.

Notice that the coordinates (12,3) are not a solution, since they mean that $x = 12$ and $y = 3$. When you substitute these numbers in the equation $y = 4x$, you do not get a true sentence. It is not true that $3 = 4(12)$ or $3 = 48$.

The set of all the solutions to an equation is the graph of the equation. Because two points locate any straight line exactly, you need to find only two solutions to an equation to find its graph. For example, the line through the points (3,12) and (5,20) is the graph of $y = 4x$.

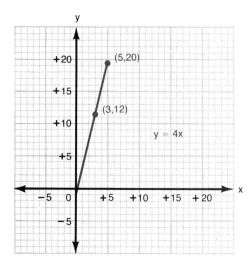

Generally, however, you should find three points to draw a graph. While two points locate the line, you may have made a mistake in finding one of them. By finding the third point, you check yourself.

Here is how to graph the equation $x + 2y = 8$. Substituting any number for x or y produces an equation with one variable. When you solve this equation, you then have a value for x and a value for y. For example, if you substitute 2 for x in $x + 2y = 8$, you get $2 + 2y = 8$. This can be solved in the ordinary way.

$$2 + 2y = 8$$
$$2 + 2y - 2 = 8 - 2$$
$$2y = 6$$
$$y = 3$$

Now you know that the point where $x = 2$ and $y = 3$, or (2,3), is a solution to the equation and a point on the graph. To find another point, you can substitute either another value for x or another value for y. Here is the work if 1 is substituted for y.

$$x + 2y = 8$$
$$x + 2(1) = 8$$
$$x + 2 = 8$$
$$x + 2 - 2 = 8 - 2$$
$$x = 6$$

This result means that the point (6,1) is a point on the graph and a solution to the equation $x + 2y = 8$.

You should find a third point as a check. The easiest points to find are when $x = 0$ or $y = 0$. If $x = 0$, the equation becomes $2y = 8$, which is equivalent to $y = 4$. The point (0,4) is therefore on the graph. Also, if $y = 0$, the equation becomes $x = 8$, so the point (8,0) is another solution. Here is the graph:

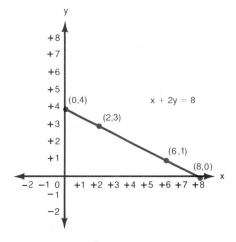

RECALLING FACTS

1. Which is the x axis, the vertical line or the horizontal line?

_____

_____

2. In the coordinates (3,5), which value does 5 represent, x or y? _____

3. How far is the point (8,2) from the x axis in units? _____

4. How can you tell whether the coordinate pair (4,6) is a solution to $4x - 2y = 4$?

_____

_____

INTERPRETING FACTS

1. In a coordinate pair, one coordinate is 0. Where would you look for the point that corresponds to that coordinate?

_____

2. If a point is in the upper right-hand region of the coordinate plane, what is the sign of the *x* value?

_____

3. What should you do if you are graphing an equation and one set of values for the coordinates doesn't fall on the line with the other two sets of values?

_____

_____

_____

_____

SKILL FOCUS

A. Give the coordinates of each of the points shown on the following graph.

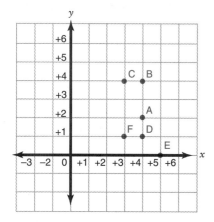

1. A _____
2. B _____
3. C _____
4. D _____
5. E _____
6. F _____

C. Match each graph with the correct equation. Write the letter of the correct graph on the line.

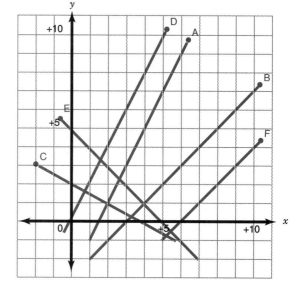

1. $y = 2x$ _____
2. $x - y = 3$ _____
3. $x + y = 5$ _____
4. $2x - y = 3$ _____
5. $x - y = 6$ _____
6. $x + 2y = 4$ _____

B. For each set of the coordinates listed below, plot and label the point on the graph.

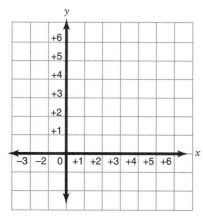

1. A (3,6)
2. B (5,1)
3. C (2,4)
4. D (2,5)
5. E (4,0)
6. F (0,3)

▶ **Real Life Connections** Describe a real-life situation in which a graph of an equation with two variables could be used. (Hint: Think of your science classes.)

Analogies

An **analogy** is a comparison. It shows that the relationship between two words is similar or that the relationship between one pair of words is similar to the relationship between another pair of words. For example, the relationship between *lazy* and *energetic* is similar to the relationship between *tiny* and *gigantic*. In other words, *lazy* is the opposite of *energetic*, as *tiny* is the opposite of *gigantic*.

One way to express an analogy is to use words.

Lazy is to *energetic* as *tiny* is to *gigantic*.

Another way to express this analogy is to use dots for the words *is to* (:) and *as* (::).

lazy : energetic :: tiny : gigantic

This word relationship shows antonyms. Other relationships can show part-to-whole (handle : pot :: faucet : sink) or synonyms (lie : deceive :: kind : considerate).

Read the incomplete analogies below. On the line, write the word from the choices on the right that completes the analogy.

1. toe : foot :: finger : _____   **a.** arm **b.** hand **c.** leg

2. seldom : frequently :: never : _____   **a.** occasionally **b.** rarely **c.** always

3. spout : pitcher :: nozzle : _____   **a.** summer **b.** hose **c.** lariat

4. dense : sparse :: Rhode Island : _____   **a.** Nevada **b.** California **c.** New York

5. maestro : concertmaster :: boss : _____   **a.** orchestra **b.** band **c.** supervisor

6. month : year :: day : _____   **a.** week **b.** hour **c.** second

7. quart : pint :: minute : _____   **a.** meter **b.** pound **c.** second

8. sandal : sombrero :: moccasin : _____   **a.** cap **b.** shoe **c.** shirt

9. city : village :: skyscraper : _____   **a.** farmer **b.** cottage **c.** land

10. dollar : dime :: decade : _____   **a.** year **b.** week **c.** day

11. occasional : constant :: infrequent : _____   **a.** seldom **b.** often **c.** always

12. building : story :: ladder : _____   **a.** rung **b.** climb **c.** height

13. spice : food :: wit : _____   **a.** salt **b.** conversation **c.** cooking

14. unusual : exotic :: ordinary : _____   **a.** different **b.** rare **c.** commonplace

15. branch : tree :: arm : _____   **a.** body **b.** fingers **c.** leg

16. stimulating : boring :: old : _____   **a.** dull **b.** new **c.** sick

Reading a Car Loan Application

Once you have a driver's license, you may be interested in buying a car. Because a car is one of the most expensive items that you will ever purchase, you should think about how you will pay for one before you buy it.

If you haven't saved up enough money to buy a car with cash, you will need a car loan. As long as you have a secure job and good credit, a bank will lend you the money that you need. When you borrow money from a bank, you have to pay a charge called the interest rate. Interest is the cost of using the bank's money. When you borrow money to pay for an item, the item costs more.

You don't have to pay the money back to the bank all at one time. Instead, you pay it back over a certain amount of time, known as the term of the loan, in installments, or monthly payments.

The car that you buy is collateral for the loan. In other words, if you miss payments, the bank can repossess the car—or take it from you—and sell it to get its money back.

Study the sample car loan application on page 175. Notice that the application asks for information about you, your car, and your finances.

A. Complete each sentence by using the information from the car loan application.

1. The amount of the loan is _____, and the applicant has _____ months to pay the loan back.

2. Judith Gordon is _____.

3. The applicant is borrowing the money from _____ to buy the car.

4. The applicant is applying for a loan at the same bank where he has a _____ account.

5. The applicant prefers to make his monthly car payments on _____.

6. Looking at the Motor Vehicle or Boat Purchase section of the application, you can tell that the applicant owned a car before purchasing the 1996 Dodge. You know this because _____.

7. If the applicant had to pay only the principal at a rate of $300 a month, then it would take him _____ months to pay back the car loan.

8. This applicant already owes a debt to _____. To date, he has paid back _____, which has taken him _____ months. He still has to pay _____.

9. If a husband and wife, mother and daughter, or even two friends apply together for a loan, they make what is known as a joint application. The two people would then be responsible for paying back the loan. You can tell that this is not a joint application because _____.

B. Circle the letter next to the phrase that correctly completes each sentence.
   1. The applicant is ____.
      a. Benjamin James Gordon   **b.** James Gordon Benjamin   **c.** Gregory Gordon

2. The applicant currently lives at ____.
   a. 5001 Westwood Drive, Gaithersburg, Maryland
   b. 300 E. Capitol Street S.E., Washington, D.C.
   c. 1830 Corcoran Street N.W., Washington, D.C.
3. It appears that the applicant moved to his current address when he ____.
   a. moved out of his father's home
   b. started working at the City Cable Company
   c. started working at the R.F. Rogers Company
4. The applicant's monthly installments for this loan will be ____.
   a. $200   b. $200 plus interest   c. $300 plus interest
5. To pay off his debt to Miles Furniture, it will take the applicant ____.
   a. 20 more months   b. 30 more months   c. 50 more months

CAPITOL BANK

PURPOSE OF LOAN	I HEREBY MAKE APPLICATION FOR A LOAN OF	CASH DESIRED	REPAYABLE IN NO. OF MONTHS
Car Loan		$7,200	36

APPLICANT

FIRST NAME	MIDDLE	LAST NAME
Benjamin	James	Gordon

CIRCLE DAY OF THE MONTH YOU PREFER TO MAKE PAYMENT
5   10   15   20   25   (30)

SEND MAIL TO ☑ HOME ADDRESS   ☐ BUSINESS ADDRESS

PRESENT ADDRESS NUMBER & STREET	APT. NO.	DATE OF BIRTH
1830 Corcoran Street N.W.	6C	9/4/72

CO-APPLICANT

CITY	STATE	ZIP CODE	☐ OWN ☑ RENT	YEARS THERE
Washington D.C.		20009		2 1/2

FIRST NAME	M.I.	LAST NAME

SOCIAL SECURITY NO.	NO. DEPENDENTS INCLUDING SELF	HOME TELEPHONE
079/48/2673	1	(202) 362-4983

ADDRESS

PRESENT EMPLOYER (FIRM NAME)	TYPE OF BUSINESS
City Cable Company	TV Cable

SOCIAL SECURITY NO.	DATE OF BIRTH

ADDRESS	SUPERVISOR'S NAME
300 E. Capitol St., S.E., Wash., D.C.	Sarah Morgan

NAME AND ADDRESS OF NEAREST RELATIVE NOT LIVING WITH YOU
Judith Gordon
4290 N. 29th St., Arlington, VA

POSITION	LENGTH OF SERVICE	BUSINESS TELEPHONE
Installer	2 1/2 yrs.	(202) 543-0066

TELEPHONE
(703) 525-6521

LIST ALL OTHER INDEBTEDNESS BELOW. IF NONE, LIST CREDIT REFERENCES. LIST FOR BOTH APPLICANTS ONLY IF HE/SHE WILL BE CONTRACTUALLY LIABLE. ATTACH SEPARATE SHEET IF NECESSARY. *(INDICATE BY CHECK MARK LOANS LISTED BELOW TO BE PAID OFF WITH PROCEEDS OF THIS LOAN)

NAME AND ADDRESS OF CREDITOR	ACCOUNT NO.	ORIGINAL AMOUNT	UNPAID BALANCE	*	MONTHLY PAYMENT
Miles Furniture 908 25th Street, N.W. Washington, D.C.	A60043	$2,500	$1,000		$50.00

COMPLETE THIS SECTION FOR MOTOR VEHICLE OR BOAT PURCHASE

AUTO LOAN PURCHASE PRICE	IDENTIFICATION OTHER	DRIVER'S OPERATORS LICENSE NO.	STATE
$ 11,400		G-488-291-337-892	Washington, D.C.

THE FOLLOWING INFORMATION MUST BE TAKEN FROM DEALERS ORDER FORM OR REGISTRATION CERTIFICATE

DOWN PAYMENT	NEW OR USED	YEAR	MAKE OR TRADE NAME	MODEL	BODY STYLE	NO. CYLS.	VEHICLE IDENTIFICATION NO.
$ 2,000	new	1996	Dodge	Neon	sedan	6	79430438

TRADE IN	SELLER'S NAME	LICENSE PLATE NUMBER
$ 2,200	City-Wide Dodge	

AMOUNT TO BE FINANCED	ADDRESS	
$ 7,200	2291 Massachusetts Ave., Washington, D.C.	230 KLB

INSURANCE AGENT (NAME AND ADDRESS)   Louise Silber   919 Rockland Pike, Arlington, VA

BANK REFERENCE	BANK	ADDRESS			
	Elgin Bank	1852 Connecticut Avenue	✓ SAVINGS / ✓ CHECKING #	011890673-5	
	Capitol Bank	350 E. Capitol Street, S.E.	✓ SAVINGS / CHECKING #	14-201098-7	

APPLICANT'S(S') PREVIOUS ADDRESS(ES)/EMPLOYER(S) IF LESS THAN 3 YEARS AT CURRENT ADDRESS/EMPLOYMENT

PREVIOUS HOME ADDRESS NUMBER & STREET	CITY	STATE	ZIP CODE	☐ OWNED ☑ RENTED	YEARS THERE
5001 Westwood Drive	Gaithersburg, Maryland		20760		2

PREVIOUS EMPLOYER FIRM NAME	POSITION	LENGTH OF SERVICE	BUSINESS TELEPHONE
R.F. Rogers Company	repair person	1 1/2 years	301-628-5322

NUMBER & STREET	CITY	STATE	ZIP CODE	TYPE OF BUSINESS
19 Rockland Road	Gaithersburg,	Maryland 20760		TV sales & service

5/6/96	X Benjamin J. Gordon X
DATE	SIGNATURE(S) OF APPLICANT(S)

Context Clue Words

The following words are treated as context clue words in the lessons indicated. Lessons that provide instruction in a particular context clue type include an activity requiring students to use context clues to derive word meanings. Context clue words appear in the literature, social studies, and science selections and are underlined or footnoted for ease of location.

Word	Lesson						
abut	37	effective	11	life expectancy	28	recession	19
adjacent	37	emporium	18	lush	38	repudiated	2
alpha particles	20	environs	10	materialized	1	scowled	1
amenities	10	exasperated	18	mechanization	28	sheaf	1
animated	18	expertise	43	mesa	36	smelter	44
antics	36	extinct	11	monitor	3	solvent	27
archaic	27	fathom	43	nucleus	20	stations	10
beta particles	20	fossil fuels	44	nurtured	37	strategic	2
bizarre	45	grazier	10	obstacle	43	stratified	38
blue-collar	19	hatter	36	outback	9	tentative	43
boisterous	9	impoverished	2	pesticides	44	toxic wastes	44
descend	3	indigenous	2	plumage	36	trajectories	36
desolateness	38	innovative	27	pollutant	44	transition	45
despair	27	intricate	9	predicament	3	unique	11
discrete	11	inverted	29	predominant	38	utilized	28
disheveled	18	isolation	9	productivity	28	virtual image	29
distinguish	45	isotopes	20	pylons	1	white-collar	19
drastic	3	labor force	19	quays	37		
		leaches	45	real image	29		

Concept Words

In lessons that feature social studies, science, or mathematics selections, words that are unique to the content and whose meanings are essential to the selection are treated as concept words. Many of these words appear in boldface type and are often followed by a phonetic respelling and a definition.

Word	Lesson						
algebra	39	convex mirror	29	half-life	20	proton	20
atomic mass	20	coordinate plane	46	herb layer	38	quaternary	
atomic number	20	deciduous forest	38	herbivore	11	consumer	11
atoms	20	decomposers	11	hibernation	3	radioactive dating	20
axes	46	desert	38	Krummholz	45	radioactive decay	20
base number	30	diameter	21	lens	29	radioactivity	20
biomes	38	dormancy	3	lichens	11	radius	21
canopy	38	droughts	38	molecule	20	refracted	29
carnivores	11	ecosystem	11	mutualism	11	secondary	
center	21	electrons	20	negative exponents	30	consumer	11
circle	21	element	20	neutron	20	shrub layer	38
circumference	21	epiphytes	38	nucleus	20	spectrum	29
commensalism	11	equation	39	omnivores	11	symbiosis	11
compounds	20	expanded notation	30	parasitism	11	taiga	45
concave lens	29	exponent	30	per	12	tertiary consumer	11
concave mirror	29	factor	30	permafrost	38	timberline	45
coniferous forest	38	food chain	11	plane mirror	29	tropical rain forest	38
conifers	45	food webs	11	predator-prey	11	tundra	38
consumers	11	gamma rays	20	primary consumer	11	understory	38
convex lens	29	graphs	46	prism	29	variable	39
		grassland	38	producers	11		